BLACK INTELLECTUAL THOUGHT IN EDUCATION

Black Intellectual Thought in Education celebrates the exceptional academic contributions of African American education scholars Anna Julia Cooper, Carter G. Woodson, and Alain LeRoy Locke to the causes of social science, education, and democracy in America. By focusing on the lives and projects of these three figures specifically, it offers a powerful counter-narrative to the dominant, established discourse in education and critical social theory—helping to better serve the population that critical theory seeks to advocate. Rather than attempting to "rescue" a few African American scholars from obscurity or marginalization, this powerful volume instead highlights ideas that must be probed and critically examined in order to deal with prevailing contemporary educational issues. Cooper's, Woodson's, and Locke's history of engagement with race, democracy, education, gender, and life is a dynamic, demanding, and authentic narrative for those engaged with these important issues.

Carl A. Grant is Hoefs-Bascom Professor of Education in the Department of Curriculum and Instruction at the University of Wisconsin, Madison.

Keffrelyn D. Brown is Associate Professor in the Department of Curriculum and Instruction at the University of Texas at Austin.

Anthony L. Brown is Associate Professor in the Department of Curriculum and Instruction at the University of Texas at Austin.

BLACK INTELLECTUAL THOUGHT IN EDUCATION

The Missing Traditions of
Anna Julia Cooper,
Carter G. Woodson,
and Alain LeRoy Locke

*Carl A. Grant, Keffrelyn D. Brown,
and Anthony L. Brown*

 Routledge
Taylor & Francis Group

NEW YORK AND LONDON

First published 2016
by Routledge
711 Third Avenue, New York, NY 10017

and by Routledge
2 Park Square, Milton Park, Abingdon, Oxon, OX14 4RN

Routledge is an imprint of the Taylor & Francis Group, an informa business

© 2016 Taylor & Francis

The right of Carl A. Grant, Keffrelyn D. Brown, and Anthony L. Brown to be identified as authors of this work has been asserted by them in accordance with sections 77 and 78 of the Copyright, Designs and Patents Act 1988.

Library of Congress Cataloging in Publication Data
Black intellectual thought in education : the missing traditions of Anna Julia Cooper, Carter G. Woodson, and Alain Leroy Locke / by Carl A. Grant, Keffrelyn D. Brown, and Anthony L. Brown.
pages cm
Includes bibliographical references and index.
ISBN 978-0-415-64190-6 (hardback) -- ISBN 978-0-415-64191-3 (pbk.) -- ISBN 978-0-203-08130-3 (e-book) 1. African Americans--Education. 2. African American intellectuals. 3. African American philosophy. 4. Education--United States--Philosophy. 5. Multicultural education. 6. Education--United States--History. I. Brown, Keffrelyn D. II. Brown, Anthony L. III. Title.
LC2717.G72 2015
371.829'96073--dc23
2015014584

ISBN: 978-0-415-64190-6 (hbk)
ISBN: 978-0-415-64191-3 (pbk)
ISBN: 978-0-203-08130-3 (ebk)

Typeset in Bembo
by Saxon Graphics Ltd, Derby

Printed and bound in the United States of America by
Edwards Brothers Malloy on sustainably sourced paper

CONTENTS

PREFACE

[W]hat is a luxury for the nation as a whole [knowing your group history] becomes a prime social necessity for the Negro.

The Negro digs up his past, Arthur Schomburg (1925)

The chief method used in writing *Black Intellectual Thought in Education* was digging, digging, and more digging to locate the *Thoughts*, and to know the imperative that drove Anna Julia Cooper, Carter G. Woodson, and Alain LeRoy Locke to make the personal and professional sacrifices they did for their academic life projects. We were humbled by their total life stories: honors, courageous deeds, promotions of others before self; each aspect of their lives. In our archival digging we often paused, not to catch our breath, but to give deserved attention to other African American scholars whose work and contributions are victims of historical distortion, omission, and inaccuracies in US textbooks and other places where historical information is shared. It is a challenge to stay on task when you come upon life stories that whisper: "Stop for a moment with me. I too have a story that should be told." There are so, so many stories, some written, most often in excellent penmanship in old bibles, on the back of envelopes, borrowed stationery and binders about so many events from yesteryear that tell of the struggles of Blacks to get an education: their desire to help and support families; their community's academic and social success; and stories that speak to a love of country and the ways in which they contributed to the growth and development of American democracy.

We celebrate the exceptionalism that Cooper, Woodson, and Locke brought to education, social science, and American democracy. Our digging has taught us that this *thing*: courage, ambition, smartness, agency, hope in the democratic ideal, etc. resided in the mind and body of many African Americans of yesteryear.

It continues to be a great loss to American democracy that these stories are not known, because they are filled with deeds and services toward the common good and not simply words of promise. John Adams spoke wisely when he posited, "Liberty cannot be preserved without general knowledge among the people." (1765). *Black Intellectual Thought in Education* is a major part of the general knowledge of America.

The digging for *Black Intellectual Thought* started with an observation at the 2012 annual meeting for the American Educational Research Association (2012) in Vancouver, Canada. It was observed that none of the many exhibitors, including all of the leading education publishing houses, had a book by a historic Black scholar on education. There was *John Dewey on Education, Piaget on Education*, etc., but no book by a Black scholar on education. When an inquiry was made at the exhibits, it was mostly greeted with a polite smile and "No, sorry we don't have that … yet." Sometimes there was searching through the catalog of books, but the concluding statement was the same, "Sorry." However, one publisher replied: "What do you want to do about that?" The response was easy: "Correct the omission!" Thus we began the journey to write *Black Intellectual Thought in Education*.

Generally, there is no such thing as the perfect time for such an opportunity to come calling, especially one that would require an unusual amount of digging-up. But a line from Paulo Coelho (2002), *The Devil and Miss Prym*, speaks well to such moments:

> When we least expect it, life sets us a challenge to test our courage and willingness to change; at such a moment, there is no point in pretending that nothing has happened or in saying that we are not yet ready. The challenge will not wait. Life does not look back.

Now, three years later, and two weeks before the 2015 AERA annual conference in Chicago coincidentally titled "Toward Justice," *Black Intellectual Thought in Education* is ready to be sent to Routledge. Or more accurately it is ready to send to Catherine Bernard and Anna Clarkson, who were the ones who un-dauntingly replied, "What do you want to do about that?"

Well we did something about that! The kind of digging we did was special, and needed us to give it special care, time, and attention. Black stories from long ago are not all carefully codified, filed, stored, and readily accessible. Deep digging is required to locate them, time is needed to engage with the story-makers, so that their story, and their history of engagement with race, democracy, education, gender, and just living life is told, for their service to African American people and America in general demands respect and an authentic narrative.

Carl A. Grant, Madison, WI
Keffrelyn D. Brown, Austin, TX
Anthony L. Brown, Austin, TX
April, 2015

ACKNOWLEDGMENTS

Throughout the book-writing journey you come upon many that give you encouragement, suggestions, and feedback about the manuscript. Now is our time to acknowledge in print all of their great help.

Carl's Acknowledgments

Alexandra Allweiss was exceptional in every way with suggestions, feedback, encouragements, and editorial corrections. SUPER, SUPER THANKS Alex. Graduate students in the *Black Intellectual Thought in Education* in Madison were super helpful with ideas about the title and offering feedback. My brothers Alvin, Shelby, and Ernest (now deceased) would always start conversations with: "How is the book going ... are you still working on the Black Intellect book?" After three years of asking that question, they will be surprised and probably thankful when I say something else. That said, I want them to know that their words were a strong source of encouragement. They would bring a smile. Similarly, my son, Carl, and daughter, Alicia, always offered a positive word when I was writing. Thanks, guys, and grandkids Gavin and Amaya, who became good and patient captives when there was a piece of Black intellectual thought I wanted to share with them, as I said: "You won't learn this in school." Thanks, you are great kids. Catherine Bernard and Anna Clarkson ... what can I say ... you two are wise and socially aware. ... Thanks much for this fabulous opportunity. Last, but in no way least, MERIT at UW—if it is in print and I asked for it they delivered. Thank you, much appreciated.

Keffrelyn's Acknowledgements

This project has been a labor of love—literally. It was conceived, nurtured, and brought to life alongside the birth of my second child. This was not the best timing and I thank our editor, Catherine Bernard, for her belief in this work and her patience in allowing us time to bring it to life. I also want to thank my colleagues and friends in my area—cultural studies in education (CSE). I am lucky to work alongside you, Noah De Lissovoy and Luis Urrieta. You are brilliant scholars and teachers and most importantly, kind, generous people. I am glad to call you comrades, friends in the struggle. Thanks also to our CSE students and specifically those I work closely with in an advising role. You all are bright, passionate, and burgeoning with ideas that I eagerly await watching you bring to life and to our field! Since graduate school I have met many people who have provided me with various opportunities, support, wisdom, and kind words. There are too many to name, but I would like to send a shout out to a few that I have recently met and some that I met well over a decade ago: Wayne Au, Kristin Buras, Amy Kraehe, Jamel Donnor, Adrienne Dixson, Rodney Hopson, Rich Milner, Tyrone Howard, Marcelle Haddix, Arnetha Ball, Cynthia Tyson, Alfredo Artiles, Valerie Kinloch, Maria Franquíz, Christine Sleeter, Na'ilah Nasir, Dave Gilborn, Sonja Lanehart, Juan Guerra, Lyn Corno, and Lin Goodwin. I also want to thank Chris Davenport and Juliet Seignious for always being there, knowing and remembering.

I also want to thank my Church of Christ at East Side family, especially Sharon Jackson, Gail Williams, Iris Williams, Marilyn Deen, and Debra Watson for checking in on me and just understanding the challenges of working and parenting while seeking to cultivate a real spiritual foundation for myself and my home. I also recognize the friendship and fellowship of Megan Mosby, Coquice Moffett, Pam Davis, Ketema Mitchell, Tarcia Jones, and Jackie Francis. Thanks for the baby shower (along with Gayle Ervin), the prayers, and of course, the laughs!

I want to thank my extended family members in Houston, New Orleans, Jackson MS, and Ann Arbor MI. Hanging out with you all at family vacations and other events has offered a needed respite from work and a place to talk about all of the ideas that invigorate me around race, culture, and Blackness. A special thanks goes to my grandmother—Mama Dee, for all of your love and fabulousness during your serious illness; my Auntie Debbie and Uncle Simon for your generosity, love, and fabulous holiday hangouts in New Orleans; and my cousin Danaeha for your love, support, and hospitality. I also want to thank my cousins Darryl Gilbert (for our recent long talk) and Dwight Gilbert for his monthly check-ins presumably to school me on effective parenting, but really, I think, to keep me on track and accountable with my writing. I got it done! I love you guys and your beautiful families (Maria, Julia, Damon, and Dylan). Thanks also to Anthony's parents who both passed in the process of completing this manuscript: Carol Brown and Roy Brown. Thanks for raising a beautiful human being,

Anthony, and for embracing me in your lives as if I were you own daughter. Thanks too to Darren for your well-wishes and positive words over the years.

Finally to Anthony: what can I say? You are a God-send, a help-mate, my soulmate. I am blessed to have you in my life as a collaborator and partner. You are sharp, insightful, and always full of ideas. But most importantly, you take care of me, our children, and our home. You love me and us more than you do yourself and your work. But most importantly, you love and know God. I know this. Thank you for loving us and me. My love for you is never-ending.

Anthony's Acknowledgments

I first want to thank my mother (Carol Anastasia Brown) and father (Roy E. Brown) and my big brother (Darren C. Brown) and all my grandparents, aunts, uncles, and cousins for surrounding me in a world filled with love, knowledge, respect, honor, and support.

My parents' love and support was profound. Now they each have passed, and I do all I can to pass this kind of love on to Keff, Kanaan, and Kythe. As Teddy Pendergrass once said: "It's so good … lovin' somebody, and that somebody loves you back." Thanks Mom and Pop!

I also cannot say enough about my wife, best friend, and my colleague: Keffrelyn. I learned how to be loved from my parents, but I learned about what it means to be *in love* when you came in to my life in 1998. You are everything to me! Our work together over the years has made me smarter and wiser. I marvel at what you do as a scholar and your love, support, and mentorship through our past projects and this project has made an indelible mark on my life. And what you do to elevate the lives of our family is astounding. You know how to take a bird's eye view to assess our lives together and think about what's best. To see Kanaan and Kythe thrive is all your doing. Thanks Keff!

I want to also take this time to thank Catherine Bernard for your patience and support through this project. I also would like to thank Ryan Crowley, Billy Smith, and LaGarett King for reading sections of our book. Thank you for your support and friendship.

And I would like to acknowledge all my friends and colleagues such as Noah De Lissovoy, Luis Urietta, David Gillborn, Tyrone Howard, Christian Davenport, Rich Milner, Rodney Hopson, Alfredo Artiles, Vivian Gadsden, Adrienne Dixson, Na'ilah Nasir, Bill Tate, Christine Sleeter, Arnetha Ball, Joao Paraskeva, Jamel Donnor, and Wayne Au. I would not be here today if it were not for your intellectual and personal support.

Keffrelyn and Anthony's Acknowledgments

Across the field we are often recognized as "The Browns." It is true that we are partners—both in work and in life—so it makes sense that we would offer acknowledgments together. Indeed if it were not for key people in our lives we would not have the opportunity to do the work we do collaboratively. We want to first thank Keffrelyn's (both of ours, really) parents: Herman and Linda Brown. Your unending support and tireless energy overwhelm us. We thank you for every drive you have taken, every diaper you have changed, every meal you have cooked, every inspiring text sent, phone call made and, in the case of Herman—every page of this manuscript read! We thank you for every single thing you do to make our lives as a family work. We love you and appreciate you more than any words could capture. We also thank our extended family: Jamaj, Cherí, Jaelyn, and Jyle Hamilton. We love you and appreciate your support and encouragement. Thanks for taking care of the children like they are your own and for always being there when we need you. Thank you for always checking in on us, stepping in to help out with the children and just being the supportive people you are. Thanks also goes out to our longtime church family: Ernest and De Shondra Booker, Ben and Danica Sumpter, Bruce and Tanda Maxwell, Derrick and La Juanda Hannah. It is a blessing to know you, fellowship and raise children with you, while also working alongside you to instill a love of Blackness and Black history in our children. Thanks so much to our colleagues and friends across the department whom we have both worked closely with or collaborated with since our arrival in 2006: Louis Harrison, Allison Skerrett, Jenn Adair, Chris Brown, Deb Palmer, Ramon Martinez, Jim Hoffman, Nancy Roser, Jo Worthy, Beth Maloch, Cinthia Salinas, and Katie Payne. We also want to send a shout out to our village (and their families) at UT-Austin—Kevin Cokely, Gigi Awad, Julian Vasquez Heilig, Mark Gooden, Angela Gooden, Terrance Green, and Brandalyn Green. You make working in the College of Education a family affair. We love you all and cherish the time we spend together. We also want to acknowledge our colleagues, administrators, and staff at UT-Austin, in the College of Education, the Department of Curriculum and Instruction, and in the Department of African and African Diaspora Studies. A special thanks goes to Randy Bomer, the current chair of our department for his support of our scholarship and research. Thanks to the wonderful staff in 406-Jim Maxwell, Ann Ford, Patricia Nenno, Linda Williams, Olivia Becerra for all of your assistance in getting the daily work done. We would like to also thank Dr. Ida Jones from the Moorland-Spingarn Research Center at Howard University for your assistance with our archival research for this project.

We also thank our Cultivating New Voices (CNV) family for providing a needed respite and well-spring of inspiration. To Carl Grant and Gloria Ladson-Billings, you continue to stand as emblematic role models of what it means to be a scholar, *par excellence*, for the long haul. You are also both beautiful people who care deeply for your work, your families, and the world in which we live. We are blessed to have had the opportunity to learn from you and work alongside you both in the struggle.

Last, but definitely not least, and the most important reason why we work so hard and do what we do, to our children: Kanaan and Kythe. You two are the light of our lives, the twinkle in our eyes! It is true that having children changes you: they make us more human. You two have changed us for the better. We are more loving, more patient, more understanding, and more generous than before you arrived. And even as we try to write these words now and you clamor to get us off our computer we are sustained by your energy and the unceasing love we have for you both. Thank you for keeping us grounded and for allowing us to make a small contribution to changing the world that we know both of you will someday make a mark upon.

INTRODUCTION

Critical social thought plays a significant role in shaping how scholars conceptualize issues of power and difference in K–12 and higher education. Researchers and theorists employ critical social thought to illuminate that schools are microcosms of a broader ideological and structural base that reproduces inequities in schools. Through the ideas and philosophies of critical social thought, scholars explore the internal structural mechanisms that work in concert with the broader economy to reproduce a stratified working class, while also curtailing students' and communities' life chances (Apple, Au, & Gandin, 2009; Darder, Baltadano, & Torres, 2008). Critical theories also enable scholars to understand how the school curriculum produces racialized master scripts that only privilege the experiences and epistemologies of dominant groups (Brown & Brown, 2010; Grant, 2011). Overall, the conceptual tools offered by critical social thought provide in-depth analytics around issues of power, agency, difference, and identity.

As a way to make sense of the varied contexts that reproduce inequities, critical educationalists have drawn from numerous theories and theorists. The mainstream field of education draws from the work of Karl Marx (De Lissovoy & McLaren, 2003), Basil Bernstein (Apple, 2002), Pierre Bourdieu (Mills, 2008), The Frankfurt School (Darder et al., 2008), Michel Foucault (Popkewitz, 1999), Antonio Gramsci (Buras, 2008), and numerous other mostly European White male scholars to illustrate the complex and implicit ways that schools reproduce inequities. These scholars and schools of thought could be thought of as "the canon" of critical social thought.

We are not suggesting that being European, White, and male should lend itself to a dismissal of this work. However, it should call into question how critical educationalists, deeply concerned with the ideological production of knowledge have reproduced their own version of a dominant discourse. In other words, while the intent has been to use critical social thought to shed light on educational inequities, the use of specific theories and theorists reified a dominant Eurocentric discourse. This project stems from this contradiction in the field and the myopic way of interrogating inequality and power. As a way to trouble this knowledge construction, we draw from the resources of thought in Black intellectual traditions relevant to education.

Our attention to Black intellectual thought is not to privilege this body of work, but to offer a counter narrative to the dominant discourse and to call for similar bodies of work from other groups. The lack of acknowledgment to Black intellectual thought is not a new issue nor is it an issue only in the field of education (also see Mills, 1997 and Gordon, 2006). For example, education theorist Beverley Gordon (1993) gave attention to these issues some twenty years ago. The following words express her concerns:

> It is of signal importance that while there is a voluminous literature written about the education for African Americans in the first decades of this century, the extensive literature written *by* African-American scholars and educators on this subject is neither represented nor referenced in the dominant educational literature.
>
> (Gordon, 1993, p. 266)

Gordon's assertions about the educational literature still ring true today. While there have been some efforts to use Black educational thought, the ideas from this body of literature have largely been overlooked.

The purpose of *Black Intellectual Thought in Education* is to bring African American intellectual contributions to bear on the prevailing and current education problems facing schools, colleges, and society today. This is not an attempt to rescue these scholars from obscurity or marginalization, but to bring to the reader's attention *ideas* that are useful for examining past and enduring educational concerns. Some of the scholars covered in this project are fairly well known but their work is narrowly conceived in the educational literature, while others cited have received little to no attention in the educational literature, yet the volume and philosophical rigor of their scholarship provides important insights to our most enduring concerns in education.

Conceptualizing Black Intellectual Thought

What is Black intellectual thought? Black intellectual thought at its core is counter hegemonic. Through a variety of genres, African Americans recast the existing master narratives that positioned Black people as sub-persons (Mills, 1998) and/or people who offered no intellectual, social, aesthetic, cultural, or historical value to American life. White narratives therefore did not include Black people as deserving full citizenship in the U.S. experiment in democracy. As a result,

Black intellectual thought emerges out of an imaging by Black people of their full potential in spite of normative White domination. African American history and culture serves as the well-spring of Black intellectual *thought* and *experience*; the combination of both *thought* and *experience* informing Black people's ways of thinking.

Philosopher Lewis Gordon (2006) argues that because experience is part of the "complex world of communication and sociality" (p. 31) it requires multiple levels of interpretation. However, he maintains that when experiences are interpreted without the input of the person's experience, this produces what he calls "epistemic colonization" (p. 31), where the process of *knowing* Black experience must be established through White theorizing.

Simply put, according to Gordon (2006), within this context, Black people need White people to interpret and give legitimization to their experiences. Black experience could not be knowable until they have been interpreted through the discourse of White theorists. Gordon (2006) further states,

> The more concrete manifestation of this relationship is familiar to many Black intellectuals. In most academic institutions, including some, unfortunately, in regions dominated by people of color, the following formula holds: Colored folks offer experience that White folks interpret. In other words, formulating theory is a White affair. Paraphrasing Arthur de Gobineau, theory is White and experience is Black.
>
> (p. 31)

As a result, Gordon explains that Black experiences can only be interpreted through White scholars such as "Martin Heidegger, Jacques Lacan, Jacques Derrida, or Michel Foucault instead of through the thought of Anna Julia Cooper, W.E.B DuBois, C.L.R. James, Richard Wright, Ralph Ellison " (2006, p. 31). Similarly, educational thought has suffered from the "epistemic colonization," whereby White scholarly discourse implicitly becomes the privileged body of knowledge even for examining Black experiences. In effect, Black intellectual thought is doubly marginalized by not being used to address Black experiences or the broader experiences of schooling across racial and cultural boundaries. Therefore, Black intellectual thought serves as a core set of ideas and philosophies to give meaning and interpretation to not only African American experience, but also to other broader issues of power and difference across space and time.

This leads us to the next important and overlapping criterion of Black intellectual thought, which is the unity between *experience* and *thought*. We conceptualize *Black intellectual thought* as orientations of thought, expressed and interpreted through ideas and lived experience; what Thomas Holt (1995) refers to as *everydayness*. Phillis Wheatley, David Walker, Frederick Douglass, and Sojourner Truth each wrote from what they saw and experienced as Black people in the US. We argue from these experiences, that important ideas and orientations of thought took form about the human condition, particularly within a societal space philosophically derived from Modernist ideals of democracy and natural rights.

So in essence, Black intellectual thought is both *experience* and *thought*. The inseparable link between experience and thought provides a useful epistemological framework, where experiences are formed within a context, yet carefully able to transcend space and time and serve as a mode of thought to long-standing issues of power and difference. This is the constructed seat of the problem to Black intellectual thought— where *experience* is seen as antithetical to *thought*. From the traditions of Black intellectual thought and particularly the ideas of Cooper, Woodson, and Locke, is an acute attention to the existential and material reality of being Black in America, while employing Western disciplinary discourse and the Black cultural forms to give meaning and interpretation to a time and place, and developing a framework for deconstructing enduring educational and social issues. Philosopher Lucius Outlaw (2005) illuminated this point when he explicated the meaning and usage of Black intellectual thought with what he calls "critical social thought for Black folks." He states,

> The turn must be made to the life-worlds of people of African descent—in all of their ambiguities, complexities, contradictions, and clarities, to our concrete life praxes—in search of our distinct orientations with regard to the matters to be addressed in a revolutionary transformation of the U.S. social order. Such orientations are given, for example, in mediated folk tales, religious practices, political language and practices prevalent during various times and under various conditions, music, poetry, and languages of common currency. [...] [T]he meanings they hold, in symbolic and/or explicit form, contain fundamental orientations.
>
> (Outlaw, 2005, p. 8)

According to Outlaw, Black intellectual and educational thought contains *fundamental orientations* that traverse the contextual spaces in which the ideas derived and took form. We gather from Cooper, Woodson, and Locke *thoughts* told through their experiences as African Americans in America.

Approaches to Black Intellectual Thought in Education

This project draws from, yet differs theoretically from, the existing literature in education that uses Black intellectual thought. There have been at least five different ways in which Black intellectual thought surfaces in the field of education. There first has been a referencing of Black scholarship in order to make a larger claim about the historical context of African American education (Watkins, 1993, 2006). For example, as a way to articulate the issues germane to African American education after Reconstruction, scholars duly note the Du Bois and Washington ideological debates (Anderson, 1988; Watkins, 1993). The second way in which Black intellectual thought receives attention is to cite an idea that reflects a perennial concern in African American education (King, 2005; Ladson-Billings & Tate, 1995). The more common examples are to use Carter G. Woodson's notion of "miseducation" or Du Bois' "double consciousness" to address contemporary educational concerns (King, 2005). The third approach is via biography. Through providing a biographical sketch, scholars discuss different aspects of a scholar's intellectual project (Goggin, 1994). The fourth approach, while only sparingly addressed in the educational literature, is to provide an in-depth and nuanced understanding of a Black scholars' body of intellectual thought (Alridge, 1999, 2008; Banks, 1992; Brandon, 2009; Dei & Simmons, 2010; Lynn, & Bridges, 2009; Taliaferro-Baszile, 2009). Finally, while rare, there has been some application of Black intellectual thought to highlight cross-cultural concerns in education (Brown & De Lissovoy, 2012; Greene, 1993; King, 2005). De Lissovoy (2007, 2012, 2013) for example, draws on the work of Frantz Fanon and W.E.B Du Bois as a theoretical tool to decouple enduring issues of capital and power. In addition, Maxine Greene's (1993) and Carl Grant's (2011) use of Black novelists and thinkers to speak to wider concerns of pluralism and curriculum in the US provides another example of scholars' uses of Black intellectual thought. However, some issues have remained, pertaining to the uses of Black intellectual thought in education.

The first is that Black intellectual thought remains subsumed within the historical and ongoing issues *only* related to African Americans. For example, when curriculum historians and theorists (Kliebard, 2003; Pinar et al., 1995) speak of the Progressive Era and curriculum, African American ideas and philosophies are rarely located within the larger curricular discourse of this era (Brown & Au, 2014). The second concern is to place Black intellectual thought only in the context of Black issues. There is little to no literature that speaks to the work of Anna Julia Cooper, Carter G. Woodson, and Alain Locke as offering important intellectual ideas to wider and cross-cultural concerns in education. The third concern is to either locate all discussions about African American intellectual thought to a few scholars or only provide partial descriptions of their ideas. This kind of canonization and over-generalization of Black intellectual thought has in effect silenced some of the most important ideas pertaining to issues of multiculturalism, pluralism, egalitarianism, and pedagogical theory.

As a result, we maintain that the inclusion of Black intellectual thought serves three purposes to this project. The first is that it provides a foundational discourse to long-standing ideas in education, such as culture, race, knowledge production, and pedagogy. The second is that it helps to broaden the existing narrative of curriculum history in the US (see Brown & Au, 2014), by locating ideas and contributions within the wider story of curriculum and education in the US. Third and finally, we argue that Black intellectual thought can help to interrogate contemporary theories in education.

Selection of Authors

There are two specific reasons why we chose to focus on these theorists. First, we wanted to focus on African American scholars whose ideas have been visible but under-theorized within the field of education. For example, while Carter G. Woodson has received some level of recognition, the scope and depth of his work remains fixated on a few ideas and contributions (e.g., mis-education and Negro History month). So the intent of this volume is to address some of the not so common educational theories and pedagogies taken from these authors' bodies of work and illustrate how their ideas inform contemporary discussions about curriculum, race, and culture. Second, we wanted to focus on theorists who provide a significant and/or lengthy body of scholarship to educational issues. Take for example the work of Anna Julia Cooper and Alain Locke whose work was quite extensive and relevant for its time. They each published numerous articles and essays about culture, democracy, education, values, and pluralism.

While the significance of Woodson, Cooper, and Locke has direct implications to historical and contemporary ideas about race, curriculum, and pedagogy; their work is only sparsely employed in critical educational thought. For example, two significant volumes in curriculum studies (Pinar et al., 1995) and multicultural education (Banks & Banks, 2004) give little to no attention to the significance of their work. Each of these authors has written numerous essays and historical studies that provide important and cutting-edge ideas about culture and race that have not been fully acknowledge in educational theory. This volume addresses this gap by providing substantive attention to Woodson's, Cooper's, and Locke's ideas, including how their orientations of thought are foundational to enduring concerns, as well as speak to contemporary theoretical concerns.

Outline of the Chapters

The first chapter of this book outlines the historical contours and foundations of Black educational thought. We argue that Black educational thought emerged out of wider Black ideological discourses concerned with the racial status of African Americans in the US. We maintain that Black educational thought took form through three different spaces: the experiential, collective, and ideological. Through the detailing of experience, African Americans wrote candidly and descriptively about the conditions of oppression and social change. We maintain however, that ideas and experiences also took form within collective spaces, where social and cultural movements (e.g., Harlem Renaissance, Chicago Realism, Civil Rights Movement, Black Power Movement, etc.) helped to shape the discourse about African American social realities. Then through the creation of Black political ideologies, African American ideas and cultural expressions were contained within a common body of philosophical thought. In this section of the chapter, we also lay out the most prominent ideologies of Black thought, including their application to educational issues.

The next three chapters highlight the work of Anna Julia Cooper, Carter G. Woodson, and Alain Locke. While each chapter takes a slightly different approach to each author's ideas, there are some core commitments across them. The first is that each chapter focuses heavily on the *ideas* and *thinking* of each author relevant to education. As we note in each chapter, we are not the first to use the work of these scholars, however, we find that in education their ideas have been under-theorized. Each chapter gives attention to two guiding questions: *What are the core orientations of thought that define each scholar's work? How are these orientations of thought useful to making sense of past and enduring issues in education?* In taking up these questions, each chapter takes a different approach.

This is in part due to the different ways each author's archives are organized, the author's style of writing, and their differing standpoints. Anna Julia Cooper's ideas took form from the standpoint of a Black woman and as an advocate for Black people and all Americans to have the full benefits of citizenship in a democracy. Woodson tended not to write in a disciplinary fashion tied to theoretical discourse. His writing mostly spoke to the condition of "miseducation," including how his myriad curriculum projects rejected the existing paradigms of Black people's history; whereas, Alain Locke was a philosopher and social theorist who wrote exhaustively about issues of race and culture in the context of Western philosophical thought. Nonetheless, each chapter focuses on the *orientations of thought* that each author brought to bear on enduring issues of curriculum and pedagogy.

The Epilogue ties together the conceptual threads that bind these authors together. We circle back to the question of why these authors' ideas are useful and important to interrogating complex educational issues. *Black Intellectual Thought in Education* as a whole brings to light the overarching silence in the field of education, while employing the authors' ideas to trouble and deconstruct enduring questions of culture, difference, and curriculum.

References

Adams, J. ([1854[1765]). A dissertation on the canon and feudal law. In John Adams and Charles Francis Adams. *The works of John Adams, second president of the United States: With a life of the author, notes and illustrations, Volume 9*. New York: Little, Brown and Company.

Alridge, D. P. (1999). Guiding philosophical principles for a DuBoisian-based African American educational model. *The Journal of Negro Education, 68*(2), 182–199.

Alridge, D. P. (2008). *The educational thought of W.E.B. Du Bois: An intellectual history*. New York: Teachers College Press.

Anderson, J. A. (1988). *The education of Blacks in the South, 1860–1935*. Chapel Hill, NC: University of North Carolina Press.

Apple, M. W. (2002). Does education have independent power? Bernstein and the question of relative autonomy. *British Journal of Sociology of Education, 23*(4), 607–616.

Apple, M. W., Au, W. & Gandin, L. (2009). *The Routledge international handbook of critical education.* New York: Routledge.

Banks, J. A. (1992). African American scholarship and the evolution of multicultural education. *The Journal of Negro Education, 61*(3), 273–286.

Banks, J. A. & Banks, C. A. M. (2004). *Handbook of research on multicultural education.* San Francisco, CA: Jossey-Bass.

Brandon, L. (2009). Remembering Carter Goodwin Woodson (1875–1950). In E. Maleski (Ed.). *Curriculum studies handbook—next movement.* New York and London: Routledge.

Brown, A. L. & Au, W. (2014). Race, memory and master narratives: A critical essay on U.S. curriculum history. *Curriculum Inquiry, 44*(3), 358, 389.

Brown, A. L. & Brown, K. D. (2010). Strange fruit indeed: Interrogating contemporary textbook representations of racial violence towards African Americans. *Teachers College Record, 112*(1), 31–67.

Brown, A. L. & De Lissovoy, N. (2011). Economies of racism: Grounding education policy research in the complex dialectic of race, class, and capital. *Journal of Educational Policy, 26*(5), 595–619.

Buras, K. (2008). *Rightist multiculturalism: Core lessons on neoconservative school reform.* New York and London: Routledge.

Coehlo, P. (2002). *The Devil and Miss Prym.* London: HarperCollins.

Darder, A., Baltadano, M. & Torres, R. (2008). *The critical pedagogy reader.* (2nd ed.), New York and London: Routledge.

Dei, G., & Simmons, M. (2010). *Fanon & education: Thinking through pedagogical possibilities.* New York: Peter Lang.

De Lissovoy, N. (2007). Frantz Fanon and a materialist critical pedagogy. In P. McLaren and J. L. Kincheloe (Eds.), *Critical pedagogy: Where are we now?* (pp. 355–370). New York: Peter Lang.

De Lissovoy, N. (2012). Education and violation: Conceptualizing power, domination, and agency in the hidden curriculum. *Race Ethnicity and Education, 15*(4), 463–484.

De Lissovoy, N. (2013). Conceptualizing the carceral turn: Neoliberalism, racism, and violation. *Critical Sociology, 39*(5), 739–755.

De Lissovoy, N. & McLaren, P. (2003). Educational "Accountability" and the violence of capital: A Marxian reading. *Journal of Education Policy, 18*(2), 131–143.

Holt, T. C. (1995). Marking: Race, race-making, and the writing of history. *The American Historical Review, 100*(1), 1–20. doi:10.2307/2167981

Gordon, B. M. (1993). Toward emancipation in citizenship education: The case of African-American cultural knowledge. In L. Castenell and W. Pinar (Eds.), *Understanding curriculum as racial text: representations of identity and difference in education.* New York: SUNY.

Gordon, L. (2006). African-American philosophy, race, and the geography of reason. In L. Gordon and J. A. Gordon (Eds.), *Not only the master's tools: African-American studies in theory and practice.* Philadelphia, PA: Temple University Press.

Grant, C. (2011). Escaping Devil's Island: Confronting racism, learning history. *Race Ethnicity and Education, 14*(1), 33–49.

Greene, M. (1993). The passions of pluralism: Multiculturalism and the expanding community. *Educational Researcher, 22*(1), 13–18.

King, J. (Ed.) (2005). *Black education: A transformative research and action agenda for the new century.* Mahwah, NJ: Lawrence Erlbaum Associates.

Kliebard, H. M. (2004). *The struggle for the American curriculum, 1893–1958.* New York: RoutledgeFalmer.

Ladson-Billings, G. & Tate, W. (1995). Toward a critical race theory of education. *Teachers College Record, 97*, 47–68.

Lynn, M. & Bridges III, T. (2009). Critical race studies in education and the "endarkened" wisdom of Carter G. Woodson. In L. C. Tillman (Ed.), *The SAGE handbook of African American Education* (pp. 339–351). Thousand Oaks, CA: SAGE Publications.

Mills, C. (2008). Reproduction and transformation of inequalities in schooling: The transformative potential of the theoretical constructs of Bourdieu. *British Journal of Sociology of Education, 29*(1), 79–89.

Mills, C. W. (1997). *The racial contract*. Ithaca, NY: Cornell University Press.

Mills, C. W. (1998). Revisionist ontologies: Theorizing White supremacy. In C. Mills (Ed.), *Blackness visible: Essays on philosophy and race*. Ithaca, NY: Cornell University Press.

Pinar, W. F., Reynolds, W. M., Slattery, P. & Taubman, P. M. (1995). *Understanding curriculum: An introduction to the study of historical and contemporary curriculum discourses*. New York: Peter Lang.

Popkewitz, T. (1999). Reviewing reviews: "RER," research, and the politics of educational knowledge. *Review of Educational Research, 69*(4), 397–405.

Outlaw, L. T. (2005[1944]). *Critical social theory in the interests of black folks*. Lanham, MD: Rowman & Littlefield.

Schomburg, A. (1992[1925]). The Negro digs up his past. In A. Locke (Ed.), *The new Negro: an interpretation* (pp. 231–237). New York: Arnon.

Taliaferro-Baszile, D. (2009). In Ellisonian eyes, what is curriculum theory? In E. Malewski (Ed.), *Curriculum studies handbook—the next moment* (pp. 483–495). New York and London: Routledge.

Watkins, W. (1993). Black curriculum orientations: A preliminary inquiry. *Harvard Educational Review, 63*(3), 321–338.

Watkins, W. (Ed.) (2006). *Black protest thought and education*. New York: Peter Lang.

1

BLACK INTELLECTUAL THOUGHT
A Cacophony of Experiences, Movements, and Ideas

> ... as Black men (and women) of learning emerged among the victims of slave systems and systems of colonial imperialism, they would feel impelled to use whatever intellectual tools they had to fight back against derogatory stereotypes and to assemble data for the elaborations of counter-ideologies to racism and anti-Negroism.
>
> (Drake & Cayton, 1970[1945], p. 2)

Ideas for academic books are born out of the belief that the text will contribute to a genre of knowledge and understanding and hopefully influence the way readers *read* the world (Freire, 1987). The purpose of *Black Intellectual Thought in Education* is to contribute to the African American scholarly movement toward personal and collective liberation, to put to rest the eighteenth- to twentieth-century legacy of the racist appraisals that "Blacks have no traditions, are bearers of an inferior culture" (Gates, 1987, p. 25) and are still struggling to prove their worth. *Black Intellectual Thought in Education* informs the education of American students, especially those who are Black and of color and it joins other works dedicated to the scholarly examination and transmission of accurate knowledge of the history, culture, and experiences of African American people. In addition, it joins and continues the struggle engraved on the British abolitionists' anti-slavery emblem: Am I Not a Man and a Brother [Am I Not a Women and a Sister]. Written in the tradition of "racial vindication" (Drake & Cayton, 1970[1945], p. 3), this volume is a counternarrative employing intellectual models that challenge the kinds of discourses that insisted on making African Americans sub-human and continues today to portray Blacks as less than Whites. Additionally, *Black Intellectual Thought in Education* argues that Blacks from the day they first arrived in colonial America were seeking physical and mental freedom as they continuously rebelled against enslavement initiating a legacy of active resistance that continues today. Over time, the persistent agency of African Americans took shape to develop into a body of knowledge concerned with the existential and material reality of being Black in America, as well as challenging ideas that consistently marginalized, silenced, and distorted the context of Black life. Arthur Schomburg's (1992[1925], p. 1) thoughts in *The Negro Digs up His Past* reflects this sentiment:

> The American Negro must remake his past in order to make his future. Though it is orthodox to think of America as the one country where it is unnecessary to have a past, what is a luxury for the nation as a whole becomes a prime social necessity for the Negro. For him, a group tradition must supply compensation for persecution, and pride of race the antidote for prejudice. History must restore what slavery took away, for it is the social damage of slavery that the present generations must repair and offset.

Black Intellectual Thought in Education supports Schomburg's thesis that African American history must be restored so it "digs up" that history. Schomburg (1992[1925]) argued that there are many incidents and milestones in Black people's lives, as well as movements that need to be "dug up" to illuminate African Americans' intellectual and cultural contributions to humankind. Schomburg's thesis also contends that U.S. history must address the wholeness of Black people's humanity, documenting their ongoing efforts of resistance and transformation in a world imbued in White supremacy. Out of the Black histories of resistance, scholars, activists, and theorists have developed what we refer to as "Black intellectual thought" concerning the condition of being Black in America. We define "Black intellectual thought" as timeless ideas, philosophies, and pedagogies that questioned, theorized, and addressed the long-standing issues of Black life (e.g., culture, experiences) in schools and society.

This chapter provides a brief history of Black intellectual thought; and while scholars typically outline Black ideological thought as a typology or approaches, we maintain that Black thought took form in two prominent ways. First, Black intellectual thought emerged out the individual agency of courageous and thoughtful individuals who used different genres to express the context of Black oppression and resistance. Second, we argue that Black intellectual thought evolved into distinct bodies of knowledge through various social, cultural, and political movements and Black people's reading of those movements. We further argue that the multitude of Black voices located in different spaces by choice, force, or condition also shaped what we now call *Black intellectual thought*.

In the section that follows, we discuss how different individuals expressed the context of racial oppression and resistance through memoirs, poems, textbook writing, and other means of recording history and public protest. Next we follow with how the Harlem Renaissance, Chicago Realism, and Civil Rights Movements informed the political discourse of Black social change. In the remainder of the chapter we address how Black intellectual thought in education evolved over time and led to the production of distinct bodies of thought that expressed the purpose and function of Black education.

Individuals: Speaking and Expressing Truth to Power

As we noted before, foundational to Black intellectual thought are the candid discourses and personal accounts of the conditions of race in America. We argue that out of experience African Americans within different times and spaces were able to provide a cogent analysis of the conditions of oppression and resistance. It was through the experiences of bondage, freedom, resistance, and racial terror that African American thought has taken form. It is through the documentation and presentation of experience that powerfully highlights the contexts that informed the individual and collective social realities of African Americans. In the following section, we briefly provide four accounts of different African Americans: Phillis Wheatley, Frederick Douglass, Mamie Carthan Till and James Pennington, that expressed the conditions of race.

Phillis Wheatley (1773), often recorded as the first African American to publish a book of poetry in the eighteenth century, exhibited Schomburg's thesis of "digging up one's past," when she fought back against the flawed statement about the intelligence of Blacks in her poem *On Being brought from Africa to America*, "Remember, Christians, Negroes, Black as Cain, May be refin'd, and join th' angelic train." Wheatley's poems identify enslavement, not (lack of) intelligence as the cause affecting the learning conditions of Blacks. Additionally, Wheatley confronted the social damage that was cast on Blacks' skin color by publicly calling-out how Whites viewed the skin color of other humans. She wrote, "Their colour is a diabolic die" (p. 42).

Frederick Douglass' life was also a model of Schomburg's request: a commitment to group tradition that supplies compensation for the absence of Black history that has been denied, distorted or made inaccurate, racial pride, and the push back from racist damage. In his autobiography, *Narrative of the Life of Frederick Douglass, an American Slave*, and the three revisions (1845, 1855, 1881, and 1892) Douglass is among the first Black people to establish the African American group tradition of constant activism to obtain liberty and establish one's personhood. Douglass' report on the horrors of enslavement called into question the mental and dispositional humanness of those who contend that Black people were not totally human and *Narrative* is one of America's early literary contributions that tells a universal story of a human being's never-ending desire and fight to be free of oppression. It also speaks to the peaceful and militant genres of protest literature. Douglass was not one to always turn the other cheek;

he had fist-fights with the Whites who enslaved him. Douglass exclaimed before one of his fistfights: "You have seen how a man was made a slave; you shall see how a slave was made a man" (pp. 65–66).

Mamie Carthan Till, the mother of Emmett Till, uniquely contributed to group tradition when she decided that the casket of her son, Emmett, should be open at his funeral. Mamie Till wanted the world to be able to view Emmett's body and see the viciousness of his murder and the legacy of enslavement active in the 1950s. The open casket showed America the brutality fostered on Black people that U.S. history claimed were stories from long ago. Mamie Till's actions were also those of racial pride. Her actions showed that the brutality committed against her son could not negate the beauty of the humanity of the Black man.

James Pennington, who escaped from enslavement, was called the "fugitive blacksmith." Pennington became the author of the first African American history book, *A Textbook of the Origin and History of the Colored People* and other writings. Pennington's narratives include the trials and tribulations of an enslaved Black man escaping to freedom. In one story, Pennington described one of the early forms of protest used by African Americans: disinformation.

> If you ask me if I expected when I left home to gain my liberty by fabrication and untruths? I answer, no! my parents, slaves as they were, had always taught me, when they could, that "truth may be blamed but cannot be shamed"; so far as their example was concerned, I had no habits of untruth. I was arrested, and the demand made upon me, "Who do you belong to?" knowing the fatal use these men would make of my truth, I at once concluded that they had no right to it than a highwayman has to a traveler's purse. …Whatever my readers may think, therefore, of the history of events of the day, do not admire in it the fabrications; but *see* in it the impediments that often fall into the pathway of the flying bondman. See how the human bloodhounds gratuitously chase, catch, and tempt him to shed blood, and lie; how, when he would do good, evil is thrust upon him.
>
> (1849, p. 87)

An account of an individual, as an agent against racism probably was Black people's earliest form of resistance, which developed into another form of resistance that must be "dug-up" in order to give further political, social, and historical context to the scholars we discuss.

In keeping with Schomburg's analogy of "digging up our past," each of the personal accounts illustrate a vantage point or standpoint with which to interpret the realities of African Americans. In each of the cases above, African American accounts of oppression highlight the individual and collective experience of Black life. Through Wheatley's and Douglass' accounts of race they set in place an oppositional discourse to the conditions of racism during their time. Whereas, Mamie Till's decision for an open casket powerfully demonstrated the context of race in America. The casket served as a pedagogical device to make real the graphic nature of racism in the South. Additionally, Pennington, like Woodson, used the genre of textbook writing to demonstrate the varied ways in which "digging up" African American histories was in large part a documentation of experience and a counter narrative to the ideologies of White racism that enveloped Black life. In each case however, experience helped to contextualize racial oppression at the level of everydayness (Holt, 1995). These personal accounts highlight the inclinations of courageous individuals to use different ways to give meaning to the climate of race and racism in the US.

Movements: Moving Toward a Collective Imagination

Social movements also shaped the discourse and philosophies of Black intellectual thought in the US. Whether political, social, or cultural, movements collectively spoke to the realities of African Americans. Through a variety of genres, different social and political movements provided a space to express the conditions of being Black in the US. In some cases, such expressions provided a space to describe Black life beyond the White gaze. Movements also allowed African Americans to deliberate over their social realities, while defining a course of action for social change. Consistent across African American social and cultural movements is the development of a discourse to define the constraints and possibilities of social change. Through social science, history, humanities, arts, and political discourse, movements helped instill new ways of imagining Blackness.

For example, the Harlem Renaissance—The New Negro Movement from the 1920s to the mid-1930s—moved forward by numerous Black men and women, including Charles S. Johnson, Alain Locke, W.E.B. Du Bois, Josephine Baker, Jessie Redmon Fauset, Zora Neale Hurston, and James Weldon Johnson was a literary, artistic, and intellectual campaign that demonstrated the African American group tradition of agency against racial oppression and Black pride through the development of a new Black cultural identity. In addition, the Movement was in part designed to turn the beauty of art and letters loved by both Blacks and Whites into a bridge of understanding between races (Katz, 1997); and to demonstrate that Black people had the knowledge, skills and disposition in every aspect and phase of life and human development equal to any other humans. David Levering Lewis (1995) also contends that the Harlem Renaissance was "a cultural nationalism of the parlor" (p. xvii) directed by Civil Rights leaders to improve race relations because of the backlash African Americans were receiving due to the economic gains they achieved working to support World War I. Whereas the Harlem Renaissance is a term that finds its way into formal and informal discussions, it is too often reduced or characterized as the "Cotton Club or a good time in Harlem" instead of as the literary, artistic, and intellectual movement it was.

Harlem, New York, was only one of the places where African Americans fought for their manhood and womanhood and to be acknowledged and accepted as human beings capable of doing all that any people of any race can do. In Philadelphia, in 1787, free Blacks established the Free African Society, the first independent Black organization and mutual society and in 1794 African Americans, Absalom Jones, and Richard Allen, respectively established the first independent Black churches to protest against segregated seating and the right to preach in a church they had helped to construct. The Chicago Urban Realism Project (late 1930s–early 1950s), led by Richard Wright and others, created a respected place (i.e., Bronzville) within a red line community in Chicago to demonstrate their agency against the White power structure that controlled the political, social, and economic life in the city and daily practiced White privilege. In addition, Wright and others pointed out that group tradition, racial pride, and pushback on the social damages done to Blacks would not be a copy of what took place during the New Negro Movement. Instead, through literature, novels, plays, and individual and group action, they would give a "faithful representation of reality" (Campbell, 2008) of Black people's struggle against horrendous odds to achieve mental and physical liberation.

In *12 Million Black Voices*, a book also about Black life in Chicago, Richard Wright (1941, p. xix) explained the "who"—everyday Black people—of the Chicago Urban Realism Project:

> This text, while purporting to render a broad picture of the process of Negro life in the United States, intentionally does not include in its consideration those areas of Negro life which comprise the so-called "talent tenth" […] This text assumes, that those few Negroes who have lifted themselves, through personal strength, *talent, or* luck, above the lives of their fellow Blacks – like a single fish that leap and flash for a split second above the surface of the sea – are but fleeing exceptions to the vast tragic school that swim below in the depths, against the current, silently and heavily, struggling against the waves of vicissitudes that spell a common fate. It is not, however, to celebrate or exalt the plight of the humble folks who swim in the depths that I select the conditions of their lives as examples of normality, but rather to seize upon that which is qualitative and abiding in Negro experience, to place within full and constant view the collective humanity whose triumphs and defeats are shared by the majority, whose gains in security mark an advance in the level of consciousness attained by the broad masses in their costly and tortuous upstream journey.

The realistic writings and other actions involving Black people in Chicago chronicled the agency—often little actions, sometimes big actions —of the everyday African Americans. These little actions generated big actions with the Civil Rights Movement of the 1960s.

The Civil Rights Movement of the 1960s is perhaps the greatest institutionalized and publicized effort on the part of Blacks and others to demonstrate racial pride, orchestrate varying strategies of resistance, and to demand a correction to the social damages of enslavement, Jim and Jane Crow, and segregation. Nonviolent protest and civil disobedience, by African Americans and others, led to numerous changes in society including several legislative changes at the federal level (Civil Rights Bill of 1964 and the Voting Rights Act of 1965) and some positive changes and increased sensitivities by White people toward people of color in public areas of society (e.g., restaurants, movie theaters, public drinking fountains). However, Civil Rights actions in the 1960s achieved only minimal gains in changing Whites' attitudes and behavior toward the opportunities for Blacks in the work place. The 1960s legislated Black people being able to enter and sit in the restaurant but did not help them to secure the employment to earn money to pay for the entre on the menu. Hiring policies and other means to exclude Blacks or keep them in low paying positions continued, except for "the single fish that leap and flash for a split second above the surface of the sea" (Wright, 1941, page xx).

The Kerner Commission Report (1968), the document produced by President Johnson's 11-member National Advisory Commission on Civil Disorder established in July 1967 to explain the more than 150 rebellions that plagued many cities in the US between 1965 and 1968, concluded that the nation was "moving toward two societies, one Black, one White—separate and unequal" and that unless conditions were remedied, the country faced a "system of apartheid" in its major cities. The Kerner report indicted "White society" for isolating and neglecting African Americans and urged legislation to promote racial integration and to enrich slums primarily through the creation of jobs, job training programs, and decent housing. President Johnson, however, was cool to the recommendations because the Vietnam War had become a huge expense, making it difficult to establish new social programs. He was also annoyed that the rebellions in the cities were taking place during the time of the passage of the Civil Rights Act of 1964 and the Voting Rights Act of 1965 (Pach, 1968). In April 1968, one month after the release of the Kerner report, rioting broke out in more than 100 cities following the assassination of Civil Rights leader, Martin Luther King, Jr.

In 2008, on the fortieth anniversary of the *Kerner Commission Report*, several media sources and foundations released an anniversary assessment. *Newswatch*'s Lerner (2008) stated, "Still separate and unequal 40 years after Kerner" and the Milton S. Eisenhower Foundation reported "America earns a D+ in progress on race, poverty, crime and inequality. Nowhere is that failing grade more evident than in the status of minority youth" (2008, p. 2). Allie Bidwell (2015) explained the status: "Nationwide, millions of young people are in a state of limbo, neither working nor in school" (p. 1).

While the Civil Rights struggle continues, deep gratitude is graciously and duly noted for the past achievements and for the opportunities now available because of the commitment and dedication of individuals and movements. Their legacies inspire the continuation of social justice work for the privilege of each and every Black person to be able to be themselves, have a legitimate opportunity for a good life, and to escape from the racist ideology and actions of the past and participate in developing new ideas for the present and future. The momentum of this time also helped to galvanize a new vocabulary about the significance of an equitable education.

Movements and Black Intellectual Thought

Through most of the twentieth century, movements provided a vital role in shaping Black intellectual thought. Social and political movements carved out a space for expression of ideas. The context of Jim and Jane Crow and institutional racism blocked African Americans from having access to publishers willing to let African Americans' ideas and perspectives flourish. However, social movements such as Harlem Renaissance and Chicago Realism allowed Blacks to use different genres of art, speech, and the written word to give meaning and vindication to Black life and histories. The kind of local and self-contained ideas helped to produce what Dawson (2001) calls a counter public space, where African Americans were able to speak candidly to their concerns. By the 1960s however, when this form of expression was no longer insular within Black communities such as in Harlem and Chicago, African Americans' discontent and desire to be included in the American dream was expressed through their bodies: marching, boycotting, sitting in, and sometimes rioting as a form of protest. In addition, with television in homes of many Americans in the 1960s, observing the marches and protests, the racist story had to change. The advent of television changed the story line and by this point African American discontent with the White world had gone mainstream. This in turn played a significant role in how Black intellectual thought took form throughout the post-Civil Rights Era.

Ideology: The Framing of Black Intellectual Thought

From the moment Africans were enslaved and forced to sail in chains across the Atlantic, an ideology of resistance took shape. The histories of slave mutinies indicate that Africans were trying to find a way to get back to Africa and freedom. In addition, in 1619, when the first cargo of Africans arrived in the British colony of the "New World," discourses of refusal took form: through memoirs, poetry, speeches, letters, sermons, songs, and dance and rebellion. Out of the many voices came a single call—the humanization of Black life and freedom.

The contours of Black intellectual thought in education have emerged from the multiple ways African Americans have historically thought about and responded to different socio-historical contexts (i.e., Slavery, Jim Crow, lynching, segregation) facing them as a group (Dawson, 2001; Glaude, 2000; Harding, 1990; Marable & Mullings, 2000; Watkins, 1993), the control and influence of White Americans, notwithstanding. From abolitionists conventions in the 1800s

(Mabee, 1979) to the present (King, 2005; Watkins, 2006) African Americans have consistently debated, discussed, critiqued, organized, and problem-solved with viable strategies to achieve social justice through education. Dawson (2001) defines the ideas and discourses that inform African American political and educational thought and action as *Black visions*. Black visions according to Dawson (2001) are philosophies that help define the social realities (e.g., enslavement, segregation) of African Americans while also mapping a course of action (e.g., boycott, civil disobedience, separation) for social change.

In this section, we first lay out the historical trajectory of ideologies that inform educational thought for African Americans, keeping in mind that any analysis of Black thought or ideology must consider the historical contexts that inform such discourse (Dawson, 2001; Glaude, 2000). Next, we discuss some of the earliest debates and tensions found in the late nineteenth and early twentieth century (e.g., industrial-liberal arts education debates). Our attention then shifts to the early 1900s when African Americans continued to debate and discuss the problems and possibilities of Black education. Finally, we discuss how out of the differing ideas of Black education, four distinct and differing orientations of thought were formulated.

Black Intellectual Thought: A Brief History

Embedded within Black education visions are specific temporal, political, and historical contexts that make possible the shaping of ideas. Within these contexts are historical and contemporary perspectives of Black educational thought that provide: (a) an understanding of African Americans' enduring intellectual and political responses to achieve social justice through education; and (b) an understanding of the ideological tensions embedded in theories about Black education.

Early Conceptions of Black Ideology: Race Uplift and the Germination of Black Thought

After Reconstruction there was a strong desire for African Americans to seek universal education, particularly in literacy (Anderson, 1988). The belief was that if African Americans were to learn how to read and write they could become self-reliant. An ideology of self-help and racial uplift guided this pursuit for education. *Racial uplift*, an ideology for social change, emerged out of the Black church (Gaines, 1996). Beauboeuf-Lafontant (1999) argues that racial uplift developed from African and Christian theological notions of the individual being connected to the collective along with the assertion that the individual (i.e., Black Americans) had a moral and spiritual responsibility to serve the race. Within this context, African American educators were exhorted to help their race by providing the social and academic tools needed to serve the people. However, despite the common goals of *racial uplift*, educators, scholars, and activists deployed different and competing approaches for "uplifting the race." Some of the more prominent racial uplift philosophies came from the following scholars and activists whose work was situated within the early twentieth century debates: Booker T. Washington, W.E.B Du Bois, Nannie H. Burroughs, and Fannie Jackson Coppin.

The Washington/Du Bois Debates: An Enduring Ideological Struggle

The most prominent voice of *racial uplift* in the late nineteenth century was the educator Booker T. Washington. In 1881, Washington started his illustrious tenure as the president of the Tuskegee Institute in Alabama, where he immediately implemented his philosophies of self-help (Dunn, 1993). Washington's education philosophy, also called the *Tuskegee model*, emphasized economic self-reliance agricultural and vocational training and development. His emphasis was on industrial, or what he called "hand training," which was premised on the idea that through doing and experience African Americans would gain the ability to become self-reliant and independent. He believed that African Americans could develop a strong economic base through the acquisition of practical skills (Dunn, 1993).

Washington's education vision asserted that Black people must learn through experience and develop tools (e.g., vocational and industrial trades) that would solve their own problems (Dunn, 1993; Gyant, 1988). He rejected education that was too theoretical, arguing that such education would not serve the difficulties associated with Black progress (Washington, 2000[1901], 1904). He advocated that Black people should be patient and in time they would earn their place next to White people.

From his education vision, he saw the role of the teacher as a model or example of how to properly train the African American masses to achieve the goal of self-reliance. Washington (1896, p. 2) wrote:

> The seven millions of colored people of the South cannot be reached directly by any missionary agency, but they can be reached by sending out among them strong selected young men and women, with the proper training of head, hand, and heart, who will live among these masses and show them how to lift themselves up. The problem that the Tuskegee Institute keeps before itself constantly is how to prepare these leaders.

For Washington (1896), teaching was an act of guiding and modeling proper training, as well as an opportunity for students to actively engage in the skills to foster self-reliance.

While few scholars and educators were in disagreement with the ideas of *self-reliance* and *self-sufficiency*, many diverged ideologically about the kind of education necessary to achieve such goals, as well as what the ideas of *self-reliance and self-sufficiency* meant to the larger political goals for *uplifting the race*. For example, during the early twentieth century, several notable educators, activists, and scholars discussed the limitations to Washington's program. Starting in the late nineteenth century and early twentieth century, scholars began to question the merits of vocational-based education approaches, arguing that education had to serve a greater purpose beyond vocational training. These scholars suggested that education must consider the social and political implications of Black education.

Clearly one of the strongest voices of opposition to Washington's vision was W.E.B. Du Bois. In 1902, in the *Atlantic Monthly* article "Of the Training of Black Men," later published in the *Souls of Black Folk*, Du Bois (1902) questioned the merits of industrial education and Washington's philosophy of education. Du Bois, like Washington, found that the legacy of enslavement assisted in the development of negative habits and behaviors that impeded the progress of Black people.

For Du Bois (1902), the condition of Black people caused by enslavement required a particular orientation to learning to assist in their progress. He acknowledged that the vocational and industrial education system had been quite successful at educating thousands of African Americans to become literate, well-trained, resourceful and thoughtful individuals. He stated, "To-day it is proved by the fact that four hundred Negroes, many of whom have been reported as brilliant students, have received the bachelor's degree from Harvard, Yale, Oberlin, and seventy other leading colleges." He further stated with regard to the graduates of these institutions, "nowhere have I met men and women with a broader spirit of helpfulness, with deeper devotion to their life work" (Du Bois, 1902, p. 7).

Du Bois (1902) asserted that beyond practical concerns, education must facilitate and develop individuals who will agitate the existing social order. Although he argued that the existing education institutions were successful at educating thoughtful and ambitious African Americans, he found many of them to be ideologically conservative leaders who did not assertively address African American racial injustice. To address this lack of racial consciousness, Du Bois (1902) proposed an education for African Americans that advanced political and racial progress. This idea would lay the foundation of his concept of the "Talented Tenth," which was the philosophy that approximately one-tenth of the Black population should attend elite colleges and would be "entrusted to return to African American communities to educate the masses of their race and ultimately lead the Negro out of economic, political, and social bondage" (Du Bois, 1902, pp. 29–30). In this context, Du Bois envisioned the college-educated African American teacher as a central purveyor of cultural, moral, political, and social knowledge necessary to elevate other Black Americans to challenge Jim Crow politics and White supremacy (Alridge, 1999). Du Bois' education vision for social justice expanded the conceptual meaning of Black education to include challenges to the existing social order. Other educators and scholars also helped to expand the definition and purpose of Black education during this period, calling attention to the conceptual limitations of vocational and industrial education programs.

Beyond Du Bois and Washington: Nannie H. Burroughs and Fanny Jackson Coppin

The contours of Black educational thought were not just the domain of Black men; numerous African American women provided important and often overlooked perspectives about curriculum, pedagogy, and teacher education. Two scholars and educators in particular that added to the Washington–Du Bois debates were Nannie H. Burroughs and Fanny Jackson Coppin.

Educator Nannie H. Burroughs offered a slightly different critique to industrial education, arguing that the "industrial mold" of education narrowly defined the capacity of African American talent. In 1903 in the article "Industrial education—Will it Solve the Negro Problem?" Burroughs commented on the assumptions and limitations of industrial education. This quote reflects her general sentiment:

> By industrial education I take it that you mean the development of that part of the mental and physical man that will respond to all or some special phase of manual labor. Industrial education will solve but one phase of the problem, and the Negro must have all phases of the problem solved in order to secure the key to the situation.
>
> (Burroughs, 1903, p. 188)

Burroughs (1903) believed that, before one could assume that industrial education would solve the "Negro problem," one must examine whether the Black mind, taste, feelings, habits, and interest were "naturally" adapted to a particular type of learning. She questioned the idea of whether African Americans were predisposed to *only* learn through manual labor. Burroughs (1903) found that the underlying assumption of industrial education was that African Americans lacked the mental capacity to learn beyond the "field of labor" (p. 188). Her central argument was that nothing about the Black community should confine them to the "industrial mould" (p. 188) of learning. Burroughs (1903, p. 188) stated:

> It has never been shown that the Negro's mental power must be cast in an industrial mould in order to fully respond to the biddings of his mind and the pleadings of his heart; nor have we evidence to show that the Negro makes a better citizen and a better man with an industrial education than with any other kind; nor has the Negro any evidence that an industrial education will secure for him an even brake in the race of life.

Burroughs challenged educators to consider the full capacity of African Americans. For Burroughs (1903), any "specific course of study" (p. 188) that narrowly trained them for one profession or trade would not solve the problems facing the Black race. She called for a redirection of Black education that considered the varied and individual inclinations, tastes, and feelings of the Black student. In a similar vein, Fannie Jackson Coppin conveyed an education program beyond the industrial mold.

Fanny Jackson Coppin was a strong advocate for developing Black citizens that would give back through her motto of "heed life's demands." Perkins (1982) states, "These demands included developing competence in skilled trades, teacher training, and the professions, as well as establishing independent Black businesses, newspapers and banks" (p. 188). Her education ideology focused on the psychological aspects of "consciousness," which for her was an understanding of the motivation and desire one possesses to learn and develop. She further suggested that such an education must be in coordination with a classical education. On this point, Jackson Coppin (1976 [1913], p. 316) stated:

> Our idea of getting an education did not come out of wanting to imitate any one whatever. It grew out of the uneasiness and the restlessness of the desires we felt within us; the desire to know, not just a little, but a great deal. We wanted to know how to calculate an eclipse, to know what Hesiod and Livy thought; we wished to know the best thoughts of the best minds that lived with us; not merely to gain an honest livelihood, but from a God-given love of all that is beautiful and best, and because we thought we could do it.

From this education vision, Jackson Coppin believed that African Americans called to uplift the race must possess: 1) personal power and ability to aid themselves; 2) intellectual and practical knowledge; and 3) the commitment and desire to give back to the race (Perkins, 1982). In her book *Reminiscences of School Life, and Hints on Teaching* Jackson Coppin argued that the Black teacher must have the capacity to instill a strong sense of self worth in African Americans that "effectively silences all slanders such as 'we won't or we can't do,' and teaches its own instructive and greatly needed lessons of self help" (Jackson Coppin, 1976[1913], p. 314). Jackson Coppin's (1976[1913]) education vision for social justice emphasized that African Americans possess practical knowledge and responsibility to the race, providing a conceptual balance between industrial and classical models of education. While much of the debates about Black education during this period either talked about industrial or classical models of education, Jackson Coppin's vision of African American education insisted that each model work in coordination to *uplift the race*.

Early Black Thought in Summary: A Different Kind of Social Gospel

Although the discourses about the improvement of African American education were an internal discussion among Africans Americans, the ideas that shaped Black education thought were clearly enveloped in the intellectual discourse of the progressive era. In particular, during the late nineteenth century, it was quite common to hear American scholars talk about the efforts to create a "perfect" union, what scholars refer to as *American Perfectionism*. Historian Wilson Moses (1998) defines *American Perfectionism as*, "a belief that the Christian must perform responsible civic duties in order to create a 'righteous empire' in the United States" (p. 138). By the late nineteenth century these ideas evolved into a doctrine called the "Social Gospel," which meant that individuals who were rendered as the privileged class would help to educate those less privileged to become citizens of the American body politic. In a similar fashion, African Americans supported a Social Gospel that employed Christian doctrine that would work to solve the social problems of the African American race. For example, for most of the late nineteenth century and the early twentieth debates about the education of the "Negro" focused on the most viable strategies for "making" a class of individuals that would possess qualities such as morality, hard work, cleanliness, and self-restraint. The debates among African American scholars and activists during this period were how to best achieve such goals.

Examining the philosophies of Black education from the late 1800s to the 1950s provides a sense of the varied contours of *Black intellectual thought* that took shape during each period. While there are clear commonalties, each scholar and educator provided nuanced perspectives about Black education. In the earlier period, from the 1800s to the 1930s, the common theme that surfaced within this literature was the central belief that the African American race was capable of learning and developing at the same pace as White Americans. In addition, scholars argued that education and the role of the Black teacher were the most salient aspects to the progress for the African American race. A central ideological debate across these writings was the dichotomy of mind and body or the debate of "head and hand." These discussions of "head" and "hand" focused on whether education for Black Americans should privilege academic skills that would develop the mind or whether practical needs of labor should be the central premise of Black education. During the early 1900s, Black scholars and activists critiqued industrial education and the merits of Booker T. Washington's vision, arguing that an education that only focused on the practical aspects of learning placed artificial limitations around the capacity of the African American student. Again, as this section illustrates, while there existed several arguments for how to best educate the African Americans, these debates coalesced around existing Progressive ideas of this period.

Early Twentieth Century Black Intellectual Thought

From the early 1930s through the 1950s, a number of African American scholars had called for the redirection of Black education (Woodson, 2000[1933]; Bond, 1934; Bunche, 1936). For example in 1936, the *Journal of Negro Education* issued a special volume titled *The Reorganization and Redirection of Negro Education*, in which several scholars grappled with questions about whether Black education should serve a general task of helping African Americans function within a U.S. context or whether there were cultural and social questions that must be of concern (Bunche, 1936; Holmes, 1936; Judd, 1936). In addition, each of these scholars provided critical and oftentimes unrecognized intellectual frameworks for conceptualizing contemporary questions about the "state" of Black education and the role of the Black teacher. We should note that these new ideas for conceptualizing Black education underscore the changing contours of *Black educational thought* and social justice that emerged during this period. Notable Black intellectuals began to explore how *culture, race, curriculum, pedagogy,* and *knowledge* informed the education context of African American students. The ideas of African American intellectuals such as Anna Julia Cooper, Carter G. Woodson, W.E.B. Du Bois, Ambrose Caliver, and Alain Locke highlight the important historical and intellectual foundations to contemporary concerns in Black education about issues of culture and racial identity.

From the 1930s to the 1950s, scholars continued to challenge the merits of industrial or more pragmatic-based education programs for African Americans. These challenges gave greater attention to aspects of curriculum, pedagogy, and culture. Woodson (2000[1933]) was one of the first to argue for a culturally specific curriculum that considered the traditions and contributions of Africans and African Americans. (See Chapter 2 for Cooper's contributions.) Woodson (2000[1933]), like Du Bois (1902), argued that previous education programs had been successful at "educating" thousands of African Americans, but did not adequately "educate" them for the social and political challenges African Americans faced. He described this type of education as "mis-education," which he referred to as an education that only served the needs of the individual and did not promote collective racial consciousness. Several other scholars made similar critiques suggesting that education must fulfill a political and social mission of change (Cooper, 1998[1930], Jackson Coppin, 1976, Johnson, 1940). In addition, scholars from this time found that education must serve a psychological capacity to "heal" or reconstruct damaged self-images from the ills of racism. However, some scholars argued that education should not only focus on the kind of knowledge one acquires, but on the way knowledge becomes integrated and conceptualized (Johnson, 1936; Locke, 1989[1950]). Johnson (1940) asserted that the African American child needed to acquire critical skills that could be transferred to any economic or social space. Locke (1989[1950]) was also concerned with knowledge acquisition, arguing that education must enable students to discern factual information as historically situated and culturally specific, rather than as fixed or possessing universal meaning.

During the first half of the twentieth century, no singular narrative, philosophy, discourse, or practice solely defined African Americans' efforts to achieve social justice through education. African American goals and discourses coalesced around similar and existing Progressive discussions about how to "educate" individuals to become active members of society. However, the source of tension and debate among African American scholars and activists from the late- to the mid-nineteenth-century was about how to achieve such goals and how the "educated" African American would contribute to these efforts. What is significant about these historical discourses is the plurality of ideas and strategies that come together for one goal: to improve the education and social status of African Americans.

Scholars of African American political thought maintain that although African Americans have historically shared common problems (e.g., enslavement, Jim Crow, segregation) they have employed different approaches to make sense of and respond to different historical tensions (Dawson, 2001; Glaude, 2000). Political scientist Michael Dawson (2001) maintains that the historical conditions of racism framed, and continue to frame, a distinct body of Black political thought that guides contemporary orientations to African American social justice. In the section that follows, we show how these burgeoning ideas took form into a distinct body of thought, what scholars refer to as Black ideologies or, in the case of education, Black educational thought.

Ideological Orientations of Thought in Black Education

Four African American *ideologies* (e.g., Black liberalism, Black Nationalism, Critical theory, and functionalism) have framed contemporary Black education theories. Each theory considers the socio-historical realities of African Americans and the strategies employed to address different political and education concerns. These theories provide an understanding of the common and competing education visions for Black freedom, self-determination, and "social justice."

Radical egalitarianism is one of the ideological lenses used by some African American educators to conceptualize and respond to the education needs of Black people.[1] According to Dawson (2001), some of the features of *radical egalitarianism* include: (1) "a severe critique of racism in American society" (p. 15); (2) participate in cross-cultural political alliances; (3) "active pressuring of the state to achieve Black justice" (p. 16); (4) "support for a strong central state that promotes equality combined with a respect for individual and self reliance" (p. 17). *Radical egalitarianism* draws from various discourses such as *equity, equality, democracy*, and *pluralism* to inform practices of social and education change. Dawson (2001) further notes that "This ideology [radical egalitarianism] is typified by the coupling of a severe critique of racism in American society, an impassioned appeal for America to live up to the best of its values, and support for a radical egalitarian view of a multicultural democratic society" (p. 16).

In education, radical egalitarianism provide a severe critique to racist policies and practices (Grant, 1988) and it argues that the perspectives and ideas from various ethnic groups need to be included (Banks & Banks, 1997; Gordon, 1999). Some of the earliest instantiations of multicultural education employed this approach. For example, aside from drawing attention to the material and education inequalities facing African Americans, radical egalitarism asserts that curriculum should include the cultural and historical experiences of African Americans and other historically marginalized groups (Banks, 2004; Gay, 2004; Gordon, 1999). By deploying democratic discourses such as *equality*, *equity*, and *pluralism*, multicultural educators challenged the state to extend education and social opportunities to African American children that had been excluded from the American political sphere.[2] Radical egalitarianism also leveled one of the strongest critiques against White liberal assumptions about Black culture and capacity, in that multicultural educationalists shifted the deficit discussion of the Black family to the deficit-orientated practices of schools and teachers.

Several scholars offered new and different theories for understanding how particular belief systems informed teachers' perceptions and expectations of African American students (Banks & Grambs, 1972; Gay, 1975; Grant, 1979). These scholars argued that teachers' perceptions and expectations of African American students had a huge bearing on academic outcomes (Abrahams & Gay, 1972; Banks & Grambs, 1972; Grant, 1979). In addition, attention was directed to schools' and teachers' cultural misconceptions of African American children's communication patterns. Abrahams and Gay (1972), for example, found that pathological conceptions of Black English often led to cultural conflicts in the classroom. These scholars focused on the cultural assets of Black English and how teachers can access this discourse to enhance their pedagogical practices. Banks and Grambs (1972) asserted that *White racism* had profoundly influenced African American students' self-concept. For Banks and Grambs, self-concept was defined as how one understands oneself in relation to "significant others." Grant (1979) argued that previous studies only saw socialization as a process of "socializing" the student, without any recognition of how teachers are socialized within a classroom context. He suggested that in order for schools to better serve students of color, they must understand the "reciprocal nature of socialization," meaning that teachers must better understand how their beliefs about students frame and undermine the learning environment for students of color. Thus, a defining ideological feature of a *radical egalitarianism* is to maintain a profound optimism that through intensely redressing the state and schools for equal opportunities, African American students will gain greater access to equitable educational opportunities. In summary, at the core of radical egalitarianism in education is a severe critique of the manner in which institutions reproduce inequitable outcomes. It directs the attention away from the so-called deficits of Black families. This is an important feature because in other Black ideological traditions there is a more cynical outlook to the possibilities of African Americans ever gaining equitable opportunities in a U.S. context.

Black Nationalism, for example, holds a more cynical outlook. It takes the position that African Americans can only solve their problems through the creation of self-reliant institutions and communities (Bush, 1999; Dawson, 2001; Ture & Hamilton, 1992[1967]). Black Nationalism is one of the oldest ideologies for African American social justice (Shelby, 2005). While within the Black Nationalist orientation there are varied conceptions of social justice, there are a few stable principles.[3] Philosopher Tommie Shelby (2005, p. 24) argues:

> Black nationalists advocate such things as Black self-determination, racial solidarity, and group self reliance, various forms of voluntary racial separation, pride in historic achievements of persons of African descent, a concerted effort to overcome racial self-hate and to instill Black self-love [...], the development and preservation of a distinctive Black cultural identity, and the recognition of Africa as the true homeland of those who are racially Black.

In education, *Black Nationalist orientations* that draw from such principles argue that in order for African American children to receive an equitable education, the curriculum and instruction must squarely center on the historical and cultural experiences of African and African diasporic cultural forms and histories (Asante, 1991; Murrell, 2002; Harris, 1992; Hilliard, 1995, 1997). A central philosophical principle of this approach is that education must serve to foster solidarity and racial connectedness between *all* people of African descent (Asante, 1988, 1991; Karenga, 1991; King, 2005). The Afrocentric and African-centered approaches draw from this ideological orientation. For example, Afrocentric scholar Molefi Asante (1991) states, "The Afrocentric approach seeks in every situation the appropriate centrality of the African person. In education this means that teachers provide students the opportunity to study the world and its people, concepts, and history from an African world view" (p. 171).

In this way, educators deploy racial discourses such as *we-ness, community, connectedness,* and *peoplehood* to help foster African American racial solidarity (Dei, 1994; Lee, Lomotey, & Shujaa, 1990; Shelby, 2005). Such nationalist discourse is present within many contemporary Black education theories, including Black feminist and culturally responsive pedagogies (Foster, 1997; Joseph, 1995; King, 2005). From these discourses, Black nationalists have forged an orientation of thought skeptical of liberalist strategies, maintaining that "social justice" is not defined nor measured by African Americans' "inclusion" in an American democracy, but by their ability to create self-sufficient social and education systems and systems of thought that are independent of White-dominated social structures and epistemologies (see Ani, 1994).

Other approaches to Black education draw from *critical theory* in order to provide a more thorough examination of how structures of race, class, and gender shape the education experiences of African American students (B. Gordon, 1997; McCarthy; 1988; Ladson-Billings & Tate, 1995; Watkins, 2006). A central premise of critical theory is to examine how human behavior interacts between the individual and various structures of society (Marcuse, 1964). Early critical theorists from the Frankfurt school were concerned with how capitalism functions to homogenize public opinion and privilege class interests (McLaren, 2003). However, since then, a number of education theorists have expanded its use to explore how structures of race and class interact to reproduce inequitable power relations in various sites, such as schools (Apple & Weiss, 1983; Bowles & Gintis, 1976; McCarthy, 1988).

In education, those concerned with how various structural factors (e.g., class stratification, racial inequalities, and gender oppression) influence Black education draw from different critical frameworks to expose patterns of race, class, and gender oppression in schools (Ball, 2000; Gordon, 1997; Henry, 2006; Ladson-Billings & Tate, 1995; Watkins, 2006). For example, Cameron McCarthy (1988) argues that any effort to understand the experiences of Black youth must account for the complex ways power relations reproduce varied expressions of racial oppression or what he refers to as "non-synchrony." These conceptions of power are also squarely defined within the social reconstructionists (Sleeter & Grant, 1987) and critical strands of multicultural education (see Gay, 2004). This approach to multicultural education conceptualizes the concerns of curriculum and pedagogy for African American children as imbued within intersecting relations of power and domination. In addition, this strand of multicultural education challenges majoritarian narratives found in school curriculum that silence the histories of African Americans or promote an ideology of American exceptionalism (Grant, 1995, 2011; Sizemore, 1990; King, 1992).

William Watkins (2006) maintained that African American education must reclaim and deploy Marxist political thought in order to make sense of class-based social injustices. He claims that common orientations to African American education thought rely too much on cultural theories (e.g., Black cultural nationalism) that do not take into account how African Americans' education experiences are tied to the "expropriation of labor and property ownership" (Watkins, 2006, p. 131). A more recent use of critical theory in education comes from the framework of *critical race theory*. Critical race theorists in education assert that the concept of "race" has been under-theorized in education, thus silencing the implicit and explicit patterns of racism and racial oppression that shape the inequitable education experiences of African American students (Ladson-Billings & Tate, 1995; Parker & Lynn, 2002). Ladson-Billings and Tate (1995) argue that race and racism is institutional, structured, and "deeply ingrained in American life" (p. 55) and in American public schools. Contrary to some multicultural conceptions of Black education, critical race theorists have little faith in liberalist education strategies that focus on prejudice reduction and cultural difference as a way to challenge institutionally engrained racial injustices (Ladson-Billings & Tate, 1995).

Another critical approach to Black education is apparent in the work of *Black feminist* theory. Drawing from Afrocentric and feminist ideology, "[b]lack feminist pedagogy is designed to raise the political consciousness of students by introducing a worldview with an Afrocentric orientation to reality, and the inclusion of gender and patriarchy as central to understanding of all historical phenomenon" (Joseph, 1995, p. 465). Black feminist educators contend that education must help in the effort to understand the multiple forms of raced, classed, and gendered oppressions that Black women and girls face (Dixson, 2003; Evans-Winters, 2005; Henry, 2006; Joseph, 1995). In addition, Black education feminists call for new ways for schools and students to construct and conceptualize knowledge. Gloria Joseph (1995) argues that the following four tenets guide a Black feminist pedagogy: (1) the use of dialogue in assessing knowledge claims; (2) the centrality of personal expressiveness; (3) the ethic of personal accountability; and (4) the use of concrete experience as a criterion of meaning. While the Black feminists draw from common African American discourses of liberation and social change, this framework elaborates on how concepts such as *patriarchy* and *sexism* interact with race and gender to frame the experiences of African American students.

While critical theory in Black education and political thought has employed several theories for addressing the socio-historical realities of African Americans, common across this approach is the use of political discourse skeptical of the possibilities of gaining access to equal opportunities within a context defined by various constructions of "race," class, and gender oppression. Therefore, aside, from changing and challenging different inequities, "social justice" within this framework also involves a complete restructuring of thought, governmentality, and power relations.

Some approaches have taken a more *pragmatic* orientation to Black education. From this approach, educators attempt to provide education and social practices that will enable Black children to function within U.S. society. The pedagogical vision of educator Marva Collins exemplifies this approach. Collins' education philosophy, unlike multicultural, critical, or nationalist perspectives, argues that education must provide African American children with education and social knowledge that will allow them to "properly" function in society (Collins & Tamarkin, 1982). Lisa Delpit (1995) similarly describes such functional knowledge as the culture of power or codes of rules. Within this orientation of Black education, beliefs are held that standard codes of knowledge, conduct, human interaction, and speech will enable Black students to function and succeed as U.S. citizens. This educational vision assumes that social justice occurs through African Americans' ability to master the normative technical and linguistic codes of the culture—or, as the phrase goes, "equity and excellence." In addition, this framework assumes that attention be given to practical concerns about how society is structured, as a way to consider questions of how it "ought to be." It is important to note that while indeed some aspects of nationalism and multicultural education deploy aspects of pragmatism, these orientations tend to see education as a way to challenge, rather than sustain, existing paradigms of knowledge, identity construction, and power relations.

Black Ideology in Summary

When looking across the different approaches to Black education, there certainly is a large degree of overlap. While the questions and concerns that educators have for the future of Black education are quite similar, with a common focus on education as a vehicle for social change, a closer examination offers a more complex rendering of how these discourses converge and diverge ideologically. Fundamentally, Black ideology is a way to think about and act on "common conditions" facing African Americans.

Thus to understand the discourse taken to social justice in Black education one must account for the local and historical contexts that inform their use. In other words, ideologies changed in the contexts of differing historical circumstances and the infusion of nouveau language of theory. For example, the early multiculturalist vision took form within a changing world called to desegregate schools (Grant, 1990). The urgency around integration of Black children in White settings called on multicultural educators to not only pressure the State to include the curriculum, language, and pedagogies for African American students, but to offer practical solutions to mounting racial tensions in schools (Banks, 1992). So, as ideas and politics shifted, a new discourse entered the lexicon of Black educational thought that provided a new vocabulary and sometimes a new analysis to long-standing questions of Black education.

These ideologies in some cases however, can be traced to some of the earliest conversations about Black education. Consistently across time are questions such as: Who should teach Black children? What kind of curriculum should Blacks receive? What kind of school should Black children attend? Also consistent across each of the ideologies outlined, is an impassioned commitment to justice and equity, even though the discourse used to explain each vision differs. Therefore, even despite the varied discourse of Black educational thought, consistent across each approach is that vital to Black freedom is the rethinking and reforming of education.

Black Intellectual Thought in Closing

For centuries, African American educators and scholars have debated over the purpose and type of education needed to improve the socio-historical realities of African Americans (King & Lightfoote-Wilson, 1990; King, 2005; Mabee, 1979; Perlstein, 2002; Watkins, 1993; Perry, Steele, & Hilliard, 2003; Washington, 2000[1901]). For example, while during the late nineteenth and early twentieth century there was relative consensus among African American scholars and activists that education was the most viable solution to "uplift the race," perspectives on how to best educate African Americans varied across ideological, cultural, and pedagogical lines (Boxill, 1984; Broderick & Meier, 1965; Dawson, 2001; Watkins, 1993, 2006; Woodson, 2000[1933]). During this period, several scholars debated the merits of providing a classical or industrial model for educating African Americans. This debate persisted through most of the early twentieth century, with enduring concerns over the quality and type of education African Americans should receive. Aside from concerns about curriculum, teaching resources, and teacher training, many educators were concerned with the ideological and political outcomes of receiving a particular type of education. For instance, should education only serve to meet the practical needs of African Americans or should it also help to educate African Americans to agitate the racial and political status quo in the US? Indeed, this question has persisted within contemporary discussions about the education of African Americans. For example, the Civil Rights Movement in the 1950s and 1960s marked a key historical period for African Americans to re-think the purpose of education for African Americans (Clark, 1965; Lewis, 1972). With the passing of the landmark case, *Brown v. Board*, and continued efforts to achieve social and political change through the 1960s, Civil Rights activists and educators called for new ways of thinking about the education of African Americans (Clark, 1965; Lewis, 1972; Wright, 1970). While there was agreement over the importance of education, there were key ideological differences with respect to how education should proceed. For example, while a number of African American activists had pushed for the integration of public schooling (Clark, 1965; Wilkerson, 1965; Willie, 1965), other activists drew from Black nationalists' orientations that called for the creation of separate schooling apart from the mainstream public school systems (Campbell, 1970; Ture & Hamilton, 1992[1967]). These tensions embody the different ways African Americans have historically conceptualized their socio-political realities and the different strategies deployed to achieve social and political change. From these tensions emerged a distinct ideological discourse in which African Americans have deployed to publicly express and respond to the collective concerns of a Black nation.

Black Intellectual Thought and the Black Intellectual

Emerging out of the multivocality of Black thought, some scholars' ideas seem to stand out or speak clearly and boldly to the conditions of race in ways that draw us back to their work. Some have argued that W.E.B. Du Bois' ideas have stirred this kind of allurement. In some cases, it is the way their ideas poetically describe and encapsulate the collective concerns of African Americans. In some instances, it was the ability of scholars to produce alternative curriculum and pedagogies, highlighting the intellectual agency of this time.

As we have noted in the Introduction however, this kind of attention to specific African American thought has received only limited attention. African Americans' ideas and body of work receive little special attention in journals and from book publishers. Organizations such as the American Educational Research Association (AERA) have no special interest groups committed to their scholarship. There are no dedicated websites or blogs committed to these ideas or body of work. African Amercans' work receives limited citations and few major universities offer courses that value the curricular and pedagogical contributions of their work. Without having access to all the curriculum meetings, academic journals, conferences, or access to academic appointments at Ivy League and elite public institutions, Black scholars continued to write and challenge the most depraved ideologies about Black life during this time. Despite this kind of systemic silence, Black scholars wrote volumes of work that have only received a shadow of attention in educational thought.

So in keeping with Schomburg's analogy of "digging up" history, we (the authors of this volume) proceeded to dig and dig and dig into our history and it did not take long to tap into the wells of resources provided through the intellectual thought of Anna Julia Cooper, Carter G. Woodson, and Alain Locke. We first went to the histories of education and curriculum, educational handbooks and journals, and very little was gathered from our initial site examination. For example, in the over 1400-page synoptic text *Understanding Curriculum*, Woodson is mentioned one time and Anna Julia Cooper and Alain Locke receive no attention. We soon realized that our intellectual excavation eventually required that we go to places not typically traversed in the White world of progressive and critical thought. Therefore, we turned our attention to sites of memory (Nora, 1989) not commonly referenced in mainstream educational spaces such as the *Journal of Negro History*, *The Journal of Negro Education*, *Negro Bulletin*, *The Opportunity* and archives at Historically Black Colleges and Universities. As a result, voluminous resources of thought surfaced. In the subsequent chapters, the intellectual treasures of Cooper, Woodson, and Locke fill the pages of this volume. The authors' ideas speak to miseducation, racial renaissances, pluralism, feminism, history, democracy, racism, and a whole host of others that eloquently and poignantly spoke to the conditions of education during the time of their writing.

Notes

1   African American scholars have argued that liberalism is one of the more common strategies for African Americans to achieve social justice. Although, the principles of liberalism have been challenged since the nineteenth century, the ideas of liberalism continue to occupy much of the racial and political discourses for African Americans. For a contemporary critique to liberalism in education, see Ladson-Billings and Tate's (1995) essay on critical race theory.

2   While multicultural education theories continue to draw from liberalist discourses, scholars in recent years have expanded the uses of multicultural education to involve critical theories of race, class, and gender. For example, Sleeter and Grant's (2004) *Five Approaches to Multicultural Education* employs critical theory, or what they refer to as the *social reconceptualist approach* within their framework of multicultural education.

3 There have been several instantiations of Black Nationalism to emerge within the racial politics of African Americans from the nineteenth through to the twentieth century. For a comprehensive discussion about the history and tensions of Black Nationalism, see Tommie Shelby's book, *We Who Are Dark: The Philosophical Foundations of Black Solidarity.* In education, Peter Murrell has also offered a fairly comprehensive analysis of African-centered theories in education, also referred to as *cultural nationalism.*

References

Abrahams, R. & Gay, G. (1972). Black culture in the classroom. In R. Abrahams and R. Troike (Eds.), *Language and cultural diversity in American education* (pp. 67–84). Englewood Cliffs, NJ: Prentice Hall.

Alridge, D. P. (1999). Guiding philosophical principles for a Du Boisian-based African American educational model. *The Journal of Negro Education, 68*(2), 182–199.

Anderson, J. (1988). *The education of Blacks in the South, 1860–1935.* Chapel Hill, NC: Chapel Hill.

Ani, M. (1994). *Yurugu: An African-centered critique of European cultural thought and behavior.* Trenton, NJ: Africa World Press.

Apple, M. & Weiss, L. (Eds.) (1983). *Ideology and practice in schooling.* Philadelphia, PA: Temple University.

Asante, M. (1988). *Afrocentricity.* Trenton, NJ: Third World Press.

Asante, M. (1991). The Afrocentric idea in education. *Journal of Negro Education, 60*(2), 170–180.

Ball, A. (2000). Empowering pedagogies that enhance the learning of multicultural students. *The Teachers College Record, 102*(6), 1006–1034.

Banks, J. A. (1992). African American scholarship and the evolution of multicultural education. *The Journal of Negro Education, 61*(3), 273–286.

Banks, J. (2004). Multicultural education: Historical developments, dimensions, and practice. In J. Banks, C. Banks (Eds.), *Handbook of research on multicultural education* (2nd ed.) (pp. 3–29). San Francisco, CA: Jossey-Bass.

Banks, J. & Banks, C. (Eds.) (1997). *Multicultural education: Issues and perspectives.* Boston, MA: Allyn & Bacon.

Banks, J. & Grambs, J. (1972). *Black self-concept: Implications for education and social science.* New York: McGraw-Hill.

Beauboeuf-Lafontant, T. (1999). A movement against and beyond boundaries: "Politically relevant teaching" among African American teachers. *Teacher College Record, 100*(4), 702–723.

Bidwell, A. (2015). Low-income, minority youth missing from summer work. U.S. News. Available online: www.usnews.com/news/articles/2015/01/14/low-income-minority-youths-missing-from-summer-job-programs (accessed February 7, 2015).

Bond, H. M. (1934). *The education of the Negro in the American social order.* New York: Prentice Hall.

Bowles, S. & Gintis, H. (1976). *Schooling in capitalist America: Education reform and the contradictions of economic life.* New York: Basic books.

Boxill, B. (1984). *Black and social justice.* Laham, MD: Rowman & Littlefield.

Broderick, F. L. & Meier, A. (Eds.) (1965). *Negro protest thought in the twentieth century.* New York: Bobbs-Merrill.

Bunche, R. (1936). Education in Black and White. *Journal of Negro Education*, *5*(3, 351–358.

Burroughs. N. H. (1903). Industrial education—will it solve the Negro problem? *The Colored Magazine*, *7*(3), 188–190.

Bush, R. (1999). *We are not what we seem: Black nationalism and class struggle in the American century*. New York: New York University.

Campbell, L. (1970). The Black teacher and Black power. In N. Wright (Ed.), *What Black educators are saying* (pp. 23–25). New York: Hawthorn books.

Campbell, D. M. (2008, July 14). *Realism in American Literature, 1860–1890*. *Literary Movements*. Available at: www.wsu.edu/campelld/amlit/realism.htm (accessed September 2, 2015).

Clark, K. (1965). *Dark ghetto: Dilemmas of social power*. New York: Harper & Row.

Collins, M. and Tamarkin, C. (1982). *Return to excellence in education & quality in our classrooms: Marva Collins' way*. New York: St. Martin's Press.

Cooper, A. J. (1998[1930]). On education. In C. Lemert and E. Bahn (Eds.), *The Voice of Anna Julia Cooper* (pp. 248–258). New York: Rowman & Littlefield.

Dawson, M. (2001). *Black visions: The roots of contemporary African-American political ideologies*. Chicago, IL: Chicago University Press.

Dei, G. (1994). Afrocentricity a cornerstone of pedagogy. *Anthropology & Education Quarterly*, *25*(1), 3–28.

Delpit, L. (1995). *Other people's children: Cultural conflict in the classroom*. New York: New Press.

Dixson, A. (2003). "Let's do this!" Black women teachers' politics and pedagogy. *Urban Education*, *38*(2), 217–235.

Douglass, F. (2003[1845]). *Narrative of the life of Frederick Douglass, an American slave*. New York: Barnes & Noble Classics.

Drake, St. Clair & Cayton, H. R. (1970[1945]). *Black metropolis. A study of negro life in a northern city*. Chicago, IL: University of Chicago Press.

Du Bois, W.E.B. (1902). Of the training of Black men. *Atlantic Monthly*. Available online: www.theatlantic.com/unbound/flashbks/blacked/dutrain.htm (accessed July 7, 2003).

Dunn, F. (1993). The education philosophies of Washington, Du Bois, and Houston: Laying the foundations for Afrocentrism and Multiculturalism. *The Journal of Negro Education*, *62*(1), 24–34.

The Eisenhower Foundation (2008). *What together we can do: A forty year update of the National Advisory Commission on civil disorders*. Washington DC: The Eisenhower Foundation. Available online: http://eisenhowerfoundation.org/docs/Kerner%20 40%20Year%Update,%Executive%20Summary.pdf (accessed May 25, 2015).

Evans-Winters, V. (2005). *Teaching Black girls: Resiliency in urban classrooms*. New York: Peter Lang.

Foster, M. (1997). *Black teachers on teaching*. New York: New Press.

Freire, P. (1987). *Literacy: Reading the word & the world*. South Hadley, MA: Bergin & Garvey.

Gaines, K. (1996). *Uplifting the race: Black leadership, politics, and culture in the twentieth century*. Chapel Hill, NC: University of North Carolina.

Gates, H. L. (1987). *Figures in black: Words, signs, and the "Racial" self*. Oxford, Oxford Press.

Gay, G. (1975). Cultural differences important in education of Black children. *Momentum*, *6*(3), 30–33.

Gay, G. (2004). Curriculum theory and multicultural education. In J. Banks and C. Banks (Eds.), *Handbook of research on multicultural education* (2nd ed.) (pp. 3–29). San Francisco, CA: Jossey-Bass.

Glaude, E. (2000). *Exodus: Religion, race, and nation in early nineteenth-century black America.* Chicago, IL: University of Chicago Press.

Gordon, B. (1997). Curriculum, policy, and African American cultural knowledge: Challenges and possibilities for the year 2000 and beyond. *Education Policy, 11,* 227.

Gordon, E. G. (1999). *Education & justice: A view from the back of the bus.* New York: Teacher College Press.

Grant, C. A. (1979). Classroom socialization: The other side of a two-way street. *Educational Leadership, 36*(7), 470–473.

Grant, C. A. (1988). The persistent significance of race in schooling. *The Elementary School Journal, 88*(5), 561–569.

Grant, C. A. (1990). Desegregation, racial attitudes, and intergroup contact: A discussion of change. *Phi Delta Kappan, 72*(1), 25–32.

Grant, C. (1995). Reflections on the promise of Brown and multicultural education. *The Teachers College Record, 96*(4), 707–721.

Grant, C. (2011). Escaping devil's island: Confronting racism, learning history. *Race Ethnicity and Education, 14*(1), 33–49.

Gyant, L. (1988). Contributions to adult education: Booker T. Washington, George Washington Carver, Alain Locke, and Ambrose Caliver. *Journal of Black Studies, 19*(1), 97–110.

Harding, V. (1990). Gifts of the Black movement: Toward "a new birth of freedom." *The Journal of Education, 172*(2), 28–44.

Harris, M. (1992). Africentrism and curriculum: Concepts, issues, and prospects. *The Journal of Negro Education, 61*(3), 301–316.

Henry, A. (2006). Black-feminist pedagogy: Critiques and contributions. In W. Watkins (Ed.), *Black protest thought and education* (pp. 89–106). New York: Peter Lang.

Hilliard, A. (1995). *The maroon within us: selected essays on African American community socialization.* Baltimore, MD: Black classic.

Hilliard, A. (1997). *SBA: The reawakening of the African mind.* Gainesville, FL: Makare.

Holmes, D. O. W. (1936). Does Negro education need reorganization and redirection?—A statement of the problem. *The Journal of Negro Education, 5*(3), 314–323.

Holt, T.C. (1995). Marking: Race, race-making, and the writing of history. *The American Historical Review, 100*(1), 1–20.

Jackson Coppin, F. J. (1976). To get an education and teach my people. In J. Lowenberg and R. Bogin (Eds.), *Black women in nineteenth century American life: their words, their thoughts, their feelings* (pp. 302–316). University Park, PA: Pennsylvania State University.

Johnson, C. (1940). The problems and needs of the Negro adolescent in view of his minority racial status: a critical summary. *Journal of Negro Education, 9*(3), 344–353.

Joseph, G. (1995). Black feminist pedagogy and schooling in capitalist white America. In B. Guy-Sheftall (Ed.), *Words: Anthology of African-American feminist thought* (pp. 462–472). New York: New Press.

Judd, C. (1936). The reorganization and redirection of Negro education: A critical comment. *The Journal of Negro Education, 5*(3), 517–520.

Lerner, R. M. (2008). Still separate and unequal 40 years after Kerner. *Milwaukee Wisconsin Journal Sentinel,* March 1, 2008. Available online: www.jsonline.com/news/opinion/29393709.html (accessed May 26, 2015).

Lewis, D. L. (1997[1936]). *When Harlem was in vogue.* New York: Penguin Books.

Locke, A. (1989[1950]). The need for a new organon in education. In L. Harris (Ed.), *The Philosophy of Alain Locke* (pp. 265–276). Philadelphia, PA: Temple.

Katz, W. L. (1997). *Black legacy: A history of New York's African American.* New York: Altheneum.

Karenga, M. (1991). *Introduction to Black studies* (7th ed.). Los Angeles: Sankore.

The Kerner Commission Report (1968). Kerner Commission, Report of the National Advisory Commission on civil disorders. Washington DC: US Government Printing Office.

King, J. E. (1992). Diaspora literacy and consciousness in the struggle against miseducation in the black community. *The Journal of Negro Education, 61*(3), 317–340.

King, J. (Ed.) (2005). *Black education: Transformative research and action agenda for the new century.* Mahwah, NJ: Lawrence Erlbaum.

King, J. & Lightfoote-Wilson, T. (1990). Being the soul-freeing substance: A legacy of hope in Afro humanity. *Journal of Education, 172*(2), 9–27.

Ladson-Billings, G. and Tate, W. (1995). Toward a critical race theory of education. *Teachers College Record, 97*(1), 47–68.

Lee, C. Lomotey, K. & Shujaa, M. (1990). How shall we sing our sacred song in a strange land? The dilemma of double consciousness and the complexities of an African-centered pedagogy. *Journal of Education, 172*, 45–61.

Lewis, H. (1972). Changing aspirations, images and identities. In K. Clark, M. Deutsch, A. Gartner, F. Keppel, H. Lewis, T. Pettigrew, L. Plotkin, and F. Riessman (Eds.), *The educationally deprived: The potential for change* (pp. 30–46). New York: Metropolitan Applied Research Center.

Mabee, C. (1979). *Black education in New York State: From colonial to modern times.* Syracuse, NY: Syracuse University Press.

Marable, M. & Mullings, L. (Eds.) (2000). *Let nobody turn us around: Voices of resistance.* New York: Rowman & Littlefield.

Marcuse, H. (1964). *One dimensional man: Studies in the ideology of advanced industrial society.* Boston, MA: Beacon.

McCarthy, C. (1988). Rethinking liberal and radical perspectives on racial inequality in schooling: Making the case for nonsynchrony. *Harvard Education Review, 58*, 265–279.

McLaren, P. (2003). Critical pedagogy: A look at the major concepts. In A. Darder, M. Baltodano, and R. Torres (Eds.), *The critical pedagogy reader* (pp. 69–96). New York: Routledge: Falmer.

Moses, W. J. (1998). *Afrotopia: The roots of African American popular history.* New York: Cambridge University.

Murrell, P. (2002). *African-centered pedagogy: Developing schools of achievement for African American Children.* New York: State University of New York Press.

Nora, P. (1989). Between memory and history: Les lieux de mémoire. *Representations, 26* 7–24.

Pach, C. (1968). *Kerner Commission Report. Milestone.* Available online: www.milestonedocuments.com/documents/view/kerner-commission-report-summary/context (accessed February 5, 2015). *The Kerner Commission Report* (1968)

Parker, L. & Lynn, M. (2002). What's race got to do with it? Critical race theory's conflicts with and connections to qualitative research methodology and research. *Qualitative Inquiry, 8*(1), 7–21.

Pennington, J.W. C. (1849). "Great Moral Dilemma." In Milton C. Sernett (Ed.), *African American Religious History* (pp. 81–88). Durham, NC. Duke University Press.

Perkins, L. (1982). Heed life's demands: The education of Fanny Jackson Coppin. *Journal of Negro Education, 51*(3), 181–190.

Perry, T., Steele, C. & Hilliard, A. (2003). *Young, gifted and Black: Promoting high achievement among African American students.* Boston, MA: Beacon.

Perlstein, D. (2002). Minds stayed on freedom: Politics and pedagogy in the African American freedom struggle. *American Education Research Journal, 39*(2), 249–277.

Schomburg, A. (1992[1925]). The Negro digs up his past. In A. Locke (Ed.), *The New Negro: An interpretation* (pp. 231–237). New York: Arnon.

Shelby, T. (2005). *We who are dark: The philosophical foundations of Black solidarity.* Cambridge, MA: Harvard University: Belknap.

Sizemore, B. A. (1990). The politics of curriculum, race, and class. *The Journal of Negro Education, 59*(1), 77–85.

Sleeter, C. E. & Grant, C. A. (1987). An analysis of the literature on multicultural education in the USA. *Harvard Educational Review, 57*(4), 421–445.

Sleeter, C. E. & Grant, C. A. (2004). *Making choices for multicultural education: Five approaches to race, class, and gender* (4th ed.). San Francisco, CA: Jossey-Bass.

Ture, K. & Hamilton, C. (1992[1967]). *Black power: The politics of liberation.* New York: Vintage.

Washington, B.T. (1896). The awakening of the Negro. *Atlantic Monthly.* Available online: www.theatlantic.com/unbound/flashbks/blacked/washaw.htm (accessed July 7, 2003).

Washington, B.T. (2000[1901]). *Up from slavery.* New York: Signet Classics.

Washington, B.T. (1904). *Working with the hands.* Garden City, NY: Doubleday.

Watkins, W. (1993). Black curriculum orientations: A preliminary inquiry. *Harvard Education Review, 63*(3), 321–338.

Watkins, W. (2006). A Marxian and radical Reconstructionist critique of American education. In W. Watkins (Ed.), *Black protest thought and education* (pp. 107–136). New York: Peter Lang.

Wheatley, P. (1773). *Poems on various subjects, religious and moral.* London: A. Bell.

Wilkerson, D. (1965). School integration, compensatory education and the Civil Rights Movement in the North. *Journal of Negro Education, 34*(3), 300–309.

Willie, C. V. (1965). Education, deprivation and alienation. *Journal of Negro Education, 34*(3), 209–219.

Woodson, C. G. (2000[1933]). *The mis-education of the Negro.* Chicago, IL: African American Images.

Wright, N. (Ed.) (1970). *What Black educators are saying.* New York: Hawthorn books.

Wright, R. & Rosskam, E. (1941). *12 million black voices: A folk history of the Negro in the United States.* New York: Viking Press.

2

A GREAT AMERICAN *VOICE* FOR DEMOCRACY
Anna Julia Cooper

We look back, not to become inflated with conceit because of the depths from which we have arisen, but that we may learn wisdom from experience.

(Cooper, 1892, p. 27)

Introduction

Anna Julia Cooper's educator, author, and activist life story (1858–1964) is one filled with struggle, optimism, and resiliency along with intellectual, political, and social activism. All facets of Cooper's life (activist, educator, author, optimist, "womanist," intellectual) intersected to produce a powerful crusader against race, gender, and class oppression. Education, service, spirituality, innovative leadership, and Pan Africanism are among the major ideas Cooper discussed. Race and culture, women's rights, Black feminism, and equality are topics she addressed when discussing major ideas. She approached these topics through an integrated analysis and discussion in order to better understand and explain concepts of oppression, marginalization, and inequality and broaden democracy in the US. Her mission was to challenge the system of White power and privilege, not only to lift up herself but all of humankind, with special attention to Black people and more specifically, Black women. Cooper was a religious woman and her essays spoke to the morality and ethics of the US and the people in power. Like John Adams who said, "Our Constitution was made only for a moral and religious people" (Adams, 1854, n.p.) Cooper believed that the foundation of our democracy was based upon religious values that saw all people regardless of their social condition, gender, and skin color as made in the image and likeness of God.

Cooper said:

> when the right of the individual is made sacred, when the image of God in human form, whether in marble or in clay, whether in alabaster or in ebony, is consecrated and inviolable, when men have been taught to look beneath the rags and grime, the pomp and pageantry of mere circumstance and have regard unto the celestial kernel uncontaminated at the core … when race, color, sex, condition, are realized to be the accidents, not the substance of life, and consequently as not obscuring or modifying the inalienable title to life, liberty, and the pursuit of happiness … then is mastered the science of politeness, the art of courteous contact, which is naught but the practical application of the principal [sic] of benevolence, the back bone and marrow of all religion; then woman's lesson is taught and woman's cause is won—not the White woman nor the Black woman nor the red woman, but the cause of every man or woman who has writhed silently under a mighty wrong.
>
> (p. 10)

Through her writing, lectures, and service to America's common good, Anna Julia Cooper, scholar/advocate in education, women's rights, and community service, was a multi-voice crusader for humanity governed by the tenets of equality and democracy. She was an innovative educational leader and contributor to educational theory, policy, and practice who saw oppression as structural, not natural. As a school principal, teacher, and thinker she encouraged the advancement of women through education and social progress and richly influenced the lives of countless Back people.

Mary Helen Washington (1988) contends that Cooper provided an "embryonic feminist analysis" (n.p.). She was among the first African American intellectuals to initiate theorizing about the intersections of race, gender, and class and their significance in policy, economics, education, and social science in general, including research and daily life. At a very young age, Cooper became aware that education could be of service to the academic and social growth of Black people, and she worked diligently throughout her life to prepare Black students to be successful and able to attend the nation's best colleges. She contended that educated Black people must serve their race and body politic; when asked about her life goal, Cooper posited that she was committed to "the education of neglected people" (Lemert & Bhan, 1998, p. 250). Cooper's dedication to helping students led her to become a forceful and consistent voice for the Black community during the nineteenth and twentieth centuries — from the end of enslavement through the failures of Reconstruction to the 1960s Civil Rights Movement.

The authors of this book are not the first group of scholars to discover Cooper's contribution to American culture. Cooper's work over the past two decades has been increasingly praised for its contribution to the Social Sciences, including

History, Feminist Studies, Ethnic Studies, and African American Studies. Books including *A Voice from the South* and Cooper's dissertation, *France's Attitude toward Slavery during the Revolution* ([1925]1988), as well as her letters and speeches (Lemert & Bhan, 1998) are now showing up on course syllabi. Also, books and articles that address her significance as a Black feminist scholar (May, 2007; Guy-Sheftall, 2009; Moody-Turner & Stewart, 2009) are read and discussed in college classrooms; textual analysis of her work is underway, and the cultural significance of her work is being noted. Her critiques of the representation of African Americans in the Arts are being discussed (Moody-Turner, 2009; Ndounou, 2014), and her exposure to the racial and gender difficulties that Black women (Moody-Turner, in press) had in trying to publish are being used to point out the silencing of African American women's voices in publications (Aldridge, 2008). In addition, the work of Cooper as teacher, scholar, and Womanist (Giles, 2006) is being promoted in order for her to receive the recognition she deserves (Johnson, 2007). Furthermore, there is an increase in the number of dissertation studies about Cooper (e.g., Hubbard, 2005; Browne, 2008; Lewis et al., 2008).

Cooper, according to herself, was first and foremost a teacher: *the* preeminent dream keeper. Many have heard of Cooper's *A Voice from the South, by a Black Woman of the South* (1892) and her work as teacher and principal of M Street High School. She believed in "academics first" and allowed no one to interrupt her students receiving the education they needed to become liberated men and women. Cooper maintained that "education for the human soul is to … give power and the right direction to the intellect, the sensibilities, and the will" (Cooper, 1892, p. 252).

This chapter discusses argument(s) in the three major topics of Cooper's scholarship that are interconnected through her ideas on democracy as expressed in her statement: "The cause of freedom is not the cause of a race or a sect, a party or a class – it is the cause of humankind, the very birthright of humanity." First, we outline the key biographical elements of her life that informed her ideas and work. We lay the ground for a life that traversed through racial and gender exclusion, academic preparation, and educational and community leadership. We then explore the theoretical and conceptual contribution of *A Voice from the South*. Here, we note that the prose of the *A Voice from the South* served as a counter narrative and as a pedagogical device, what we call rhetorical advocacy. Then we explore the key precepts that informed Cooper's social and educational thought, including how the ideas of race, culture, and gender inform perennial educational and social issues. We conclude the chapter with a discussion of the importance of her life and scholarship as a useful counter narrative to the enduring problems of race and schooling in the US.

The Intersection of Biography and Educational Thought

Throughout the chapter we provide descriptive details, discuss significant events, and offer anecdotes and personal interpretations about Cooper. It is in these narratives that the reasons for why she dedicated her life to "the education of neglected people" are clear; and it is from these narratives that we understand her imperative to give the Black woman the opportunity to become an equal participant in the future of the African American race and nation for "Such is the colored woman's office" (Cooper in Lemert & Bhan, 1998, p. 117).

A Voice *is Born* ...

On August 10, 1858 Anna Julia Haywood was born into enslavement in Raleigh, North Carolina to an enslaved 39-year-old Hannah Stanley Haywood, and "presumably," in Cooper's words, to George Washington Haywood, her mother's White master and rapist. Cooper held a low opinion of her father and she observed that "presumably my father was my mother's master"; and stated "if so I owe him not a sou she was always too modest & shamefaced ever to mention him" (Hutchinson 1981, p. 4). According to Hutchinson (1981), Haywood owned 271 enslaved persons. Cooper's birth occurred shortly before the Civil War. She was the youngest of three children. She had two older brothers, Rufus and Andrew Haywood, who later became free men and worked as carpenters and bricklayers. Cooper's mother's father, Jacob Stanley Haywood, was an enslaved skilled carpenter and who, according to Cooper's autobiographical account, "took part in the planning and construction of the State Capital [in North Carolina]" (Cooper, n.d).

About her mother, Cooper also said, "My mother was a slave and the finest woman I have ever known. Tho untutored she could read her Bible and write a little. It is one of my happiest childhood memories explaining for her the subtle differences between q's and g's or between b's and l's" (Hutchinson, 1981, p. 4). Cooper was very devoted to her mother and she remained a dedicated daughter until her mother's death in 1899, explaining, "self-sacrificing toil to give me advantages she had never enjoyed is worthy [of] the highest praise & undying gratitude" (Hutchinson, 1981, 5).

At the age of eight, or perhaps earlier, Cooper entered St. Augustine's Normal School. It was a school started to prepare Black people to teach other Blacks during Reconstruction. Cooper had learned to read while living with the Busbee family, a family her enslaved mother was loaned out to work for. Cooper was very smart and enjoyed helping others to acquire literacy skills. In school she excelled in her course work: language, arts, mathematics, Greek classics, science, history, and government. It was during her days at St. Augustine that Cooper's advocacy for gender rights developed. She observed that male students were able to take advanced intellectual courses such as Latin and Greek, but female students were denied access. Speaking about the gender inequity the female students at St. Augustine experienced, Cooper wrote:

> I had devoured what was put before me, and ... was looking for more. I
> constantly felt (as I suppose many an ambitious girl has felt). ... A boy,

however meager his equipment and shallow his pretensions, had only to declare a floating intention to study theology and he could get all the support, encouragement and stimulus he needed.

(Hutchinson, 1981, p. 22)

Cooper took her complaint of gender discrimination to the principal and it led to a change in school rules. Female students were given the opportunity to attend the classes they wished (Cooper, 1930). Cooper enrolled in advanced mathematics, and the writings and oratory speeches of Caesar, Cicero, and Virgil.

Cooper remained at St. Augustine as a student and then as a teacher-student for close to 14 years. She enjoyed her experiences as a teacher-student. Perhaps, more importantly, she came to understand that education/school offered a way to greatly improve her life circumstances and the circumstances of others. While at St. Augustine, in 1874, she met George A. C. Cooper, an instructor of Greek language who was in his early thirties. From Nassau, British West Indies, George Cooper was attending St. Augustine to become an ordained Episcopalian minister and completed his program in 1876. Anna, then 19, and George got married in 1877. Unfortunately, two years later, in September 1879, George died. Anna remained a widow for the rest of her life. Over the years, she took in two foster children and five orphans. Recalling her time at St. Augustine, Cooper (n.d.) wrote about its significance on her early life.

That school was my world during the formative period, the most critical in any girl's life. Its" [sic] nurture & admonition gave not only shelter & protection from the many pitfalls that beset the unwary … the whole atmosphere contributed growth & nourishment beyond the power of words to estimate … it develops in one a feeling of "belonging."

(Statement of St. Augustine's School Experience, n.d., Cooper, n.d.)

The significance of Cooper's "feeling of belonging" probably fostered during the early years of her life a positive self-esteem and self-identity (Allen & Bowles, 2012; Lee & Robbins, 1998; Nutbrown & Clough, 2009) and the ability to manage stress and disappointment, as well as success (Jacobsson, Pousette, & Thylefors, 2001), that she would encounter and have to deal with throughout the rest of her life.

In Cooper's first 21 years of life, she experienced enslavement, abundant love from a mother she dearly loved, anger toward her White rapist father, the Civil War and Reconstruction, an introduction to formal schooling, and the discovery that education had the potential to give her a better quality of life. She also learned that she enjoyed the personal and social rewards she received from teaching her Black sisters and brothers. In addition, she had the experience of being a bride and a widow and discovering that her advocacy could bring about change. These experiences were powerful lessons and would help to structure the rest of her life.

Cooper also observed the economic and social changes occurring in the US; and she saw that the personal circumstances of her life and life goals demanded that she do well in school in order to have a moderate financially comfortable life and some degree of freedom. But personal and academic success for her meant that she needed to develop ways and means to speak out against ideologies, policies, and practices that were detrimental to herself, her race, and Black women. More specifically, Cooper began to acknowledge that she had a gift: the ability to learn; and a cause—racism, sexism, and a critique of American democracy, in which she had profound interest. Browne (2008) contends:

> Working as a student-teacher and assisting both male and female adults, Cooper began to draw parallels between the power of education and individual and group uplift and empowerment. This understanding served as a basis for questioning the specific boundaries placed on her as an African American female early in life, and this questioning of the limits placed on her as an individual allowed her to conceive of the possibility of challenging such limits for all.
>
> (Browne, 2008, p. 68)

This early period of Cooper's life is what some describe as the Victorian Era (1837–1901). It was a time of transition for people, especially White people, who were emigrating and immigrating, resettling and relocating (east to west, south to north, rural to urban, urban to suburban) (Schleereth, 1991). By 1870, an enormous building boom had increased the number of millionaires and with that a more financial flourishing society. This led to the call for more of everything among the wealthy. "Too much is not enough" became the mantra, as the rich constantly sought out new ways to display their prominence in society (Yeary, 2009). But life for Black people was exceedingly difficult as the race was overwhelmed by racism, sexism, poverty, and the ignoring of the US Constitution. There was a blatant exercise of power and privilege as Jim and Jane Crow were everywhere in society and the number of lynchings rose. Although Blacks faced challenges both as individuals and as a group, the one small opportunity for any modicum of personal liberty was education. However, Blacks also understood that even upon receiving an education, the opportunity for freedom, employment, and to have a flourishing life would still be extremely difficult and in some cases impossible to achieve.

Oberlin College Years

In 1881, Cooper applied and entered Oberlin College, Ohio. Along with her application, Cooper wrote a letter to the President of Oberlin telling him about her academic preparedness for college life. She wrote:

[b]esides the English branches & Latin: Caesar's seven books; Virgil's Aeneid, six books; Sallust's Cataline and Jugurtha; and a few orations of Cicero—Greek: White's first lessons; Goodwin's Greek Reader, containing selections from Xenophon, Plato, Herodotus and Thucydides; and five or six books of the Iliad— Mathematics: Algebra and Geometry.

(Gabel, 1982, p. 8)

Cooper was successful again, just as she was when she wrote the letter requesting admittance into "boys' classes" at St. Augustine. In presenting her case, she speaks "the language" of the audience of scholars, whom she was hoping to win over. Her argument was grounded in the "high end" of Western knowledge: mathematics and knowing the authors of the Western Canon. In addition, Cooper was establishing herself as a person who belonged at Oberlin. Goodenow (1993) describes belonging in an educational environment "as being accepted, valued, included, and encouraged by others (teacher and peers) in the academic classroom setting" (p. 25).

Oberlin's motto is "Learning and Labor" and the college was renowned for being an institution that believed in progress even while facing strong resistance. By attending Oberlin, Cooper was walking on the grounds where abolitionism flourished. The Underground Railroad was a very recent memory and only 23 years before she arrived on campus, students and faculty were involved in the rescue of John Price, a fugitive slave.

Cooper excelled at Oberlin; several of her professors stated she was an accomplished scholar in Latin, Greek, and French literature and rhetoric. She was invited to teach the advanced algebra class at the tutorial academy. Breathing the air of advocacy and progress, listening to stories about the pursuit of equality, hearing of the resilience of fugitive enslaved people, and engaging in discussions of racial justice in her classes and with professors outside of classes, and being accepted into the family of Professor Charles H. Churchill (Hutchinson, 1981) became the (re)seeding and pruning of Cooper's belief system—a system that already had a natural bent toward racial justice and a special regard for Black girls and women. The Oberlin years strengthened Cooper's ideas about justice, informed her beliefs on equality for Blacks, educated her about power and privilege, and told her that she was ready to join and become part of the leadership of the national protest for racial and gender justice and a critique of American democracy.

In Cooper's graduating class in 1884 there were two other Black women who would go on to also establish a name for themselves: Mary Church (Terrell) and Ida A. Gibbs (Hunt). Church and Gibbs also took the course of study that the men took. All three women had a life career that included taking leadership in fighting for racial justice and women's rights.

The Convergence of Life and Thought

Maya Angelou wrote "You are the sum total of everything you've ever seen, heard, eaten, smelled, and forgot—it's all there. Everything influences each of us." (2011). Angelou's statement speaks to why knowing Cooper—the ideas she advocated, her family relationships and friendships, the kind and quality of education she received, the depth of her academic gifts and talents and how she employed them and for what purpose, along with how her personal struggles, success, and love of community shaped her life work—can be instructive to educators today. Simply being familiar with a scholar's signature piece is often considered homework well done. However, we believe that reading an essay or two from *A Voice from the South* will only show some of the reasons why her work is held in high esteem. Understanding how she came to be described as an interpreter of her times, a person who spoke in an authentic voice for Black people, a person who loved America and spoke to it in ways to help it actualize the tenets of democracy, and a person who described and critiqued the complexities of race, gender, and class in a unique way requires, as Maya Angelou observes, knowing about "the sum total."

Carl Rogers (1961), the eminent psychiatrist who wrote *On Becoming a Person*, offers a short remark pertinent to this chapter, "I have found it of enormous value when I permit myself to understand another person" (p. 18). C. Wright Mills' (1959) statement "On Intellectual Craftsmanship" also has meaning for this chapter because it gets at the relationship between Cooper's life and her scholarship.

> [T]he most admirable thinkers within the scholarly community you have chosen to join do not split their work from their lives. They seem to take both too seriously to allow such dissociation, and they want to use each for the enrichment of the others. ... Scholarship is a choice of how to live as well as a choice of career; whether he [sic] knows it or not, the intellectual workman [sic] forms his [sic] own self as he [sic] works toward the perfection of his craft; to realize his own potentialities, and any opportunities that come his [sic] way, he [sic] constructs a character which has as its core the qualities of the good workman [sic].
>
> (p. 1999)

Maya Angelou's statement "You are the sum total of everything ... " and C. Wright Mills' (1959) observation that admirable thinkers do not split work and life are an intersection for where Cooper lived and had office.

Voice: A Treatise on Race and Democratic Theory

A Voice from the South is a counter-narrative written by a Black woman from the South who lived the devastating experiences of enslavement, which included learning that her mother was raped by her master and father. Cooper also experienced the failure of Reconstruction and was a participant observer of early twentieth-century America industrial changes that brought economic and social growth to many White people, and migration north for many Black people. As Elizabeth Alexander states, Cooper's *Voice* "stands in a new space between the first person confessional of the slave narrative (or spiritual autobiography) and the third person imperative of political essay" (1995, p. 338). M.H. Washington states that *Voice* is "the most precise, forceful, well-argued statement of Black feminist thought to come out of the nineteenth century" (1988, p. xxvii). Cooper's position was that she entered at her convenience and where and when she wanted to, and in doing so her words and deeds deconstructed whiteness, emphasized the worth of Black people and other peoples of color, and urged through her critiques full democracy for oppressed people.

Writing her Verse: *The Conceptual Meanings of the* Voice

When Cooper graduated from Oberlin at the age of 26 she was prepared to write her *verse* as exemplified in the following lines from Walt Whitman's (1892; see Price, 2004) *Leaves of Grass*. "That you are here—that life exists and identity. That the powerful play goes on, and *you may contribute a verse*" (my emphasis) for the world to hear and see.

"Confident, poised, self-assured, and armed with a B.A., she was ready to address the inequities and indignities that Black women like her mother had experienced in enslavement and in the post-Civil War South," comments Hutchinson (1981, p. 227). In 1884, Cooper took a job at Wilberforce University as the principal of the Normal School and Chair of the Modern Language and Literature Department. At Wilberforce, Cooper taught ancient and modern languages, literature, and mathematics (Cooper, 1892). Although her stay at Wilberforce was brief, she was on a very progressive campus—the nation's oldest private, historically Black university that traced it roots backs to before the Civil War and was a station for the Underground Railroad. Cooper's year at Wilberforce allowed her to expand her knowledge about Black women's issues and racial uplift and to develop a deeper understanding of connections between religion, education, and race. The year also allowed her to enlarge her circle of friends, some of whom would remain her friends for years, including Bishop Benjamin W. Arnett, educator, member of Ohio General Assembly, and first Black man to serve as a foreman of an all-White jury to whom she dedicated *Voice*.

The following year, 1885, Cooper returned to St. Augustine and taught mathematics, Greek, and Latin. Back at St. Augustine, Cooper's advocacy for racial and gender justice was heightened. Her involvement in the African American community was kinetic in several areas including recruiting students for college and working with the North Carolina Teachers Association to achieve higher wages and better working conditions. In addition, she fought for the adoption of teaching ideas that would respond better to the academic potential of Black students (Cooper, 1892).

In 1887, Cooper earned a Master's degree in mathematics from Oberlin and moved to Washington, D.C. Soon after, she began teaching at Washington's Preparatory High School for Colored Youth.[1] She remained at the school from 1870–1892. Cooper considered it an honor to receive an invitation to teach at M Street. It was the number one college-prep high school for African Americans and had an outstanding faculty. Many faculty members had earned or were earning a place in history in spite of the cruelty of overt and systemic racism and several had earned a PhD, including Kelly Miller, Mary Church Terrell, and Carter G. Woodson. Three of the school's principals were Mary Jane Patterson, the first African American to receive a B. A. degree in 1862; Richard T. Greener, the first African American to graduate from Harvard College and who also became the dean of Howard University School of Law; and Robert Terrell, who preceded Cooper as principal. When Washington Preparatory was started its purpose was to provide students with the "incentive to higher aim and education" (Stewart, 2013, p. 32).

In 1892, five years after Cooper completed college, *A Voice from the South by a Black Woman from the South* was published. The book was a collection of Cooper's essays written between 1886 and 1892 that eloquently expressed her views about democracy, women's rights, and racial progress in multiple areas including segregation, education, and literary criticism. In the essays in *Voice* Cooper not only worked at the intersections of race, class, and gender, but according to Lindquist (2006) in working at intersections she helps us currently to appreciate and complicate the discourses on masculinities (see Connell, 1995, *Masculinities*). This is so, Lindquist (2006) thinks, because she believed that race was at the core and fundamental to the development of Western masculinities and that masculinity was integral to racial debates. Lindquist (2006) explains that Cooper saw "masculinity not only as central to the problem of gender relations, patriarchy, and sexism, but also as essential to comprehending the origins of racism, imperialism, internal colonialism, and economic exploitation central to the problem of gender relations" (p. 13). Also, Lindquist (2006) posits, Cooper argued that "masculinity intersected with race to create a White 'predominant man-influence,' what today might be called an Anglo-Saxon hegemonic masculinity, which simultaneously legitimized and connected the Woman Problem to the Negro Problem and sexism to racism" (p. 13). In addition, Lindquist (2006), in summarizing the intersections where Cooper worked, states:

> Wielding social science, theology, autobiography, literature, and history she [Cooper] posited theories of the individual and racial development of masculinities; outlined a Gospel-inspired manhood ideal based upon Simon of Cyrene; employed masculinity to theorize the race problem and its solution; and deconstructed Anglo-Saxon hegemonic. The only orthodoxy

she would have claimed was to a womanist Africana, Christian theology that espoused the equality of sex and race based upon the New Testament Gospels.

(Lindquist, 2006, p. 14)

Cooper's work at intersections illustrates how her scholarship and social contributions were born out of the "sum total" of her life and her experiences. Her essays encourage and inspire one to stay true to causes of racial uplift as Cooper did during the harsh times of the Victorian and Progressive eras. In addition, the essays in *Voice* demonstrate an "art of rhetorical advocacy" as a contribution to academic scholarship and community development. *Voice* is divided into two parts: "women issues" and "the race problem." It critiques individual and institutional racism and sexism. Cooper argues Sojourner Truth's thesis in "Ain't I A Woman," as she speaks of how sexism, racism, and authoritarianism influence Black women's participation in racial uplift. She never minces words when discussing the rape of Black women and its significance to the problems facing African Americans in the post Reconstruction period. In addition, she discusses the African American community, Western culture, as well as the intersections of Christianity and progressive reform, racial uplift, and women's liberation.

At the conceptual core of *Voice* is Cooper's belief that "the fundamental agency under God in the regeneration, the re-training of the race, as well as the ground work and starting point of its progress upward, must be the *Black woman*" (p. 62). The title of *Voice* situates the narrator, but not the topics and range and depth of scholarship. The audience for *Voice* was any-and-all who wanted to learn about the problems and issues that challenged Black people, American democracy as well as the problems and issues that many White people chose to ignore. Cooper employs a legal metaphor as a key rhetorical technique in her writing and she uses Biblical precepts and religious references in order to employ a discourse that would have familiarity with her audience. In addition, she uses scholars and leaders that her audience are familiar with from the national and local community as sources to support her statements and to bolster the message and the messenger's right to deliver it.

Voice, as Browne (2008) observes, uses all the linguistic and rhetorical tools that Cooper learned from her years of studying rhetoric and her reading of Western literature: logic and sarcasm; literary, religious and historical references; political and legal metaphors and Christian allusions. Cooper became superb at employing each and every one of these rhetorical tools. Also to complement her use of linguistic and rhetorical tools, Cooper assumed a variety of 'voices' in order to establish her racial identity, and to demonstrate that she had the knowledge to speak on race and gender issues and to critique the practice of American democracy. In addition, the examples she employed to contextualize and to enrich the texture of her argument are ones that most people have experience with or know about. For example, when discussing personal and institutional racism, she delivers the message with attention-grabbing stories that are within the life experience of the audience. In one case, Cooper tells of being forced out of the train car she was riding by the train conductor because of her Black skin. She describes the incident in a way that allows institutional racism to take on a personal face.

The years Cooper spent studying different academic subjects as well as the benefits she reaped though intellectual engagements with different people shine throughout *Voice*. Cooper took full advantage of the intellectual opportunities on each campus where she attended school or taught. She sought out the best and brightest on the campus for intellectual engagement. Whereas books, classroom instruction, and visiting lectures on the campus are fundamentally important to the growth and development of academic scholarship, Cooper additionally learned the value of engaging with people, hearing their point of view, and learning about their experiences. Such an integration of book knowledge with the understanding gained from life experiences, hers and others, was a catalyst for her dogged persistence in pointing out flaws in the exercise of democracy for everyone and for her professional and personal loyalty to the Black women.

A Counter Narrative to De Tocqueville's Imagined Democracy

Voice was and is a counter narrative to the traditional narrative that describes Blacks as racially inferior, devoid of culture, and deprived of self-worth and humanness. *Voice*, published in 1892, was a counternarrative to a well-read, highly praised assessment of democracy, including enslavement in America: Alexis De Tocqueville's *Democracy in America*.

Tocqueville's text was a study of U. S. democracy in order to understand how a stable democratic government functions. This study of equality through the struggles, strengths, and weaknesses of a democratic way of life served as a framework for discussions of daily living for White and Black people, during Cooper's day and continuing to the present. It continues to be touted as one of the two most important books on American political life, the other being *The Federalist Papers* (Hamilton, Madison & Jay [1788]1987). David Wallace-Wells pointed out in *Newsweek* that Edward Banfield (the noted political scientist who served as an adviser to Presidents Richard Nixon, Gerald Ford, and Ronald Reagan) called *Democracy in America* "certainly the greatest book ever written by anyone about America" (Wallace-Wells, 2010). In response, Gordon Wood (distinguished professor, author, and National Humanities Medal winner in 2010) added, "not only on America but also on democracy itself" (Wallace-Wells, 2010). Others also have offered up high praise of Tocqueville (e.g., historians George Wilson Pierson ([1938]1996) and Leo Damrosch, 2011).

Alexis de Tocqueville came to America in 1831 to assess the U.S. experience with democracy: to discover how government of the people, by the people, and for the people was working. He wanted to know how democracy was affecting individuals and the society where the authoritarian influence of one person over the other was replaced with egalitarianism. In France, growing up as an aristocrat with an interest in political theory, Tocqueville was motivated to discover how the concept of political equality determines relations between people. He had witnessed the failed efforts by a democratic government in France so he turned his focus to America. However, in reading *Democracy in America: Volume I* along with *A Voice from the South*, Cooper's discussion is far more inclusive and informative than Tocqueville's as it relates to an analysis of "equality," particularly pertaining to Black people.

In 1831 when Tocqueville came to America, Nat Turner — a self-educated enslaved Black man — led a rebellion that killed approximately 60 White people before his capture. In retaliation, the state of Virginia hanged Turner and executed 56 enslaved persons who were fighting for their freedom. A mob of White people also massacred upwards of 200 other Black people. The rebellion was discussed across America. It increased restrictions on both free and enslaved African Americans in the South, and particularly in Virginia. Religious meetings were only for White ministers, nor could Blacks assemble without permission. The impact of the Nat Turner rebellion on American democracy seemingly was not understood or was dismissed by Tocqueville.

Writing specifically about Blacks, Tocqueville made numerous racist statements. He contended that slavery had its justification in skin pigmentation, that the skin of Black people irrevocably condemned them to servitude. Tocqueville believed that since enslaved Blacks were born into slavery they had no sense of their own tragedy and had little cause to complain about their condition. He posited, "[A]s they [enslaved persons] cannot become the equals of the Whites, they will speedily show themselves as enemies," and "they looked hideous to our eyes and they are seen as a being intermediate between man and the brutes" (Tocqueville, 1835[2004], p. 372). Tocqueville, as Dominick LaCapra (2000) notes, was living in a time and place [France] of the "scientific" theory of stages of civilization and was probably bound up with racist presuppositions that led to Tocqueville thinking that whereas Blacks may not be biologically inferior, they were "morally" inferior and therefore oppressive colonial and imperial policies were necessary.

Anna Julia Cooper's book, on the other hand, saw democracy in America as being inclusive of people of all color. She was a fierce advocate against oppositional dualism and stressed the importance of an independent critical mind. Cooper argued, "It is not the intelligent woman *v.* the ignorant woman; nor the White woman v. the Black, the brown, and the red, it is not even the cause of woman v. man. Nay, tis woman's strongest vindication for speaking that the world needs to hear her voice" (Lemert & Bhan, 1998, p. 189). Cooper acknowledged the cultural shortcomings of the development of Blacks in Africa, but on balance, pointed out their cultural merit when she wrote "the Black side of the stream with us is pretty pure, and has no cause to blush for its honesty and integrity" (Lemert & Bhan, 1998, p. 165). She understood the importance of democratic institutions for eliminating human shortcomings as well as society's responsibility to provide opportunities for human growth and development. Cooper also knew that politics and governance in a democratic society influence the treatment by institutions of Black citizens. Cooper wrote "[o]ur form of government … must be brought to the bar to be tested" (Lemert & Bhan, 1998, p. 186). She then added, fully aware of different barriers constructed to challenge Blacks receiving an education, that she was less concerned with testing the "good atmosphere," "moral code," "rituals and religious ceremonies," "social ethics and "logic" in society. The only test of concern to her was whether social institutions produced a "man," or sound manliness on the part of the individual. Cooper described this as "the *measure of the stature of the fullness of a man*" (Cooper, 1892, p. 187; emphasis in original).

This socialized "man," Cooper argued, would then be expected to support democracy. In her essay, "Hitler and the Negro," Cooper supported this statement by the Council for Democracy: "If the world is to be a place where a free man can hold up his head, *We have to help make it so with our own blood and sweat and tears.* … This duty responsibility, and high privilege rest upon every mother's son without distinction of race, color, creed or condition" (Lemert & Bhan, 1998, p. 265; emphasis in original).

That said, Cooper did not hesitate to call out the inherent contradictions in the ways of the U.S. practice of democracy, especially concerning race and gender. Cooper highlighted the important, fundamental role of "difference" to a vibrant democracy. She noted that sameness would lead to stagnation, tyranny, and death and she pointed out the special role that women play in introducing a "gendered" dimension to democracy—of bringing the other half—care, compassion, concern, and commitment; and giving voice, representation, and justice to those who have wrongly suffered. *Voice* is a counter narrative; Cooper firmly believed that democracy meant "A man's a man" (Lemert & Bhan, 1998, p. 130). She also thought that discussion in a democratic society that undercut that idea should be brought into the light instead of ignored.

During Tocqueville's visit to the US, the enslavement of Blacks, including the fear and terror in which they lived, had to have been known to him, as well as the significant role that enslaved Black people played in America's economic growth and political unrest. However, according to Brooks D. Simpson (2013), Tocqueville never observed enslavement on a plantation and wrote his text based on observations of and discussions about African Americans living in urban areas. Whereas Blacks living in urban areas were treated harshly, the treatment was not as severe as Black life on the Southern plantations.

The narratives of both Tocqueville and Cooper recognize the good qualities and hope in America. Tocqueville states, "America is a land of wonders, in which everything is in constant motion and every change seems an improvement"

(1835[2004], p. 424). In response, Cooper posits, "We have not yet reached our ideal in American civilization. The pessimists even declare that we are not marching in that direction. But there can be no doubt that here in America is the arena in which the next triumph of civilization is to be won; and here too we find promise and possibilities infinite" (Lemert & Bhan, 1998, p. 54).

Cooper's Art of Rhetorical Advocacy

Throughout *Voice* Cooper's oratory – the art of composing and presenting a speech are exhibited along with her understanding of when, where, and how to persuade people to see the point of her argument. *Voice, American Studies* (2012) notes is:

> multi-generic: blending personal essays, philosophical and spiritual treatises, literary and historical analyses, and political polemics, among other genres. Throughout, it weds an impressive erudition with a genuine and personal tone and voice, elements that reflect Cooper's compelling oratorical style yet that exemplify the best qualities of essayists such as Ralph Waldo Emerson. It is, in short, a singular and hugely significant American book, and one that in its form and content inspires on every page.
>
> (*American Studies*, 2012, p. 1)

Cooper shows no fear in choice of topics and with each topic she exhibits historical and present-day command of it, as well as a carefully developed narrative that at times shows how discursive and material forms of power work together to maintain inequality. Cooper does not rush through her story, but brings readers along with a compelling commentary that, for example, explains the dynamics of internalized oppression and the need for a decolonized imagination. Her knowledge of the disciplines she studied in school benefits her oratory and enables her to speak back to power.

Cooper's art of rhetorical advocacy is a valuable contribution to academic scholarship, especially to social justice and multicultural advocates. It begs to be studied and modeled. Arguably it begins with an observation made by Mills: "[T]he most admirable thinkers within the scholarly community ... do not split their work from their lives ... they take both too seriously to allow dissociation and they want to use each for the enrichment of the other" (1959, p. 198).

Cooper places responsibility upon her readers and listeners to make meaning from her speeches and publications. She hopes that her readers and listeners have a strong commitment to democracy. She speaks to all groups and she particularly tells Blacks, "Don't let them argue as if there were no part to be played in life by Black men and Black women" (Lemert & Bhan, 1998, p.132).

In her presentations Cooper contextualizes her argument, takes into account the moment the audience is living in, establishes dialogic relationship with the people, and invites them into her oratory. Cooper also employs sociological imagination to grasp history, biography, and the relations between the two and to speak pointedly to the audience (Mills, 1959). Mills states, "No social study that does not come back to the problems of biography, of history and of their intersections within a society has not completed its intellectual journey" (1959, pp. 2, 3).

Mostly, Cooper speaks to and for the people who are marginalized. She states, "It would be subversive of every human interest that the cry of one-half the human family be stifled" (Cooper, 1892, p. 107). Browne (2008) argues, Cooper's task in *Voice* was multifaceted: demonstrate familiarity with Western culture and a mastery of the English language to establish intellectual authority; use this authority to undermine the master narratives of White supremacy and sexism; and, if need be, deliver the message with a "bite."

Cooper's Art of Rhetorical Advocacy was also powerful, because, as Vivian May (2004) observes, it acts at the intersections—the intellectual crossings of disciplines including literature, economic, theology, science, and political theory—and encourages the bringing together of philosophical inquiries that are often pursued separately (epistemology, ethics, ontology, and aesthetics). In addition, Cooper links theory to action and posits that experience and social location is epistemologically and politically significant.

Thematic Threads of Cooper's Thoughts

Since the publication of *Voice,* pre-kindergarten through college education has embraced numerous changes that make classroom life better for students of color, females, and students who are "othered." However, in this third section we include topics that Cooper's writing and teaching dealt with that are still troubling educators and influencing students' life chances: Naming and Identity; Cooper's Postcolonial Thought: Another Critique of Anti-Democracy; Gender Equality and Black Women: An Intersectional Critique and The Black Woman as a Moral Barometer; and Black Women: Race or Gender First?

Naming and Identity

Anna Julia Cooper stood firm against having people's life experiences, ways of reasoning, and how they made sense out of the world defined and named by others. She strongly believed in the significance of knowledge acquired through lived experiences. She believed that no one racial or ethnic group of people should define the ideologies, frames, labels, and standards for knowing and learning. V.M. May writes that Cooper insisted:

> "that the acts of self-naming and of articulating collective (but not homogenous) African-American political, ethical, and aesthetic standpoints

are essential to realizing the fullest meaning of freedom. Rather than have the meaning of reality, the pathways of knowing, or the nature of the self named by other, Cooper pushes for the right of all humans to participate in creating and defining new paradigms of knowing and being that draw upon the race and gender-specific particularities of lived experience, of cultural memory, and of complex legacies of resistance.

(2007, p. 41)

Through essays and speeches Cooper spoke about the dignity and humanity of Black people, and although she criticized Black men, she spoke of their worth and appreciated them as men. She took a strong stance against names, symbols, signs, and stereotypes employed by Whites to trash the human quality of Black people and to tear down the manhood of Black men. May further contends that Cooper unhesitatingly countered White men's use of a mantle of false objectivity to rationalize and reinforce racism, sexism, and the human character of Black people. She challenged the prejudgment of African American character throughout her essays, including "The Negro's Dialect" (1930s) and "The Ethics of the Negro Question" (1902). Innuendos about Blacks being shiftless, sullen, or childlike, Cooper contended, were racist preconceptions that comprise a "nightmare vision" with no basis in "objective reality." Cooper (1892) knowingly said truth must be infinite and not limited to "one little creature's finite brain" (p. 193).

Although Cooper died in 1964 she was a witness to the beginning of the Civil Rights Movement in 1954 and the protest not only to end racial segregation and discrimination but to have Black people accepted and appreciated as human. Cooper's life served as a counter-narrative to the social construction of race and Blacks as inferior, and we can be fairly certain from her writing that she would have applauded a sign carried in the 1968 during a Civil Rights protest in Memphis, Tennessee. "Wearing sunglasses, a young Black man holds a sign with bold print in full view of the camera that states: 'I AM A MAN.' The word 'AM' is underlined. He's not just stressing the word 'AM,' he's insisting on it! Around him, there are other African Americans with similar signs, black ink on white paper. Some look into the camera lens, some stare ahead, defiantly as they march" (Matthew, 2014, n.p.). In the 1960s, African Americans demanded a right that they had long been denied. A right they had fought and died for since the colonial period (1607–1783): the right to control how they are identified, and the right to be recognized and treated as human beings. Who names, identifies, and says what is and what is not is central to racial equality and quality of life in the United States.

Today, normative ideologies continue to name and identify Blacks negatively as they did in Cooper's day. Although gains have been made that improve the quality of life for African Americans throughout society (including in education), racial legacies from the past and racial biases today stand in the way of the total acceptance of Blacks as equal men and women to Whites. In many U.S. schools, the children of African American families continue to be educated by a system that uses ideologies, frames, and labels that thwart their academic success. Cooper's response to negative ideologies and framing was to write and/or produce plays and skits that positively framed, identified, and named African Americans for M Street High School students, and told of Black people's history and contributions to the American way of life.

Moody-Turner (2013) tells us that Cooper had a strong opposition to mainstream America's idea that framed Black people as in need of an education that would "civilize" them. Instead, Cooper contended that Western civilization needed to be examined for its biases and false and misleading assumptions that were based upon flawed scientific reasoning. "She [Cooper] went to work interrogating, or 'de-naturalizing,' the assumptions underlying the discourses of civilization, while also working to expose the biases encoded in the prevailing epistemologies employed to study and analyze Black 'folk' and Black folklore" (Moody-Turner, 2013, p. 89). Also, Moody-Turner posits that Cooper encouraged African American writers to develop a literary tradition that would include the everyday experiences of Black people and push back on distorted misrepresentations of Black people in the mainstream literature. For Cooper, "the politics of cultural representation were intricately tied to issues of equality, social justice, and democracy" (Moody-Turner, 2013, p. 89).

In addition, Cooper understood that the politics of representation are important to politics and education. At M Street, School teachers used students' experiences to validate them personally and Black people as a group. In doing so they helped students to develop a critical consciousness about dominant representations that was vital to creating people who could engage and transform society. In addition, they told students to bring their stories and theorized them from lived experiences. To students it became "truth from the people's perspective."

Cooper's Postcolonial Thought: Another Critique of Anti-Democracy

Postcolonial studies are defined as the analysis of the politics of knowledge through examining the relations of political and social power that seek to maintain colonial power structures (Gilbert & Tompkins, 1996). This definition accurately describes the research that Anna Julia Cooper conducted for her dissertation.

Cooper was a post-colonist but more famously known as the only woman to speak at the first Pan-African Congress in London in 1900, thereby proving to a gender-biased world and African men that women – Black women — could be thinkers and advocates for human rights. The cutting edge essays in *Voice*, written at a time of severe racism and gender exploitation in the US, argue for racial progress, dignified resistance to racism and gender bias, the dignity of Black women, education of neglected people, service to the Black community, and the hope of democracy. All of this was meaningful enough to place Cooper deservedly as one of the keynote speakers at the Congress and be recognized for using post-colonial ideology and methodology. Her dissertation, *France's Attitude toward Slavery during the Revolution* ([1925]1988), should situate her among the early, esteemed post-colonists. Cooper did not believe that African countries needed the "extension of civilization" as colonialism implies. She was militantly against ideological justification of the self-ascribed racial and cultural superiority of Western countries over non-Western countries. In lectures and essays, such as "The African Character," Cooper derided Hegel's contention that some cultures are in need of Christian-European guidance in order to develop.

In her dissertation, Cooper ([1925]1988) was examining the causes of the Haitian struggle for racial equality and liberation from France. Cooper argued that the French were overlooking the "colonial question" – the resistance and agency of the enslaved and free Black Saint-Domingueans in France's emergent democracy. In addition, they were refusing to acknowledge all three countries (only two were generally acknowledged) involved in "The Age of Revolution": (1) the American revolution of 1776 that declared "all men are created equal," (2) the French declaration of 1879 that announced "men are born and remain free and equal in rights," and (3) the Haitian constitution of 1805 that stated "equality in the eyes of the law is incontestable." Cooper contended that dominant discourses were silent about the Haitian revolution because, if they were not, attribution of the Haitian fight for racial equality would need to be included as central to the "modernity that took shape in the Western Hemisphere" (Fischer, 2004, p. 273). In addition, Cooper argued there is no natural hierarchy among humankind and contended that race was socially constructed.

Vivian May (2007) notes that in 1925, Cooper introduced in her dissertation ([1925]1988) a challenge to France's democratic premise — *Men are born and remain free and equal in rights* — in regard to Haiti ("their" colony). Cooper, May argues, found evidence of sanctioned ignorance and beliefs in White supremacy through the use of words and certain evidence in historiography (archival documents and records) that had been used to marginalize the role of enslaved Blacks in their liberation. Cooper underscores the actions of enslaved Black people and "gens de couleur" (mulattos) in Saint-Domingue's (Haitian) revolution as relevant to constructing a "more dimensional and inclusive understanding of history and humanity" (May, 2007, p. 179). Also May (2007) contends that Cooper illustrated the tensions between the revolutionary ideas and actual practices of France's government, and argued that France's declaration of Enlightenment and the Age of Revolutions must be considered within the context of a transatlantic framework that takes into account how "capitalism emerged in concert with colonialism as a racially exploitive economic system" (pp. 179–180).

Cooper acknowledged that France took official action against enslavement:

[I]t was in France that the first flash of the philosophic ideal capable of awaking the entire world burst forth. Montesquieu, Rousseau, Voltaire,

Filangieri and Raynal thundered the most forcefully against the odious traffic [enslavement]. It was in France that official acts striking a death blow to the most unjust of institutions would be announced for the first time. The honor of having voted the deliverance of the slaves in all the French colonies belongs to the National Convention of the French Republic.

(Cooper [1925]1988, p. 283)

Cooper then argued that the monetary greed of the planters and merchants in Saint-Domingue and the economic hardship in France (e.g., bankruptcy, idle workers, lack of food) caused France to continue with the colonial evil of enslavement in Saint-Domingue, therefore rebuking their noble declaration that "Men are born and remain free and equal in rights" (Marquis de Lafayette, 1789, p.1)

Cooper believed that history must attend to its marginal spaces and silenced stories (May, 2007, p. 904). She also noted how French citizens responded during the economic crisis: "They showed themselves as self-centered as they could possibly be" (Cooper, 1892, p. 288). In other words, Cooper pushed back on the propaganda that colonialism and enslavement in Haiti had a unidirectional power dynamic and argued in her Sorbonne thesis ([1925]1988) that the Haitian and French revolutions were dialectical. In addition, she pointed out shortcomings between French theories and France's application of democracy. Cooper contended that the political uprisings in the two countries developed through a complex transatlantic consciousness and not via the intellectual debate and political unrest in France.

In articulating her postcolonial analysis, Cooper pointed out gross misrepresentations and inaccuracies in French history. She did so by analyzing the powerful interpretive norms and biases put forth by the French, along with examining the relationship between political and social power that worked to maintain French belief in its superiority of ideas and voice. This ideology served to maintain the status of France in the eyes of the world and in history.

Cooper's thoughts on Pan-Africanism and anti-colonial studies are resurfacing at an important time in history. As the entire world connects through transportation, electronic communication, economics, trade, and cultural activities — and ordinary people look toward the future — many in the global community want to better understand their histories. People everywhere increasingly demand scholarship born out of the full range of human experiences and authentic and accurate accounting of past histories and deed. Cooper's ground-breaking work, *France's Attitude toward Slavery during the Revolution* ([1925]1988), serves as a post-colonialist model for such undertakings.

Gender Equality and Black Women: An Intersectional Critique

Gender equality and Black women are two topics that consumed a great deal of Cooper's attention. In discussing gender equality she paid attention to both equality between men and women, and gender and racial equality for Black women. She pushed back against racism and White male patriarchy, and simultaneously told White women they were wrong for not being inclusive of Black women and treating them equally. Cooper offered a good deal of insight into the "race or gender first?" question. As time has passed, Black women have added related strands to this question — strands that include critiques of the Black male patriarchy and adoption of phrases like "Blackhood" that take into account both male and female. In addition, Cooper argued that Black women were the moral barometer of America.

Gender Equality: The Black Woman as a Moral Barometer

Cooper argued for action and material change for Black women and in doing so she clearly demanded a policy and practice change in their education, along with funds to support the change. Cooper posited that women should develop their intellectual capacity in order to be self-reliant, have the capacity to earn a living, and contribute in all areas of society. Her life and work were guided by Christian values, and she believed that the teachings of Jesus provided a rationale for gender equity. She drew from religion and history to make arguments for equality. Cooper posited that the Christian Church was an authoritative source and guide for the development of women: "[T]he source of the vitalizing principle of women's development and amelioration is the Christian Church so far as the church is consistent with the teaching of Jesus" (1892, p. 57). She added, "By laying down for women the same code of morality, the same standard of purity as for men … [Jesus] has given men a rule and guide for the estimation of woman as an equal, as a helper, as a friend, as a sacred charge to be sheltered and cared for with a brother's love and sympathy" (Cooper, 1892, p. 57). Cooper argued that history discloses that societies that have promoted the status of women advance more rapidly than societies that see women only as wives and mothers. She asserted that the "position of women in society determines the vital elements of regeneration and progress" (1892, p. 57).

Cooper's thesis did not advocate reverse sexism but was founded on "a priori grounds." She explains that the social promotion of women is not because a "woman is better or stronger than a man, but from the nature of the case … it is she who must first form the man by directing the earliest impulses of his character" (Lemert & Bhan, 1998, p. 59). Cooper's observations were written at the time when the "norm" argued that women were irrational, and men were the objective knowers, that a woman's contribution to knowledge was to serve men as a muse or object of worship. Such misrepresentations about the way knowledge is discovered, who discovers it, and the role of women in its discovery Cooper argued were sexist and grounded in unequal power relations designed to further patriarchy.

Importantly, Cooper's argument for gender equality based upon Christian beliefs and her contention that women's enhanced position in society improves

ɔ are gaining attention today as a crusade to roll back reproductive
1en's choices has gained momentum, furthered by numerous
ion (e.g., closure of abortion clinics) to control women's rights.
g, explained in the *Kwanzaa Guide* (2014), gives America:

> [A] way of measuring the progress of women and the Women's Movement
> as well as the quality of American society. Measured against her writings,
> the discussion and debate around women and their status is impoverished.
> Being a mother, for example, was just one possibility of womanhood for
> Cooper. She saw women as the necessary compliment to men, worthy of
> the same, if not more, social investment given their dual task as mothers
> and workers.
>
> (*Kwanzaa Guide*, 2014, p. 2)

Anna Julia Cooper's words speak compellingly to men, women, and policy makers
today. She states: "We need men who can let their interest and gallantry extend
outside the circle of their aesthetic appreciation," and "We need women who are
so sure of their own social footing that they need not fear learning to lend a hand
to a fallen sister" (Lemert & Bhan, 1998, p. 64). To policy makers and those in
power Cooper says they need to be people – men and women — "who do not
exhaust their genius splitting hairs on aristocratic distinctions and thanking God
they are not as others; but earnest unselfish souls, who can go into the highways and
byways, lifting up and leading, advising and encouraging with a true catholic
benevolence of the Gospel of Christ" (Lemert & Bhan, 1998, p. 64).

In today's context Cooper is arguing for America to have a discussion, debate,
and practice on women's issues worthy of its greatness. From the *Kwanzaa Guide*:

> Cooper's writings, insights, and the qualitative decline of the nation is
> correlated with the debasement and degradation of women. Elected
> officials, members of political parties, policy makers, and power brokers,
> for whatever political or social purpose, are dancing on the margins of
> women's rights and career dreams, and are enveloped by their own make-
> believe world of women. For Americans to achieve a full democratic
> society, their reality must take precedence over political joisting, for
> women cannot be fooled.
>
> (*Kwanzaa Guide*, 2014, p. 3)

In addressing women's rights, Cooper was inclusive; she advocated and welcomed
all of humankind. But she also knew how Black women had been not only
marginalized but often shut out and abused by both White men and women, and
had been politically and socially silenced by African American men. Charles
Lemert wrote in the Introduction to the 1998 edition of *Voice*: "Though
Sojourner Truth's idea (i.e., the triple oppression of Black women) is well

understood, Cooper's *Voice* was the first systematic working out of the insistence that no one social category can capture the reality of the colored woman" (Lemert & Bhan, 1998, p. 14). Cooper understood Truth's meaning of "woman" and the political, economic, and cultural assumptions attached to the word for Black women in comparison with White women (Elkholy, n.d.). Because of this understanding of difference and Black women's subjugation to intersecting oppressions (e.g., race, class, gender), Cooper believed they had a unique and invaluable outlook about society. She argued that rather than being suppressed, it is the voices of these women that need to be front and center as society moves forward. To Cooper, the Black woman was America's moral and ethical barometer because White men were corrupt and selfish people who enslaved Black people and tore Black families apart. Too often Black men were acting for themselves and modeling after White men in their support of patriarchy. Cooper critiqued White women for being selfish and enjoying or going along with the narrow standard of beauty that people admired. She did not think that White women had stepped up to include and respect their Black sisters and many White women went along with enslavement.

Cooper affirmed "Black woman's moral superiority to White civilization, whose 'blasé world-weary look characterized the old washed out and worn out races which have already, so to speak seen their best days" (Lemert & Bhan, 1998, p. 2). She also took into account a growing and developing nineteenth-century America:

> To be a woman in such an age carries with it a privilege and an opportunity never implied before. But to be a woman of the Negro race in America, and to be able to grasp the deep significance of the possibilities of crisis, is to have a heritage, it seems to me, unique in the ages.
>
> (Lemert & Bhan, 1998, p. 117)

Cooper then added:

> In the first place, the race is young and full of the elasticity and hopefulness of youth. All its achievements are before it. ... There is a quickening of its pulses and a glowing of its self-consciousness. ... Something like this ... is the enthusiasm which stirs the genius of young Africa in America; and the memory of past oppression and the fact of present attempted repression only serve to gather momentum for its irrepressible power. ... She [Black women] must stamp weal or woe on the coming history of this people.
>
> (Lemert & Bhan, 1998, p. 117)

Whereas, America is more than one hundred and twenty years older than when Cooper made the statement above, for Black Americans their achievements are still before them. With the election of Barack Obama, and in spite of Bloomberg

Politics polling (2014) that reports the majority of Americans — 53 percent — say that interactions between White and Black communities have deteriorated since he [Obama] took office in 2008, many younger African Americans are feeling the quickening of self-consciousness. Also, many young Black women, much like Cooper, recognize the responsibility they have to take advantage of the opportunity before them to lift themselves and Black people to a higher level.

It was likely that Cooper began to formally advocate a Black feminist position with a speech on the role of Black women in racial and social progress at a Convocation of Clergy at the Protestant Episcopal Church in 1886 (Cusick, 2009). In the speech, *Womanhood: A Vital Element in the Regeneration and Progress of a Race*, Cooper critiqued the Black leaders —men and women—for their selfishness and ambition. She bluntly denounced those who "exhaust their genius splitting hairs on aristocratic distinctions and thanking God they are not as others." Instead, she lauded as true leaders, the "earnest, unselfish souls, who can go into the highways and byways, lifting up and leading, advising and encouraging" (Lemert & Bhan, 1998, p. 64).

Cooper took advantage of this platform for speaking. She next presented programs to support Black women and explain the different types of oppression they faced. She argued that because of these oppressions, the improved status of Black women in educational programs was needed immediately. In addition, Cooper advocated that working class and poor Blacks needed education and more job opportunities. Her final remarks were aimed at Black male clergy. She spoke to them about the importance of personal sacrifice for the good of the people, along with the need for community advocacy. Throughout her speech, Cooper maintained an authoritative voice. She wanted men to take notice of the wisdom in her plan and to realize that their past efforts were falling short. In her conclusion, Cooper spoke about how the Protestant Episcopal Church had ignored the majority of Black people's needs, failing to attend to their customs and traditions. The church, Cooper believed, had been mute about Black women's needs and used stories about the achievements of a few individual Blacks as cover for ignoring the larger Black community.

It was at the Convocation that Cooper made what many say is her signature statement: "Only the BLACK WOMAN can say when and where I enter, in the quiet, undisputed dignity of my womanhood, without violence and without suing or special patronage, then and there the whole Negro race enters with me" (Lemert & Bhan, 1998, p. 31). Six years later (1893) at the *World's Congress of Representative Women*, held as part of the Columbian Exposition in Chicago, Cooper struck another chord for Black Feminism. To begin, no women were on the program, but White women challenged their omission and were granted permission to speak. The permission did not extend to Black women, who then protested on their own behalf. After constant demands to World Congress officials, the Black Women were allowed to have speakers as part of the "exotic people" exhibit.

Five women were granted permission to speak: Fannie Barrier Williams (who was appointed to supervise Black women's contributions and to whom Cooper would direct her remarks), Sarah J. Early, Hallie Quinn Brown, Frances Harper Black, and Anna Julia Cooper (Logan, 2006). When Cooper spoke, she did several significant things. First, she responded to Fannie Barrier Williams, who likely was given her oversight position because she was northern, had light skin, and was from the affluent class. Next, Cooper described the progress of the Black woman since enslavement. In her speech, *The Intellectual Progress of the colored women in the United States since the Emancipation Proclamation: A response to Fannie Barrier Williams* (1893), Cooper highlighted the oppression of Black women. Her opening line set the tone: "The higher fruits of civilization cannot be extemporized, neither can they be developed normally, in the brief space of thirty years (after enslavement). It requires the long painful growth of generations" (Lemert & Bhan, p. 201). Cooper (1893) argued that "the severest persecution and oppression – enslavement – could not kill-out (African Americans) or even sour their temper. ...Without money and without price they poured their hearts' best blood into enriching and developing of this country" (Lemert & Bhan, 1998, p. 179). Throughout *Voice*, Cooper wrote with longing and steadfast devotion for complete democracy for African Americans. She pointed to the many ways— regardless of condition (e.g., enslavement) and occasion (e.g., Revolution War, Civil War)—that the dedication and loyalty of the Black race had contributed to the development and growth of America.

Since the 1960s and 1970s, with a focus on race and racism, attention has increasingly turned to theorizing and framing the examination of systems of oppression faced by Black people with an intersectional analysis. Cooper's observations about the overlapping of race, gender, and class and their connection to domination and exploitation are not only prophetic but suggest that her theorizing and framing about the impact of power and authority on oppressed people may be useful for current scholars grappling with the inclusion of LGBTQ issues. When examining the intersections of gender, race, class, colonialism, and imperialism, scholars can benefit from the inclusive nature of her work. Cooper argued that "The cause of freedom is not the cause of a race or a sect, a party or a class—it is the cause of humankind, the very birthright of humanity" (Lemert & Bhan, 1998, p. 182).

Peggy McIntosh's (1988) *White Privilege and Male Privilege* discusses how White males and females have benefited from racism, including how White women do not recognize their "unearned skin privilege" (1988, n.p.). McIntosh's work references Cooper's essay, "Woman versus the Indian," in which she tells about Black women who were forcibly ejected from [train] cars and removed from seats, their garments rudely torn and their bodies wantonly and cruelly injured. Long before contemporary analyses, Cooper described the unearned skin privilege of White women. She wrote about scenes at railway stations when White women disembarked from trains. When a White woman would step off, a White train conductor would place a stool for her to step on, and then take the women's hand, satchel, and bag. He performs this "gentlemanly and efficient" task in order to prevent her from having to take a long step down. With a polite, "thank you" or nod, the woman was on her way, never giving particular notice to the courtesy because it was an expected way for White women to be treated. However, when Black women disembarked from the train carrying a satchel and bag, and facing the challenge of a long step down to the pavement, White conductors simply, and without the gentlemanly efficiency accorded to White women, turned their backs and folded their arms—not to perform other duties but to degrade Black female skin. About the unearned skin privilege of White women and the denial of simple courtesy to Black women, Cooper wrote: "The feeling of slighted womanhood is unlike every other emotion of the soul" (Lemert & Bhan, 1998, p. 92). Cooper's message about White privilege throughout *Voice* is one that points out how "Whites are taught to think of their lives as morally neutral, normative, and average, and also ideal," as McIntosh also observes (1988, n.p.).

What then would eliminate White privilege, that continues to be openly discussed, at least since the publication of *Voice* and now discussed in social science literature; and does Cooper's work offer suggestions given the tenacity of White privilege? Elkholy argues:

> to break free from racist ideology may not be such an easy task for Whites, as it threatens the very foundations of their pride and self-love ... the legacy of cultural resources from which a White identity is drawn, are steeped in practices of racial oppression and domination. Consequently, relinquishing racism means not only giving up the actual privileges and benefits that are associated with being White, but may involve shunning one's ties to a cultural history upon which White personal esteem and sense of self are grounded.
>
> (Elkholy, n.d., p. 13)

With such a tap root in the psyche and behavior of Whites, in order for White privilege to be eliminated there has to be a recognition of its state of being and a tool kit of effective measures to repudiate practices that arise from enacting, embodying and animating whiteness (Elkholy, n.d.). Cooper, speaking on the point of repudiating White privilege, argued:

> American [aka White] women need to have a clearness of vision as well as a firmness of soul ... and ... "to wheel into line" other women; the American woman not only gives tone directly to her immediate world, but her tiniest pulsation ripples out and out ... into society.
>
> (Lemert & Bhan, 1998, p. 304)

Carby's (1987) statement "White women are made visible because they are the women that White men see" (p. 302) speaks to the patriarchy that enables

American women's tiniest pulsation to ripple out into society. Cooper suggests that since the White woman is responsible for American manners or the respectful equal attention it gives to "the othered" throughout society, it is the responsibility of the White woman to teach America respect for others.

A strong case can be made that Cooper's essays and public speeches placed her among the early group of women who explain the connection between racism and patriarchy and that it "laid the ground work for the Black feminist movement [that among other things] served as a corrective for male dominated leadership in the Civil Rights and Black Power Movements" (*Kwanzaa Guide*, 2010). Cooper's (1892) hope and belief in the Blacks woman's ability to transcend race and gender inequality, marginalization because of her skin color, and put downs from her Black brothers, as these oppressions operated as interlocking forces, is a powerful testimony that Cooper's confidence was expressed:

> With all the wrongs and neglects of her past, with all the weakness, the debasement, the moral thralldom of her present, the Black woman of to-day stands mute and wondering at the Herculean task devolving upon her. But the cycles wait for her. No other hand can move the lever. She must be loose from her hands and set to work.
>
> (Lemert & Bhan, 1998, p. 62)

Black Women: Race or Gender First?

African American women still hear, "Do you identify by your gender or race first?" Cooper recognized the Black women's dilemma in 1892. She stated, "The colored woman ... is confronted by both a women question and a race problem, and is as yet an unknown or unacknowledged factor in both" (Lemart & Bhan, p. 134).

Cooper's question about the priority of race or gender has generated several strands of research in the academic press including studies on the intersectionality of gender, class and race (see for example, Evangelina Holvino, 2008; Emir Kamenica and Iatamar Simonson, 2008). When Cooper wrote about race, gender, and class, her analysis tended to point out how these different systems of oppression were dominating Black people and were severely unjust to African American women. Patricia Hill Collins (2000) in *Black Feminist Thought* wrote about how systems of oppression (e.g., race, class, gender) intersected to form "the matrix of domination and/or matrix of oppression" and negatively influenced Black women's social and personal lives. Collins enhanced the analysis of the oppression of Black women started by Sojourner Truth who argued that there is no speaking about "women" as if they have a universal experience and that the concept of "woman" is influenced by a race and class ideology. Collins' scholarship also helped to crystalize African American women as agents of knowledge. Cooper's (1892) essays gave greater attention to Truth's observation that no one social category can capture the reality of African American women and Collins' continuation of the analysis of the systematic oppression of Blacks has promoted a fundamental paradigmatic shift in how the oppression of Black women and other women of color is analyzed, thereby increasing Black women's emerging power as not only agents of knowledge but as sources of power (e.g., according to an article by Sarah Wheaton in the *New York Times* (2013) in 2012 66 percent of eligible Blacks voted in the presidential contest and only 64.1 percent of Whites turned out to vote. In addition Wheaton states "The increase in Black turnout was driven in significant part by more votes from Black women" (Wheaton, 2013, n. p.). Collins' analysis has also influenced the race or gender priority question in that it has served to promote Black and Afrocentric feminist thought; and, as Hyman (1990) observes, a reconceptualization of family.

According to Hyman (1990):

> Black women's experiences as bloodmothers, othermothers, and community other mothers reveal that the mythical norm of a heterosexual, married couple, nuclear family with a nonworking spouse and a husband earning a "family wage" is far from being natural, universal and preferred but instead is deeply embedded in specific race and class formations.
>
> (Hyman, 1990, p. 2)

In addition, Hyman (1990) posits:

> Black women's actions in the struggle or group survival suggest a vision of community that stands in opposition to that extant in the dominant culture. The definition of community implicit in the market model sees community as arbitrary and fragile, structured fundamentally by competition and domination. In contrast, Afrocentric models of community stress connections, caring, and personal accountability.
>
> (Hyman, 1990, p. 2)

Many Black women have rejected the generalized ideology of domination advanced by the mainstream in order to preserve the idea of family and community common to their homes. As such, the vision of community sustained by many African American women in conjunction with African American men addresses the larger issue of reconceptualizing power. Hyman (1990) connects the reconceptualization to the family and community thesis to the race or gender priority question when she states:

> Approaches that assume that race, gender, and class are interconnected have immediate practical applications. For example, African-American women continue to be inadequately protected by *Title VII of the Civil Rights Act of 1964*. The primary purpose of the statute is to eradicate all

aspects of discrimination. But judicial treatment of Black women's employment discrimination claims has encouraged Black women to identify race or sex as the so-called primary discrimination.

(Hyman, 1990, p. 3)

Then, quoting Scarborough: "To resolve the inequities that confront Black women the courts must first correctly conceptualize them as 'Black women,' a distinct class protected by *Title VII*" (Hyman, 1990, p. 3). Hyman then states "Such a shift, from protected categories to protected classes of people whose Title VII claims might be based on more than two discriminations, would work to alter the entire basis of current antidiscrimination efforts" (1990, p. 3). If Scarborough's (quoted in Hyman, 1990) idea comes to pass, will it put to rest the race or gender priority question? The authors of this book think not, because levels of domination operate on multiple levels: personal, community, and systemic and each level is interpreted by individuals in different ways, and whereas (arguably) most Black women do not have too much difficulty pointing out how they are a victim of race, class, or gender—this same level of analysis does not carry over to understanding some other Black women's subordination, including how they are impacted by race or gender, thereby promoting race over gender or gender over race. Cooper's contribution to the discussion is that she was full-throated in calling attention to the debate during her day and illuminating the extra burden that Black women face. White women do not have to make decisions on whether their priority is race or gender. Scholars who write on "White women" and who have not addressed this point will find several discussions of the "difference and privilege afforded White women" in *Voice* useful in theorizing and discussion. In addition, they will find that Cooper was forthright with her White sisters about their neglect of their Black sisters. In *Woman versus the Indian*, Cooper (1892) tells a story of a White woman who believed in helping to elevate her Black sisters and Black people "so long as they understand their place" (Lemert & Bhan, 1998, p. 88). That said, Cooper was not mean spirited toward White women. In her 1893 speech in Chicago, *Women's Cause is One and Universal*, Cooper argued:

The colored woman feels that woman's cause is one and universal ... and not till the universal title of humanity to life, liberty, and the pursuit of happiness is conceded to be inalienable to all; not till then is woman's lesson taught and woman's cause won—not the White woman's, nor the Black woman's, not the red woman's, but the cause of every man and of every woman who has writhed silently under a mighty wrong.

(Lemert & Bhan, 1998, p. 205)

Toward a Cooperian Vision of Education

At a young age, when she attended St. Augustine's Normal School, Cooper viewed education as a liberating agent, a way to escape from institutional and personal racism and sexism. May (2010) contends that Cooper believed that all forms of education, be they classical, professional, or vocational, full-time or part-time, should be sites of liberation. For Cooper the economic benefits achieved from education were important, but developing one's personhood, becoming liberated men or women, was the major purpose of education, and then other life possibilities would follow. Besides being a liberating force, Cooper posited that education should take into account the whole humanity of a Black person and was essential to the development of Black people's full intellectual capacity, as well as their social and emotional development; and was needed to advance the African American community. Cooper (1892) also believed that education was "the safest and richest investment possible to man. It pays the largest dividends and gives the grandest possible product to the world a –man (sic)" (Cooper, 1892, p. 168).

Political Agency and Evolution of Cooper's Education Vision

There are few places where the race and culture of Blacks is debated more than in the education of Black children. Laws (e.g., *Plessy v. Ferguson*), legal mandates (e.g., busing), Supreme Court decisions (e.g., *Brown*), individuals (e.g., Governor George Wallace), and events (e.g., school closings in Chicago in 2013) are only a few. Of significance to the understanding of race and culture in the education of Blacks is M Street High School in Washington D.C. There a controversy swirled around Anna Julia Cooper over the curriculum and the academic ability of Black children. The curriculum controversy was ignited in the debate between Booker T. Washington and W.E.B. Du Bois. On September 18, 1895, Washington delivered the *Atlanta Compromise* speech, which was a doctrine for racial solidarity, accommodation, and self-help. In the speech, Washington told Blacks to go slow, accept discrimination for the time being, and strive to lift themselves up through hard work and material prosperity. Washington argued that Blacks should study crafts in schools and learn industrial and farming skills. He counseled Blacks to cultivate the virtues of patience, enterprise, and thrift. Accommodation, Washington contended, would lead to Whites giving Blacks respect and subsequently, full U.S. citizenship. Du Bois ([1903]2005), on the other hand, argued that Washington's ideas would serve only to cause Whites to further oppress Blacks and would primarily serve White power and privilege. He contended that Washington's ideas were a request for Blacks to give up political power, as well as their fight for civil rights and access to quality higher education. Du Bois argued that Blacks must be assertive in obtaining their freedom throughout the country. He advocated political action and argued in "The

Talented Tenth" that social change for Blacks could be accomplished by developing small groups of college-educated African Americans (PBS: Public Broadcasting System, 1995; Du Bois, [1903]2005)).

In Washington D.C. the White-controlled school district and many Whites in general wanted Cooper—who was mostly using a classical academic curriculum and successfully placing graduates in prestigious colleges such as Harvard, Yale, and Amherst—to change to the vocational/industrial curriculum proposed by Washington. Cooper was opposed to this idea. She stated "[T]he American Negro is capable of contributing not only of his brawn and sinew but also from brain and character" (Lemert & Bhan, 1998, p. 213). Cooper's resistance to the industrial/vocation curriculum led to a political fight that lasted close to two years.

Cooper was verbally attacked in the media, and questions were raised by the Washington, D.C. Board of Education about her moral integrity. She was accused of having a relationship with one of her foster male adult children. Publicly, questions were raised about the appropriateness of the curriculum for Black students. Two graduating seniors were denied permission to graduate by the White superintendent because each had not passed a math exam taken during their sophomore year, but were nevertheless allowed by Cooper to graduate. Thus, her leadership as principal of the school was challenged.

Cooper temporarily survived the political assault with the help of colleagues and friends who strongly supported her innovative leadership and endorsed her use of an academic curriculum. However, she was summoned to a hearing about her leadership. There she delivered a strong testimony about her leadership ability, including data about the increasingly positive reputation the school had acquired under her guidance. She pointed out the placement of M Street High School graduates in leading colleges and universities and strongly defended the employment of an academic curriculum. Her opponents, however, would not give up. Four months later, a new committee to oversee M Street School was convened and took their concerns about M Street High School and Cooper's leadership to the congressional committee in charge of the District of Columbia schools. The strategy of attack by Cooper's opponents was to argue that she and some Black members of the school district convinced the Black assistant superintendent to sign the certificate of graduation for the two students who had not passed their math exam. Thus they had not followed official Board of Education procedure because it was argued that Percy Hughes, who was director of both the Black and White schools, was the only one who had the authority to sign the graduation certificate, and he had not done so. Therefore Cooper had violated District rules and regulations.

The congregational hearing resulted in a change in organizational procedures and establishment of a new board of education to handle policy and procedures. The hearing also led to the appointment of Percy Hughes as Superintendent of the D.C. school system. One of the first actions of the new board was to review all of the teachers employed by the district in order to decide who, if anyone, should be fired or not rehired. Cooper and three teachers were not rehired.

Standing up for and believing in the academic ability of her students—more so than accepting the score on a math test, employing innovative leadership, and using an academic curriculum that placed M Street High school students in the best colleges in the country—cost Cooper her job as principal. More significantly it cost many African American male and female students the opportunity to acquire the quality of education needed to pursue their dreams and career ambition. Furthermore, they lost the opportunity to validate their self-worth by successfully competing with their peers at the nation's finest colleges and universities.

The battle Cooper fought—not to have African American students segregated into a curricular program that was not in their best interest to challenge their academic talents—still continues today in schools across the US where Black students attend. African American students, especially males, are unfairly relegated to special education classes with regularity. In 1998, the U.S. Department of Education identified disproportionate minority representation in special education as an issue that was supported with exhaustive documentation (Artiles, 1998; Chin and Hughes, 1987; Grant, 1992; Patton 1998). In 2002 the Council for Exceptional Children noted the unfair representation of African American students in many districts across the country who were still disproportionally over-represented in special education classes; for example, in 2014 a report released by the Annenberg Institute posited that "the over-representation of African-American boys in special education classes has long been a widespread national problem, often related to a greater willingness on the part of the nation's overwhelmingly White, female teaching staff to peg behavior problems in Black males as some sort of disability" (Annenberg Institute, 2014, p. 2). Blanchett (2006) concluded that the disproportionate representation is in the context of White privilege and racism that is maintained disproportionally at all levels (e.g., the individual, institutional, educational, research, policy, and practice levels) and that teachers are inadequately prepared to deconstruct their privilege.

In addition to not providing African American students with an academic curriculum and by placing them disproportionately in special education programs, Black students are "tracked" into lower level classes. According to Pedro Noguera (2007), a school that uses a tracking system has obstacles in place (not encouraging Black students, promoting a deficit ideology about Black students) that often prevent African American students from entry into more rigorous classes. Further, schools in urban areas where Blacks attend often do not have "honor classes" or have fewer honor classes than in White suburban areas. In an article by Teresa Wiltz for the Maynard Media Center on Structural Inequity, it was reported that, "Students of color are also less likely to be given advanced-level coursework" (Wiltz, n.d.) This happens so often that students of color are held to lower academic expectations and Black students are placated and not pushed. They are given an "A" for work that should receive a "C."

The current battle for African American students to receive a challenging academic curriculum continues today with the same overt hideous theme that Anna Julia Cooper faced at M Street High School: many in the dominant society have difficulty accepting African Americans as fully intellectually developed, capable of competing and performing as any other living human being. Curriculum programs, designated classrooms, and other grouping strategies have been used and continue to be used to remove African American students from the mainstream of learning. Cooper offered two comments in 1892 that are relevant today: "We are not just educating heads and hands; we are educating the men and women of a race" and "The time has come ...when the educators of Negroes must see that one narrow pattern cannot meet the demands of this people whose life is as varied and whose needs are as various as the life and needs of the American people" (Lemert & Bhan, 1998, p. 252).

The Educational Thought of Anna Julia Cooper: A Closer Look

Bonnick (2007) contends that Cooper's vision of education was redemptive and should be "seen as a powerful inaugural formulation of an anti-racist pedagogy, detailing the concomitant understanding of the interconnection of race, gender, and class that others have built upon" (Bonnick, 2007, p. 179). Also, Cooper (1892) argued that schemes of education should have regard for the whole man (as we noted above) not a special class or race of men, but man as a paragon of creation, possessing in childhood and even in youth almost infinite possibilities for physical, moral, and mental development (Cooper, 1892, p. 258). As such, Bonnick (2007) argues, Cooper used education to navigate and transcend the negation of Black self-formation and contended it is located in "the traditions of resistance that emerged to reconstruct the generative experience of rupture which characterizes the forced incorporation of Black people in Western modernity" (Bonnick, 2007, p. 180). Central to Cooper's advocacy of education as redemptive and within the tradition of Black resistance, for Cooper it was the vehicle to address the exclusion and marginalization of Black women, and she linked racial uplift to the education of girls. In addition, Cooper's "redemptive vision" of education took strong exception to pathological characterizations of Black people as mentally incapable and not valuing education. Cooper needed little motivation to speak out against sneering malicious statements such as:

> Were Africa and the Africans to sink tomorrow, how much poorer would the world be? A little less gold and ivory, a little less coffee, a considerable ripple, perhaps where the Atlantic and Indian Ocean would come together—that is all; not a poem, not an invention, not a piece of art would be missed from the world.
>
> (Henry W. Beecher, quoted in Cooper, 1892, p. 161)

Cooper (1892), in response to such statements, wrote:

> Professing a religion of sublime altruism, a political faith in the inalienable rights of man as man, these jugglers with reason and conscience were at the same moment stealing heathen from their far away homes, forcing them with lash and gun to unrequited tool, making it a penal offence to teach them to read the word of God—begetting of their own flesh among those helpless creature and pocketing the guilt increase, the price of their own blood in unholy dollars and cents.
>
> (p. 207)

In her essay "What Are We Worth?" Cooper explains how an accumulative impact of historicized racial structures have shaped and continue to shape the conditions under which Black people lived; a point that was lost on many critics (e.g., Henry W. Beecher) about the intellect of African American people. Summarily, Cooper "rejected the racialization of Black life as biologically deficient and its methodological study of Black life as the systematic measurement of the inherent flaws of the character and culture" (Bonnick, 2007, p. 183).

About the schooling of Black students, Cooper (1892) said:

> We must, whatever else we do, insist on those studies which by the consensus of educators are calculated to train our people to think, which will give them the power of appreciation and make them righteous. In a word, we are building men, not chemists or farmers, or cooks, or soldiers, but men ready to serve the body politic in whatever avocation their talent is needed.
>
> (Lemert & Bhan, 1998, p. 47)

Ursuline Brooks, a former student at M Street High stated: "We were taught that our lives were to be lives of service and uplift to our race and our country" (quoted in Moore, 1999, p. 93).

Cooper, like many of her female colleagues during the time of legalized segregation, believed that she had a special responsibility to educate African American students and the Black community (Harley, 1982). Cooper saw education as a service to Black people. Bonnick (2007) posits:

> It is out of the lived experience of neglect that the critical reflexivity of Cooper's philosophical objective to situate education in the service of neglected people created a pedagogic space of rescue within which the self-authentication of the Black child could find expression. Education was to become a crucial instrument, inextricably linked with the creation of a new pedagogic imperative to fight the ontological insecurity of Black existence.
>
> (Bonnick, 2007, p. 180)

In performing her service, Cooper, as Collins (2000) posits, saw herself as a social change agent; a change agent who believed in the worth of every Black person and who was committed to giving each and every Black student the educational opportunity to succeed. Cooper (1892) argued that the bricklayer's and farmer's children as well as the children of the nurses and lawyers should have a curriculum that suited their ability. Cooper taught students until they got it; she believed in their ability, but understood that some students needed more attention than others. Gabel (1982) describes one of Cooper's former students speaking to this effect: "I was a member of [Mrs. Cooper's] Latin class ... I remember her ... put[ing] her whole heart and complete dedication into the performance of her job of teaching, *demanding* attention and participation from her students" (Gabel, 1982, p. 66; emphasis in original). The same student continues, "[s]he showed the young girls that it was possible to be a lady and a scholar" (Gabel, 1982, pp. 66–67). Cooper contended that female students are major receivers of the dividends from education, pointing out that schools [globally] have marginalized and/or denied women/girls full access to the educational opportunities. As the principal of M Street High School "[s]he allowed her teachers to take as much time as they needed to make sure students understood thoroughly" (Stewart, 2013, p. 48). Cooper believed that "If a child seem poor in inheritance, poor in environment, poor in personal endowment, by so much the more must organized society bring to that child the good tiding of social salvation through the school"(Cooper, 1892, p. 259).

Today, schools in the US continue to marginalize the female; and African American females are ignored throughout the curriculum. This arguably leads to achievement gaps and creates other social, psychological, and economic gaps (Kurpius, 2004; Tutwiler, 2005 and NCES, 2003). Baratelli et al.'s (2007) study, "Positioning toward Mathematics and Science Learning: An Examination of Factors Affecting Low-Income, African American Girls," reports on the marginalization of African American sixth grade female students and points out issues in schooling that affect Black girls. Baratelli et al. (2007) contend that positionality (e.g., where students are seated and relationship with the teacher) is important to classroom learning. Positionality is compounded by the gender and race of the students and teacher and it can influence the power dynamics in the classroom. Baratelli et al. (2007) report that their study is consistent with other research that reports African American girls are marginalized in math and science classes; and that they are aware of factors, such as positionality, that challenge their success in math and science. Also, African American girls know that they have been given a deficit academic label and they know that the girls who attend magnet schools live in better homes and receive a better education. In addition, African American girls are aware that their schools are less attractive and cared for than the schools of the girls who live in the "burbs." Issues of marginalization and denial of a quality education for African American girls, Baratelli et al. (2007) contend, undermine their development into womanhood and thereby stifle their contribution to humankind.

Cooper on Curriculum

For Cooper, teaching and the curriculum was about preparing Black people for the problems in life they would face and not constructing them as a problem. Humanistic education, Cooper believed, with its attention to the development of the whole child (e.g., knowledge, character, judgment, disposition, taste) steeped in Greek, Latin, and other classical subjects was the course of study to prepare "neglected people" to believe in themselves, and push back on the propaganda that they were inferior and should advocate for full citizenship. Cooper's choice of a humanistic curriculum more so than a science curriculum was probably born out of her positive belief in the worth of all people and the high regard she had for all members of her race. Throughout her essays and dissertation, she implicitly and explicitly celebrates all of human kind. Cooper clearly understood that Blacks' many years of enslavement had allowed Whites to totally construct and normalize them in any and every dehumanizing way possible; perhaps with one exception that was tightly controlled: Blacks' physical ability. Cooper understood that her affirmation of her own humanity and her preparation to live the life she chose, and not a life chosen for her, came from studying a humanistic curriculum and articulating a humanistic message. Bonnick (2007) argues that Cooper's, and other Blacks', pedagogic commitment to humanistic education "came from knowing their own humanity and those to whom they belong" (p. 186).

Over her tenure as a student, teacher, and principal, Cooper dealt with a number of curriculum issues. Perhaps the largest one was the academic/classic and vocational/industrial debate discussed above. However, the curriculum issue closest to Cooper's heart arguably was the issue of boys and girls being able to take the same course of study. Another curriculum issue that Cooper dealt with was the inclination to label Black children in general as lazy, instead of first examining the teacher quality and standards set by White text books and administrators. At M Street, Cooper saw actively engaged students who eagerly learned when treated with respect and when given direction and guidance. A curriculum issue that caused notable upset in Cooper was in the literature course, which included negative narratives about African Americans. Cooper (1892) stated, "What I hope to see before I die is a Black man honestly and appreciatively portraying both the Negro as he is, and the White man, occasionally, as seen from the Negro's standpoint." Cooper believed "that truth from each standpoint should be presented" (Lemert & Bhan, 1998, p. 35).

Today, with many arguing that students should follow a STEM (science; technology; engineering; maths) curriculum and the knowledge that social justice for Black people and other people of color has not been realized and the knowledge that many Black people are still struggling to see themselves as a "whole person" we wonder what Cooper would say about STEM. Would she tell African Americans to take STEM and then do what she did at St. Augustine and Oberlin and make a case for a change in the course of study that satisfies their needs? Would she argue for the STEM curriculum to include the arts and humanities? Or would she encourage girls, especially African American girls, to learn their science, mathematics, and technology and not to take a backseat to boys and to challenge the silencing of the cultural dimension of STEM. An article written by Celia Islam in the *Huffington Post*, speaks to why Cooper may say to African American girls, consider STEM but follow your interest. Islam (2013, n.p.) states:

> In a country in which the average woman still earns 77 cents for every dollar that a man earns, and in a country in which the majority of single parents are single mothers, getting more women into STEM could both reduce the gender wage gap and ensure that single mothers don't have to struggle to put food on the table. Not only are there currently more jobs in STEM than in any other industry, but most of these high-tech jobs are high-paying, as well.

We contend that first Cooper would welcome a discussion of curriculum that considers academics: humanities and science. She would be pleased that African Americans are not being systematically channeled to a course of study that mainly prepares them to work as service employees and therefore contributes to keeping them feeling as second class citizens because of economic disparities, which for many Blacks supports the legacy of inferiorization. On the other hand, she would insist that African Americans be aware of the application of STEM, making certain that knowledge acquired from math, science, and technology (e.g., Bell Curve, tests, and measurement) is not used to work against (e.g., objectification of) Black people as it has on occasions in the past and continues to do so. That said, we believe that Cooper would encourage African American students who have a proclivity to STEM to take up and excel in the course of study. Cooper understood that education operates both discourses of redemption and discourses of stratification and exclusion. Therefore, she was aware of the structural limitations within which education operates, but nonetheless she pursued pedagogic goals that would transgress educational neglect and its sociogenic roots by seeking to transform racism in school and society.

Cooper's theorizing on curriculum pushes back against the neoliberal thesis in State standards that contend the dominating activity in curriculum is the preparation of students for citizenship and work. Such essentializing of curriculum narrows the idea of the purpose of curriculum away from educating "men and women" for a well-rounded life, having the knowledge and skills to give services to the community and employing a curriculum that benefits all racially diverse male and female students as Cooper advocates. As educators update State Standards, reviewing the writing of Cooper will remind them that not all Americans agree with the ideas that only citizenship and work define the purpose of schooling.

During Cooper's time, quantitative research and measures were the yardstick used to evaluate the quality of research and arguments; and research and arguments that were not based on quantitative assessments were not given much attention. Cooper, with her acceptance and promotion of the use of personal knowledge and her argument that it should be considered alongside and not distinct from traditional forms of knowledge, was one of the early proponents of qualitative research. Cooper argued for "qualitative" methodology, not only because she believed in the importance of stories and other literary devices in promoting knowledge and understanding, but she believed that scientific methodology and quantitative measures often obscure prejudice and bigotry more than they uncover facts. She was wary of "the habit of generalization and deductive logic … used by statisticians and Social Science Research compliers" (May, 2012, p. 35). Researchers today who are conducting studies that use qualitative research may wish to view the writings of Cooper; she strongly challenged objectification and pointed to flawed theories of racial inferiority to make her case. In so doing, Cooper called attention to how societal institutions, such as the Supreme courts in the Dred Scott decision, used and supported flawed reasoning. Cooper contends that "weakness" and "strengths" "are socially enforced," and, therefore, not inherent.

A curriculum and teaching strategy in use in many schools, Place-based education (PBE) is consistent with Cooper's ideas about students using new school learnings to satisfy community needs and the importance of the school curriculum taking into account students' knowledge and interest in order to promote their intrinsic motivation. PBE tenets use curriculum to empower community members to improve the quality of life and their community; immerse students into their local heritages, cultures and landscapes; and it provides students with opportunities to use their newly learned knowledge to solve local problems (Promise of place, n.d.). Proponents of PBE will find Cooper's theorizing about students' learning and their application of knowledge meaningful.

Cooper on Teaching

Cooper was noted for saying that "Teaching has always seemed to me the noblest of callings" (*Negro College Graduates' Questionnaire*, n.d. cited in Johnson, 2007). As a teacher and principal, Cooper believed that teachers should be broadly educated—i.e., well-versed in the matters of the world and cognizant of the events and circumstances in their community. She believed that Black teachers should be the most enlightened individuals in the community and should, therefore, be educated to disseminate a broad range of information as well as have the knowledge and skills to help students achieve higher order thinking and life skills. M Street High School was well constituted to prepare students for college academic and social life. It had an outstanding faculty, several teachers had doctorates, and all were aware of the race and gender struggle that Black students would face.

When Cooper took over as principal, the school's college preparatory program was changed and expanded to better meet the academic needs of the students and to prepare them for college (Johnson, 2007). The changes led to many of the M Street students being accepted at elite colleges and universities. In addition, M Street was accredited by Harvard University (Robinson, 1981, p. 6, quoted in Johnson, 2007). Throughout the time Cooper was principal, Gabel (1982) states, "[s]uperior instruction was fostered by insistence on high standards of scholarship" and provisions were employed for "special tutorials to prepare promising students for college entrance examinations" (p. 49).

Cooper was a big believer in the arts as a teaching tool. She used drama to help students learn history, language, culture, and democracy and about Africans Americans' experiences and their service to the US (Ndounou, 2014). Cooper wrote and produced *Christmas Bells: A One-Act Play for Children*. The play is a story of three young African American sisters, Hannah, 11, Nannette, 8 and Annikins, 4, preparing for Christmas without their mother at home because she is working and their father, a soldier, is also away from home. He is fighting for democracy overseas. Because the family lacks economic means, the three girls are forced to celebrate Christmas and gift-giving by making their own gifts for each other instead of purchasing them. Ndounou (2014) writes: "The short play links concepts of democracy, Christianity, and the effects of the war on all of the nation's citizens represented by references to the absent parents as well as the rationing of sugar" (p. 35). Hannah explains to Nanette and Annikins, "democracy is what the Christ Child wants everywhere in the world" (p. 35). The play, as Ndounou points out, tells the audience about Black Americans' economic, political, and social hardship and their significant role in America's fight for democracy. All activities and events at M Street served as curriculum and pedagogy to teach students and community members about U.S. history and African Americans' role and patriotism in that history as well as in other subject matter disciplines. In addition, the school staged events designed to prepare students for college and to inform community members about how they could engage in racial uplift.

Cooper's dramatic performances would transcend the Black/White binary. They included different genres of music and dance, a mix of White and Black historical figures, references to famous Western works of arts, and employed language and visual clues to make connections between historical work and Black racial pride (Ndounou, 2014).

The plays and other school events encouraged community members to go to M Street and to consider it *their* school. In addition, Cooper wanted the community to know that she believed that the school knowledge students learned should be of service to their community. She stated:

> The youth must be taught to use his trigonometry in surveying his (sic) own and his (sic) neighbor's farm; to employ his (sic) geology and chemistry in finding out the nature of the soil … [and] to apply his (sic) mechanics and physics to the construction and handling of machinery.
>
> (Lemert & Bhan, 1998, p. 176)

Unfortunately, Cooper's teaching and curriculum methods have received little attention from those responsible for educating students who attend schools in urban spaces. M Street High School, located in the urban area of Washington, D.C. and several other schools years ago in the US consistently produced academically, socially, and civically successful African American students. Why the history of these schools has not been examined is concerning and speaks to how ideas from Black history and culture continue to be unrecognized and unutilized.

Cooper as a Cultural Worker in the Community

Throughout her life, Cooper was a strong supporter of community activities. From the time she arrived in Washington D.C. to take a job at M Street, Cooper engaged in school-community activities and offered leadership and direction to the Black community. Cooper argued that it took the family, community, state institutions, and the individual to educate (develop) the person. The house she purchased became the home for two foster children and eventually her mother when she was older. The house also became a regular meeting place for friends and community members to discuss art, literature, and music. Cooper held a night school for poor students in the living room of her home. She was a big believer in the home and, as Charles Lemert notes:

> [E]verything she did seemed always to issue from or return to her home. Nothing better expressed Cooper's sense of her life's work than the ways she used and effectively redefined her home … a figurative as well as a literal hearth of domestic warmth for cosmopolitan life of many accomplishments.
>
> (Lemart & Bhan, 1998, p.7)

In writing about home Cooper stated:

> A stream cannot rise higher than its source. The atmosphere of homes is no rarer and purer and sweeter than are the mothers in those homes. A race is but a total of families. The nation is the aggregate of its home.
>
> (1892, p. 63)

Cooper believed (as we noted above) that one of the roles of M Street was to help improve the social and economic conditions of the community and she held high expectations for parents and valued their commitment to the education of their children in spite of the racial and economic challenges they were facing.

In the 1890s, when the Women's Club movement was developing, Cooper became an active member within this middle class organization that promoted education for young children and the moral, religious, social, and economic well-being of women and children. Cooper was also very active in getting the Settlement House Movement started. In her essay, "The Social Settlement: What it Is, and What It Does" (1913), Cooper—a longtime member, trustee, and supervisor in the program—said of its purpose, "It is an attempt to carry into the city slums the incarnate Word, the idea of better living, the ideal of high thinking, embodied or energized in earnest and resourceful men and women who LIVE THERE" (Lemert & Bhan, 1998, p. 216).

In addition, Cooper was involved with organizations such as the Mu-So-Lit and Bethel and regularly participated in activities of Literary Clubs, the American Negro Academy, and the A.M.E. Church. Cooper founded the Colored Women's League of Washington in 1892, and seven years later helped open the first YWCA chapter for Black women in response to the National Office of the YWCA unwillingness to allow women of color into the organization. Another important facet of Cooper's community outreach was to speak at events within the D.C. Black community and to speak to the world community at conferences such as the Chicago World Fair (1983), the second Hampton Conference (1894), the American Negro Academy in Washington, D.C. (1897), and the first Pan-African Conference in London (1900).

Speaking at the first Pan-African Conference, Cooper voiced criticism about the emergence of apartheid in South Africa. Often when speaking in the U.S. one of Cooper's topics was offering a counter-narrative about the lives of enslaved people and debunking the romantic myth of the old South and that enslaved people were ignorant, happy, and needed the Whites to take care of them. Another way Cooper participated in community engagement was to write articles for newspapers and professional journals.

Looking across Cooper's life resume, a take-away is that Cooper always gave in an extraordinary way to global, national, and local communities. She was a leader and a worker, inspirational and caring, and saw Community as an important part of her life and the lives of Black people.

Conclusion

Since 1976 when Alex Haley published *Roots*, a saga of an enslaved family stolen from Africa, which also aired as a television mini-series in 1977, African Americans, and people in general, have engaged in research to re-discover their past—principally to learn about their ancestors (i.e., who they were, where and why they lived as they did, and what happened to them). For many Black people, "Slavery is a memory of something we cannot remember, and yet we cannot forget" (Jones, 2014, n.p.). *Black Intellectual Thought in Education: The Missing Traditions of Anna Julia Cooper, Carter G. Woodson, and Alain LeRoy Locke* agrees with Jones' statement, but knows that additional reasons other than simply "wanting to know" are a driving force. The major purpose for engaging in research includes continuing the drive to liberate and educate a people who are still seeking the full bloom of "life, liberty and the pursuit of happiness"; recognizing and honoring the people, institutions, and places that remain unknown, and whose story will probably never be told because of the US's racist past; enriching and enlarging the body of academic scholarship and research in education and the social sciences.

During her life, Anna Julia Cooper produced an amazing, first-of-its-kind body of work that stood on the democratic pillars of freedom, liberation, and acceptance of the humanity of Black people. In developing her scholarship, Cooper produced a powerful chain of inquiry into numerous social and political areas (e.g., schooling, working of the church, liberty, democracy) for Black and White people during the nineteenth and twentieth centuries. Cooper still has much to say to People of Color and White people today—especially those who advocate for social justice and multiculturalism.

Cooper would be the first to point out that quality research stands on the shoulders of past research and history that is accurate, inclusive, and as free as possible of omissions, biases, and distortions. Cooper would also be the first to argue, as this book argues, that for decades mainstream researchers read history and searched for research data and ideas only from mainstream historians and researchers and they ignored, discounted, and often silenced other possibilities. They, therefore, provided a flawed report, along with a biased analysis and discussion that has devastated Black people, socially, psychologically, economically, and politically. The voice of Anna Julia Cooper (along with the voices of many other scholars of color) has been ignored in mainstream research, reporting, and discussions as the nation continues to struggle with ideology, policy, and practice in regards to Black people and the education of students of color.

Cooper's life work was about helping African Americans as a people to gain all of the rights and privileges that White people have, including the opportunity unimpeded by racism for "life, liberty and the pursuit of happiness" and to be accepted as five-fifths (5/5) men and women. Cooper's day-to-day passion was to successfully educate African American children and families and to help lift up the Black race. Cooper was not naive; she understood the burden of the "cross" she chose to bear. She was unwavering in her protest against people who denied her people, and people in general, equality and fairness and "the full blessing of American life." Cooper had primary source knowledge of the tyranny Black people experienced on a daily basis as well as primary knowledge of the belief among many White people that a Black child was "worthless" or at best not as good as a White child. This belief has changed for the better over the decades, but the flawed ideology upon which it was constructed is a long way from being completely eliminated from the minds and behaviors of some White people as it is nuanced in what Joyce King (1991) calls "dysconscious racism," and as Mahzarin R. Banaji and Anthony Greenwald (2013) reference as "blind spots." From her days as a very young child, when she made the ABCs (schooling and education) her life's work, she was an academic and social warrior. She was celebrated somewhat during her life, but never received the recognition and celebration she deserved. It is encouraging to know that in recent years, scholars from all disciplines and of different identities (race, gender, class) are using her scholarship. Cooper, like so many others who were blessed with a great mind and a caring disposition, put forth ideas that have significance for today's problems and issues and for the enduring problems and issues of the past that continue to challenge the US.

Obituary: Washington Post, *February 27, 1964*

Anna Julia Cooper, writer, teacher and school administrator who celebrated her 105th birthday in August, died Thursday in her sleep at her home, 201 T. St. NW. The daughter of George Washington Haywood, a slave, Mrs. Cooper married the Rev. George A. C. Cooper, an Episcopal minister in Raleigh, N.C., in 1877. After her husband's death two years later, Mrs. Cooper moved north to become one of the few Negro women college graduates in the country when she received her Master's degree from Oberlin College in 1884. … After teaching Latin for several years at Dunbar, Mrs. Cooper received her Ph.D. in Latin from the Sorbonne in Paris in 1925, also publishing that year, in French, "Le Pelemage de Charlemagne." … Mrs. Cooper is survived by two great-nieces, Regia Bronson and Marion Goodwin, and a nephew, Andrew Haywood, all of the T St. address.

Note

1   The school changed its name to M Street High School from 1892–1916, and then to Dunbar High School from 1916 onwards.

References

Adams, J. & Adams, C. F. (1854). *The works of John Adams, second president of the United States: With a life of the author, notes and illustrations*, Vol. 9. New York: Little, Brown and Company.

Alexander, E. (1995). "We must be about our Father's business": Anna Julia Cooper and the in-corporation of the nineteenth-century African-American woman intellectual. *Sign, 20*(2), 336–356.

Aldridge (2008). D. P. (Ed.). *Our last hope: Black male–female relationships in change.* Bloomington, IN: Author House.

Allen, K. A. & Bowles, T. (2012). Belonging as a guiding principle in the education of adolescents. *Australian Journal of Educational & Developmental Psychology, 12*, 108–119.

Angelou, M. (2011). *O, the Oprah Magazine*, April 2011. Available online: www.oprah. com/spirit/How-to-Write-a-Poem-Maya-Angelous-Advice (accessed May 25, 2015).

Annenberg Institute for School Reform & Center for Collaborative Education (2014). Available online: www.ccebos.org/Executive%20Summary_final_pages.pdfity for Equity: Enrollment and Outcomes of Black and Latino Males in Boston Public Schools (accessed 22 December 2014).

Artiles, A. (1998). The dilemma of difference: Enriching the disproportionality discourse with theory and context. *The Journal of Special Education, 32*, 32–36.

Banaji, M. & Greenwald, A. G. (2013). *Blind spot*. New York: Delacorte.

Baratelli, A., West-Olatunji, C., Pringle, R., Adams, T. and Shure, L. (2007). Positioning toward Mathematics and Science Learning: An Examination of Factors Affecting Low-Income, African American Girls. Available online: www.eric.ed.gov/?id=ED496526 (accessed 24 May 2015).

Blanchett, W. J. (2006). Disproportionate representation of African American students in Special Education: Acknowledging the role of white privilege and racism. *Educational Researcher, 35*(6), 24–28.

Bonnick, L. (2007). In the service of neglected people: Anna Julia Cooper, ontology, and education. *Philosophical Studies in Education, 38*, 179–197.

Browne, E. T. (2008). Anna Julia Cooper and black women's intellectual tradition: Race, gender and nation in the making of a modern race woman, 1892–1925. Doctoral dissertation. University of California, Department of History.

Carby, H. (1987). *Reconstructing Womanhood: The Emergence of the Afro-American Woman Novelist*, New York: Oxford University Press.

Chin, P. C. & Hughes, S. (1987). Representation of minority students in special education classes. *Remedial and Special Education, 8*, 41–46.

Collins, P. (2000). *Black feminist thought: Knowledge, consciousness, and the politics of empowerment*. New York: Routledge.

Connell, R. W. (1995). *Masculinities*. Berkeley, CA: University of California Press.

Cooper, A. J. (1892). A Voice from the South, by a Black Woman of the South. In C. Lemert and E. Bhan (1998). *The voice of Anna Julia Cooper: Including a Voice from the South and other important essays, papers, and letters*. New York: Rowman & Littlefield.

Cooper, A. J. ([1925]1988). Slavery and the French Revolutionists (1788–1805) (translation of Cooper's doctoral thesis, *France's Attitude toward Slavery during the Revolution* [L'attitude de la France à l'égard de l'esclavage pendent la revolution]. Lewiston, NY: Edwin Mellen Press.

Cooper, A. J. (1930). The humor of teaching, *The Crisis, 37*(10), 393–394.

Cooper, B. (2014). "Not going to lie down and take it": Black women are being overlooked by this president. *Salon*. Available online: www.salon.com/2014/06/17/not_going_to_lie_down_and_take_it_black_women_are_being_overlooked_by_this_president/ (accessed 17 June 2014).

Council for Exceptional Children (2002). Addressing Over-Representation of African American Students in Special Education. Arlington, VA: Council for Exceptional Children.

Cusick, C. M. (2009). Anna Julia Cooper, Worth, and public intellectual. *Philosophia Africana, 12*(1), 21–41.

Damrosch, L. (2011). *Tocqueville's discovery of America*. New York: Farrar, Straus and Giroux.

de Lafayette, M. (1789). *Declaration of Rights of Man and of Citizen.*

Du Bois, W. E. B. ([1903]2005). *Souls of Black folks.* New York: Simon & Schuster.

Elkholy, S. N. (n. d.). Feminism and race in the United States. *Internet Encyclopedia of Philosophy.* Available online: www.iep.utm.edu/fem-race/print (accessed 31 December 2014).

Fischer, S. (2004). *Modernity disavowed. Haiti and the cultures of slavery in the age of revolution.* Chapel Hill, NC: Duke University Press.

Gabel, L. (1982). *From slavery to the Sorbonne and beyond: The life and writings of Anna Julia Cooper.* Northampton, MA: Smith College.

Gilbert, H. & Tompkins, J. (1996). *Post-colonial drama: Theory, practice, politics.* London and New York: Routledge.

Giles, M. S. (2006). Dr. Anna Julia Cooper, 1858–1964: Teacher, scholar, and timeless womanist. *The Journal of Negro Education, 75*(4), 621–634.

Goodenow, C. (1993). The psychological sense of school membership among adolescents: Scale development and educational correlates. *Psychology in the Schools, 30,* 70–90.

Grant, P. (1992). Using special education to destroy black boys. *The Negro Educational Review, 63,* 17–21.

Guy-Sheftall, B. (2009). Black feminist studies: The case of Anna Julia Cooper. *African American Review, 43*(1), 11–15.

Haley, A. (1976). *Roots.* New York: Doubleday.

Hamilton, A., Madison, J. & Jay, J. ([1788]1987). *The Federalist papers.* London: Penguin.

Harley, S. (1982). Beyond the classroom: The organizational lives of Black female educators in the District of Columbia, 1890–1930. *Journal of Negro Education, 51*(3), 254–265.

Holvino, S. (2008). Intersections: The simultaneity of race, gender and class in organization studies. *Gender, Work and Organization.* Available online: www.chaosmanagement. com/images/stories/pdfs/GWO%20Simultaneityfinal5-08.pdf (accessed 7 July 2014).

Hubbard, L. C. (2005). An Afrocentric study of the intellectual thought of Anna Julia Cooper. Temple University, Philadelphia, PA: Doctoral dissertation, Temple University, Department of African American Studies.

Hutchinson, L. D. (1981). *Anna Julia Cooper: A voice from the South.* Washington, DC: Smithsonian Institution Press.

Hyman, U. (1990). Black feminist thought in the matrix of domination. Available online: www.runet.edu/~lridener/courses/BLKFEM.HTML (accessed 26 December 2014).

Islam, C. (2013). Closing the STEM gender gap: Why is it important and what can you do to help? *Huffington Post.* October 10. Available online: www.huffingtonpost.co/celia-islam/closing-the-stem-gender-g_b_3779893.html (accessed May 25, 2015).

Jacobsson, C., Pousette, A. & Thylefors, I. (2001). Managing stress and feeling of mastery among Swedish comprehensive school teachers, *Scandinavian Journal of Education Research, 45*(1), 37–53.

Johnson, K. (2007). The educational leadership of Anna Julia Haywood Cooper. Available online: www.advancingwomen.com/awl/winter2007/annajcooper.htm (accessed 6 September 2024).

Jones, B. T. (2014). Journey to Tanzania. Available online: http://avatanzania.blogspot. com/2014/05/slavery-is-memory-of-something-we.html (accessed 17 February 2015).

Kamenica, E. & Simonson, I. (2008). Racial preferences in dating. *Review of Economic Studies, 75,* 117–132.

King, J. (1991). Dysconscious racism: Ideology, identity, and the miseducation of teachers. *Journal of Negro Education, 60*(2), 133–146.

Kurpius, S. E. (2004). Encouraging talented girls in math and science: Effects of a guidance intervention. *High Ability Studies, 15*, 85–102.

Kwanzaa Guide (2014). What Anna Julia Cooper can teach America and the Women's Movement. Available online: http://kwanzaaguide.com/2014/03/what-anna-julia-cooper-can-teach-america-and-the-womens-movement/ (accessed 28 December 2014).

LaCapra, D. (2000). *History and reading: Tocqueville, Foucault, French Studies.* Toronto: University of Toronto Press.

Lee, R. M. & Robbins, S. B. (1998). The relationship between social connectedness and anxiety, self-esteem, and social identity. *Journal of Counseling Psychology, 45*(3), 338–345.

Lemert, C. & Bhan, E. (1998). *The voice of Anna Julia Cooper: Including A Voice from the South and other important essays, papers, and letters.* New York: Rowman & Littlefield.

Lewis, C. W., James, M., Hancock, & Hill-Jackson (2008). Framing African American students' success and failure in urban settings: A typology for change. *Urban Education, 43*, 127–153.

Lindquist, M. A. (2006). "The world will always want men": Anna Julia Cooper, womanly Black manhood, and "predominant man-influence." *Left History,* 11(2), 13–46.

Logan, S. W. (2006). Frances, E. W. Harper, "Women's political future." Available online: http://archive.vod.umd.edu/civil/harper1893int.htm (accessed May 30 2015).

McIntosh, P. (1988) *White privilege and male privilege: A personal account of coming to see correspondences through work in women's studies.* Working paper no. 189, Wellesley College Center for Research on Women, Wellesley, MA 02181. Available online: www.iub. edu/~tchsotl/part2/McIntosh%20White%20Privilege.pdf (accessed May 30, 2015).

May, V. M. (2004). Thinking from the margins, acting at the intersections: Anna Julia Cooper's *Voice from the South. Hypatia, 19*(2),74–91.

May, V. M. (2007). *Anna Julia Cooper, visionary black feminist: A critical introduction.* New York and London: Routledge.

May, V. M. (2009). Writing the self into being: Anna Julia Cooper's textual politics. *African American Review, 43*, (1), 17–34.

May, V. M. (2010). *Writing the self into being: Anna Julia Cooper's textual politics.* Athens, OH: Ohio University Press.

May, V. M. (2012). *"It is never a question of the slaves": Anna Julia Cooper's challenge to history's silences in her 1925 Sorbonne thesis.* Athens, GA: University of Georgia Press.

Mills, C. W. (1959). *On intellectual craftsmanship: The sociological imagination.* New York: Oxford University Press.

Moody-Turner, S. (in press). "Dear doctor Du Bois": Anna Julia Cooper, W. E. B. Du Bois and the gender politics of black publishing. *MELUS.*

Moody-Turner, S. (2013). *Black folklore and the politics of racial representation.* Jackson, MS: The University Press of Mississippi.

Moody-Turner, S. & Stewart, J. (2009). Gendering Africana studies: Insights from Anna Julia Cooper. *African American Review, 43*(1), 35–44.

Moore , J. M. (1999). *Leading the race: Transformation of the Black elite in the nation's capital, 1880–1920.* Charlottesville, VA: University Press of Virginia.

NCES (2003). The condition of education. National Center for Educational Statistics (NCES). Washington, DC: US Government Printing Office.

Ndounu, M. W. (2014). *Shaping the future of African American film: Color-coded economics and the story behind the numbers.* New York: Rutgers University Press.

Noguera, P. A. (2007). School reform and second-generation discrimination: Toward the development of equitable schools. Annenberg Institute for School Reform. Available online: www.indiana.edu/~atlantic/wp-content/uploads/2011/11/Noguera-School-Reform-and-Second-Generation-Discrimination.pdf (accessed December 22, 2014).

Nutbrown, C. & Clough, P. (2009). *Early childhood education: History, philosophy and experience.* New York: SAGE.

Patton, J. M. (1998). The disproportionate representation of African-Americans in special education: Looking behind the curtain for understanding and solutions. *Journal of Special Education, 32*, 25–31.

Price, K. M. (2004). *To Walt Whitman, America.* Chapel Hill, NC: University of North Carolina Press. Available online: www.whitmanarchive.org/criticism/current/anc.00151.html#chap1 (accessed October 18, 2014).

Promise of place (n.d.). Available online: www.promiseofplace.org (accessed May 25, 2015).

Public Broadcasting System (PBS). (1995) Booker T. & W. E. B. Frontline. Available online: www.pbs.org/wgbh/pages/frontline/shows/race/etc/road.html (accessed August 17, 2014).

Rogers, C. R. (1961). *On becoming a person.* Boston MA: Houghton Mifflin.

Schleereth, T. J. (1991). The everyday life in America series, Vol. 4 (Book 4). New York: Harper Perennial, Internet archive (accessed June 21, 2014).

Simpson, B. (2013). Tocqueville on slavery and prejudice. Available online: http://cwcrossroads.wordpress.com/2011/07/21/tocqueville-on-slavery-and-prejudice/ (accessed September 9, 2014).

Stewart, A. (2013). *First class: The legacy of Dunbar, America's first Black public high school.* Chicago, IL: Lawrence Hill Books.

Tocqueville, A. de ([1835]2004). *Democracy in America.* New York: Library of America.

Tocqueville, A. de ([1835]2014). *"Mon Instinct, mes opinions"* In A. H. Nimtz, Marx, Tocqueville, and race in America, p. 5. Lanham, MD: Rowman & Littlefield.

Tutwiler, S. J. W. (2005). *Teachers as collaborative partners: Working with diverse families and communities.* New York and London: Routledge.

Wallace-Wells, D. (2010). The trouble with Tocqueville. *Newsweek,* 14 April 2010. Available online: www.newsweek.com/trouble-tocqueville-70747 (accessed May 25, 2015).

Washington, B. T. (1895). Cast Down Your Bucket. (Atlanta Comprise Speech). Atlanta Cotton Exposition. https://www.google.com/?gws_rd=ssl#q=booker+t+washington+cast+down+your+bucke (accessed June 18, 2015).

Wheaton, S. (2013, May 8). For first time on record, Black voting rate outpaced rate for Whites in 2012. *The New York Times.* Available online: www.nytimes.com/2013/05/09/us/politics/rate-of-black-voters-surpassed-that-for-whites-in-2012.html (accessed December 22, 2014).

Wilberforce University, (n.d). Available online: www.wilberforce.edu/welcome/history.htm (accessed July 3, 2014).

Wilson Pierson, G. ([1938]1996). *Tocqueville in America.* Baltimore, MD: Johns Hopkins University Press.

Wiltz, T. (n.d.) Educators alarmed: Black, Latino high school students perform at levels of 30 years ago. Maynard Media Center on Structural Inequity. *America's Wire.* Available online: http://americaswire.org/drupal7/?q=content/educators-alarmed-black-latino-high-school-students-perform-levels-30-years-ago (accessed December 22, 2014).

Yeary, C. (2009). *The Victorian era in America: 1837–1901.* Available online: http://twrpcactusrose.blogspot.com/2009/09/victorian-era-in-america1837-1901.html (accessed May 26, 2015).

3

CARTER G. WOODSON AGAINST THE WORLD

A Racial Project of Freedom and Resistance

Introduction

Critical thought that transcends time and space can address ongoing educational and social issues. In education, there is a canon of scholars whose ideas have exceeded the context of their original publications. For example, if one were to use a "Gramscian," "Freiran" "Bourdieuian," "Marxian," or "Foucauldian" approach to educational and curricular problems, one would be drawing on a body of work or a set of philosophies that appear to have perennial application across time and space. The author is dead but the ideas endure. However, what allows a scholar's ideas to endure? While there is no clear-cut answer to this question, there are a few noted characteristics in academia.

Some may reference the significance of a methodology that shed new theoretical light on a social phenomenon in schools and society, such as Clifford Geertz's (1973) notion of "thick description." In some cases, enduring theories can help to challenge old thinking about race, class, gender, and sexuality. A scholar's ideas might have helped to develop new theoretical and historical scholarship for exploring educational problems, such as Michel Foucault's notion of historical genealogy. Such a theory is likely to be widely used to make sense of different aspects of education, including teacher education, curriculum, policy, and school practice. Paulo Freire's use of critical theory in education helped to create a new field known as critical pedagogy.

A prominent scholar may also help create a space to produce a clearinghouse of important scholarship, through the creation of a journal, a center, or a series of textbooks. In addition, important scholars that seek to produce new knowledge are often great teachers. They are able to convey their work in a clear and coherent fashion, thus producing new scholars that expand the original ideas with important and cutting-edge scholarship. Moreover, an area that has recently received much attention within academia is the extent to which a scholar's ideas and work is able to reach the masses.

Scholars of this magnitude tend to have a global quality that enables their ideas, philosophies, and research to speak broadly to the issues related to the human condition. We cite scholars' work for their ability to explain and deconstruct how different socio-historical contexts have encumbered the ability of humans to reach their highest potential. There is a timelessness to this scholarship that enables the researcher and theorist of education to draw on their ideas, quote their phrases, and employ their theories, no matter how far removed in time and space is the author's work. Their work inspires a new generation of theorists to explore new questions and apply their ideas to new pedagogical contexts. Over time, their ideas and names become iconic and normalized, where using their work becomes an expectation. Their ideas and body of literature become an approach where we add the suffix "–ian" to give credence to the author's ideas as a framework that could be applied to any sociological issue in schools and society.

However, what is apparent in the field of critical educational thought is that our Marxian, Freirean, Gramscian, Freudian, Deleuzian, and Foucauldian approaches are all from White males. This is not to take away from the pertinence of this work, but to highlight a blind spot in the field of educational thought that has received little interrogation—the overwhelming whiteness in the canonical thought of education. There are many historical and institutional arguments to explain why the "great thinkers" of social and educational thought are mostly White and male, but the truth remains that White males' ideas are the frames used to examine universal problems in schools and society. In the case of Marx, the context of the European proletariat became the conceptual frame for all exploitative working relationships around the globe. Again this does not take away from the significance of Marx and other great thinkers that are used to explain perennial educational issues, but it does highlight whose knowledge and ideas receive the most currency.

For example, scholars have addressed the importance of Black educational thought as a way to give coherence to the core beliefs that guide this body of work. The work of William Watkins (1993), in particular, outlines the ideologies that have had the most currency in Black educational thought; what he calls "Black curriculum orientations." What this work tends to do however, is clump Black educational thinkers into overarching ideological themes, as opposed to focusing on the details of their scholarship. The exception, however, is Derrick Alridge's (1999, 2008) thoroughly engaging work on W.E.B. Du Bois.

In a similar vein, we believe that Carter G. Woodson's ideas require this kind of attention. His experiences, ideas, philosophies, and projects help to provide a powerful framework for making sense of enduring issues such as race, culture, pedagogy, and curriculum. His work touches on all the qualities discussed above.

Most notably, Woodson provided a vocabulary and theory to explain the conditions of education, while also developing a methodology to deconstruct curriculum in a manner that was accessible to the masses. In the sections that follow we lay out the philosophical tenets and projects that define Woodson's scholarship and how his conceptions of curriculum and instruction can serve as a theoretical frame to examine enduring educational concerns.

This certainly is not the first time scholars have discussed the importance of Woodson's work. However, there appear to be three prominent ways in which Woodson's work has been addressed in the historical and Black studies literature. One prominent body of literature has focused on his biography and the evolution of his work (Apatheker, 1997; Dagbovie, 2004, 2007a, 2007b, 2011, 2014a, 2014b; Goggin, 1985, 1993; Goggin and Wilson, 1994; Pressly, 2006). This scholarship seeks to either explain the trajectory of Woodson's biography and/or outline the details of his work with the *Association of Negro Life and History* (1915) (from this point forward referred as the *Association*). Studies in this category include those by scholars who worked closely with Woodson at the *Association* and who wrote retrospectively about their experiences (Lindsay, 1950, Logan, 1945; Wesley, 1951). In addition, some scholars attempt to outline the underlying precepts of Woodson's project as it relates to aspects of education (Dilworth, 2003; Brown, King, Crowley, 2011; King, Crowley & Brown, 2011; King & Brown, 2015). A small body of literature has attempted to situate Woodson's ideas within the discourse of progressive educational history (Au, 2012; Apple, 2013; King, Davis & Brown, 2012) and critical educational thought (Brown, 2010; Dagbovie, 2004, 2007b, 2010). Scholars have also focused on Woodson as the progenitor of Black Historical Studies, pan-Africanist thinking (Fenderson, 2010; Levine, 2000; Rashid, 2005), and multicultural education (Crowder, 2005; Warren, 2007; Wiggan, 2010). However, it is Woodson's notion of "mis-education" that has received the most attention. Across a variety of fields the idea of mis-education is used to make sense of enduring educational and social issues (Strong-Leek, 2008). Even in more popular media spaces such as *Ebony, Jet*, and *Essence* magazine, Woodson's *The Mis-education of the Negro* is touted as one of the most widely read texts among the mostly Black readership of these magazines. In addition, the singer and rapper Lauryn Hill used the phrase in her popular album, *The Miseducation of Lauryn Hill* (Dagbovie, 2014b).

One of the more striking realizations is that Woodson's ideas are virtually absent from the wider or "Whiter" educational discourse of curriculum studies and curriculum (Brown & Au, 2014). With the exception of a few scholars that have called for reconceptualization of his work, Woodson's work has been ghettoized in at least two ways that are significant to this project. Woodson's ideas and work are mostly cited in journals that focus exclusively on issues related to African Americans. We do not suggest that this is a problem in of itself as Woodson's project and ideas were certainly speaking to a targeted audience— African Americans. This however, was the case for Dewey, Marx, Bourdieu, and many of the scholars that are used in a global sense. Their ideas were speaking to a specific context, yet we use them in a general sense. We contend that Woodson's work should be treated as a coherent body of thoughts and ideas that have universal application to the theorizing of critical education.

In the section that follows, we lay out the core parts to Woodson's racial project (Omi & Winant, 2015) with the *Association*. We then speak to aspects of his biography as a way to outline the personal undercurrents of his racial project. These undercurrents surface throughout this chapter to illustrate the inextricable ties between Woodson's personal convictions and the work he produced through his lifetime to what was called *the cause*. Then we lay out the core theoretical presuppositions of his work as expressed through the different projects tied to the *Association*. In addition, we lay out the defining aspects of his work as it relates to enduring issues in educational theory—we call it the *Woodsonian Vision of Educational Thought*. A core question guiding this chapter is: *How are Woodson's ideas foundational to many of the enduring theoretical concerns in education?*

Woodson's Project

Woodson's body of work produced volumes of historical studies about the experiences of African Americans in the US. Woodson produced historical and sociological scholarship about the experiences of African Americans in order to challenge existing theories. The cornerstone of the *Association* was to produce scholarly work that was empirically rigorous and theoretically sound. Woodson made every effort to ensure that the ideas and histories promoted through the *Journal of Negro History* were accurately depicted and not appealing to the belief in producing hyperbole or exaggerations about the histories and experiences of African Americans (Dagbovie, 2007a).

His body of work also has helped to set in place a new theoretical discourse, what he called "mis-education." In his seminal text *The Mis-education of the Negro*, he developed two critiques to the common educational models promoted for African Americans. First, he found that industrialized education did not provide the African American with the practical tools to gain employment. Second, he argued that classical education could only amount to "mental discipline" because of the limited opportunities given to African Americans outside of industries of labor. Woodson (2000 [1933]) examined the limitations of each program and drew attention to a larger problem he defined as the "mis-education of the Negro."

Woodson (1998 [1933]) argued that "mis-education" created the conditions for the "educated Negro" to no longer be committed to the needs of African Americans. Woodson (2000 [1933]) stated, "The 'educated Negroes' have the attitude of contempt toward their own people"(p. 1). He maintained that typical histories of African Americans helped to foster an *ideology of inferiority*. Woodson (1998 [1933]) makes this point clear through his contention that: "Students were not told that ancient Africans of the interior knew sufficient science to concoct poisons for arrowheads, to mix durable colors for paintings, to extract metals from nature and refine them for development in industrial arts" (p. 18). He concluded that the production of myths about African Americans caused educated African Americans to engender negative perspectives about themselves and Black people as a whole.

Woodson (1998 [1933]) further asserted that without giving attention to the philosophical aspects of Black education, African Americans would continue to be "mis-educated," resulting in the internalization of negative beliefs. He maintained that mis-education perpetuated class differences and community mistrust, creating a politically and socially fractured African American community. Woodson further claimed that because of this process of mis-education, the "educated" African American teacher had become nothing more than a symbol of inclusion, lacking the cultural knowledge, history, and vision necessary to uplift the race.

Woodson's critical perspective makes clear the role and expectation of Black education. He raised important questions about how systems of beliefs or, as some educational theorists have put it, the "hidden curriculum" (Apple, 1975; Giroux, 1983; Young, 1971) reproduces African American students' educational and socioeconomic conditions. Woodson (1998 [1933]) insisted that the best way to transform the dilemma of "mis-education" was through the re-development of a curriculum. This critique shifted the discourse of Black education in the 1930s to focus on the unintended outcomes of "educating" African Americans and offer new ways to conceptualize the needs of Black education.

Woodson was also able to create a space in which to produce and house important scholarship. Although Woodson never held a long-term position in higher education, his ability to remain an independent scholar was remarkable. As numerous scholars (Dagbovie, 2007a; Hine, 1986; Meier & Rudwick, 1984) explain, the creation of the *Association* helped to catalyze the professionalization of Black History. The *Association* helped to produce the *Journal of Negro History* and the *Negro Bulletin* as well as publish volumes of textbooks for elementary and secondary classrooms (Brown, 2010; Dagbovie, 2007a). It also served as a training ground for numerous Black scholars such as Rayford Logan, Lawrence Reddick, Charles Wesley, and Lorenzo Greene who each went on to produce some of the most important scholarship on Black History. The *Association* also generated new ideas about Black curriculum and history, as well as serving as an organized clearinghouse for the most important scholarship of the early twentieth century on African American history.

In addition, there are numerous examples of how Woodson's scholarship reached the masses. Some historians (Dagbovie, 2004, 2007a; Goggin, 1993) note that making his ideas and research about Black history relevant was a foundational principle in Woodson's work. His most recognized and enduring contribution to Black history and curriculum was making his scholarship accessible through the creation of Negro History Week. Lawrence Reddick (2002[1950]) described the importance of Negro History week:

> Negro History Week is, perhaps, the most characteristic creation of Carter G. Woodson. He seemed to think of it as his most successful venture. While his greatest influence upon scholars came through the pages of the Journal of Negro History and his research books, his greatest direct influence upon the public mind came through Negro History Week. This mass education program appealed to one side of Dr. Woodson's nature. The response to it from young and old, educated and uneducated, pleased him to no end.
>
> (p. 35)

Without question, *Negro History Week* was Woodson's magnum opus (Woodson, 2002 [1926]). One indicator of the importance of Negro History Week for Woodson is reflected in the number of times he wrote about the growth and significance of the event annually (Woodson, 1925, 1926, 1927, 1930, 1935, 2002[1926]).

His efforts inspired scholars who would eventually become part of the *Association*. In 1930, at the close of the Negro History Week in Washington D.C., Lorenzo Greene, one of the key scholars from the *Association*, wrote in his diary that the event made him "a confirmed and dedicated associate" (cited in Strickland, 1996, p. 1) of Dr. Carter G. Woodson. The *Negro History Week* and *Negro Bulletin* and *Home Study Program* each sought to make historical and sociological knowledge about African Americans clearly written and reachable.

As many scholars note, Woodson was an activist-scholar in the truest sense of the word (Dagbovie, 2007a; Wesley, 1951). The content and racial philosophy of Woodson's project were directly tied to the discourses and imagery that surrounded Black life and Black people. Through multiple genres, Woodson saw Black history as the content and context to produce a new conception of Black life and Black people. Woodson, however, found that the context of Black life was tied to deep humanistic and democratic concerns. The displacement of the "Negro" in the US was seen as a breach of the spoils of nationhood in the US and the basic human protections that are afforded to mankind. In the section that follows we outline how the aspects of survival and resistance undergirded his lifetime project about African American history and life.

A Short Biography of Woodson: Birth to the Association

Carter Godwin Woodson was born December 19, 1875 to James Henry and Anne Eliza Woodson (both former enslaved Africans) in New Canton, Virginia, where he was raised in a setting of "high morality and strong character through religious teachings"(p. 9). His early years mostly involved working on his father's farm, with the exception of four months out of the year when he attended a one-room schoolhouse, where his uncles John Morton and James Buchanan Riddle were his teachers. By his teenage years, Woodson eventually followed his brothers to work in the coalmines of West Virginia.

At twenty years old however, he returned to the city where his parents lived and he attended Frederick Douglass High School, where he finished his diploma in only two years. With a desire for more education Woodson enrolled in Berea College in Kentucky. He eventually completed his degree at Berea, where he then worked as high school teacher for a short while in West Virginia. He would then take a teaching job abroad through the War Department to teach in the Philippines. By 1907, Woodson had been enrolled at the University of Chicago full time, where he would earn a bachelor's and master's degree. After completing his degree he enrolled in a PhD. in History at Harvard University, where he earned his doctorate. While he was completing his dissertation at Harvard he held several teaching jobs at the Washington D.C. public schools. His main teaching position took place at the well-known M Street High School from 1911 to 1917, where he inspired many students to study Black History, including the prominent historian, Rayford Logan (Goggin, 1993).

In 1915, Woodson co-founded the Association of the Study of Negro Life in History, while he was still teaching in the Washington D.C. schools. Then after a short stint as a principal, he would eventually be hired at Howard University for his first academic appointment. However, after a series of controversial interactions with then President and board member J. Stanley Durkee, he was eventually dismissed (Goggin, 1993). He then would spend the next two years at West Virginia Collegiate Institute as a teacher and administrator before his work at the *Association* became his single-minded focus.

In a fairly short amount of time Woodson had gained three degrees, studied at the University of Paris, taught in the Philippines, and served as a public school teacher and administrator, eventually to teach at Howard University and the West Virginia Collegiate Institute. It seemed as if Woodson's early adult life had pulled him in many directions. From 1922 to his death in 1950 however, he spent his entire life committed to one mission: the illumination of Black History. In Goggin's (1993) words:

> By 1915 this son of former slaves had come a long way. Working as farm laborer, sharecropper, and coal miner, Woodson acquired an appreciation for both the Black masses and Black folk culture. [...] From the time Woodson left his parents' home to attend Berea until the time he founded the Association for the Study of Negro Life in History eighteen years later, he underwent experiences that expanded and influenced his world view and shaped his ideas about the ways in which education could transform society.

(p. 31)

While the purpose of this section is to briefly show the trajectory of his life just before the *Association* flourished, certain stories, people, and experiences would provide Woodson with the most significant narratives to serve as muses and inspiration to his life. In the section that follows we outline three contexts that would serve as a lasting narrative to his vision of educational transformation.

Biographic Muses: An Enduring Narrative of Freedom and Persistence

Carter Godwin Woodson's life was situated within the extremes of opportunity—on one end the dire circumstances of Black life while on the other end the elitism of higher education. The polarity of his experiences in seeing the gritty reality of racial exclusion as well as the ivory towers of academia created a complex biography that is intimately tied to his life's work. His biography illustrates the kind of historical narrative Woodson often shared in his curricular project—situating the context of Black achievements in the wider Black struggle to overcome the overt and hidden hand of racial oppression. Woodson's life was certainly defined within the wider context of Black oppression, as well as through the unique struggles of his life. Most strikingly, Woodson was, "the first and only Black American of slave parentage to earn a PhD in history" (Goggin, 1993, p. 1). This achievement powerfully illustrates Woodson's drive. Woodson was impassioned in his efforts to tell the story of the American Negro as they traversed the tumultuous terrain of racial prejudice and White supremacy. This larger story mirrors the individual story of Carter Godwin Woodson.

Woodson's narrative displays a life in perpetual motion. His project to produce new knowledge about Black life remained constant. In many respects, *it was his life*. He never married and never had children, so his work was the very substance of his life. With a dogged and sometimes stubborn focus, Woodson's efforts created a new discipline by challenging enduring myths told about people of African descent in the New World. When he passed in 1950, Carter Godwin Woodson had developed a voluminous catalogue of Black life, laying the foundation for a body of scholarship that indelibly impacted academia and the popular discourse of Black history. In looking at his life and accomplishments, raised in a humble coal mining community, Woodson's legend has all the makings of an American folktale. While his single-minded focus on the knowledge construction of the American Negro can give one the impression that his agency alone helped to single-handedly transform the existing racial narrative of the African Diaspora, the people and spaces from his past also provided a foundation or worldview to carry out his mission.

Two aspects of Woodson's biography would have an indelible mark on his project. The first was the stories of his uncle, father, and grandfather, who each held tight to an enduring and stubborn conception of freedom beyond the racial bondage that enveloped their lives. The second influence on his life emerged during his childhood and pre-college years, when he would be exposed to and surrounded by ideas that shaped his earliest ambitions to construct and distribute new knowledge about Black people. Collectively, these experiences set in place an identity of persistence and ambition to study, construct, and disseminate the story of the American Negro and the African Diaspora.

Woodson's family biography starts well before his birth. He was the child of parents that grew up in slavery. The lives of his parents and grandparents provided Woodson a narrative that he would carry with him his entire life. Their experiences taught him that, even within strident racial boundaries, one must persist to seek freedom and overcome the existential experience of bondage. Woodson's grandfather had a unique experience as an enslaved African. As a trained carpenter, he was able to work as a hired slave. In one sense, the conditions of hired slaves were harsher due to the difficult working conditions and the day-to-day abuse from craftsmen but, in another sense, being a hired slave provided more freedom. As a result, his grandfather often saw himself as a free man, which caused him many problems with his master (Goggin, 1993). As Goggin (1993) explained, this notion of rebelliousness and insistence to be free was also a characteristic of Woodson's uncles. Here Goggin (1993) explains the rebelliousness of George (Woodson's uncle):

> George, who worked as field slave, was purported to have been an unruly and rebellious slave and was frequently punished, even after performing all of his duties. He grew tired of punishment and began to strike back. Like his father, he got into a fight with an overseer when he believed his punishment was unjustified.
>
> (p. 3)

The other son, James Henry Woodson (Carter's father), followed his father's and brother's examples of rebelliousness. After coming close to being whipped by a farm owner for using "leisure time to his own advantage" while working as hired hand on a farm (Goggin, 1993, p. 4), James Henry rebelled and whipped the farm owner and fled to his master to plead his case. His master reprimanded James Henry for his impertinence and insisted that he not act as if he were free. James Henry responded by saying that, "he did feel free" (p. 4). James Henry would eventually make his escape to freedom in 1864, just as Union General Philip Sheridan waged his battle in the neighboring Shenandoah Valley. James Henry was keenly aware of his geographic surroundings (a trait of hired slaves) and, in pursuit of his freedom, he came upon Sheridan's troops and shared his story. James Henry guided the troops to mills and supply depots in the county, resulting in several small skirmishes with Confederate troops guarding the military supplies. These battles resulted in Union victories, after which they "loaded the confiscated provisions, burning whatever they could not carry" (Goggin, 1993, pp. 4–5). These are the stories that Woodson drew from: rebellious and unruly grandfather, uncle, and father, all of whom insisted on seeing themselves as free in the midst of slavery and bondage.

Woodson asserted that this notion of freedom was defined by one's orientation to self as a person of African descent; free to think, dream, and enact social change beyond the barriers that have been put before a people. Therefore, "freedom" shapes one's conception of self and what knowledge one acquires. In other words, the notion of mis-education denotes a lack of freedom even when provided formal education. One could not simply be free through material gain and social opportunities. Freedom required a concept of self that is tied to the broader interests of the Negro Problem. Knowledge and freedom were linked, a connection implanted in Woodson through his early experiences with Mr. Oliver Jones.

Woodson described his friendship with Mr. Oliver Jones, a Civil War veteran and co-worker, as "one of the more formative educational experiences in his life" (Goggin, 1994, p. 11). Oliver Jones ran a tearoom out of his house where coal miners spent leisure time eating ice cream and drinking tea. Woodson described his establishment as a "godsend." Woodson would describe Jones as a kind of organic intellectual who had accumulated volumes of books about Black life in his home, even though he could not read. As Woodson explained, Jones' house "was all but a reading room" (Goggin and Wilson, 1994, p. 11). He owned volumes of books about the life and achievements of African Americans. His collection had books such as J.T. Wilson's *Black Phalanx*, W.J. Simmons' *Men of Mark*, and George Washington Williams' *Negro Troops in the War of the Rebellion.* When Jones found out that Woodson could read, he asked him to read newspapers from White and Black weeklies. It was through reading these papers that Woodson gained an increased knowledge about history and economics. As Goggin and Wilson (1994) explained:

> He read "speeches, lectures, and essays dealing with civil service reform, reduction taxes, tariff for protection, tariff for revenue only, and free trade," and became knowledgeable about populist doctrines advocated by Tom Watson and William Jennings Bryan. Frequently Woodson discussed "the history of the race" with Black miners at Jones's house, and his "interest in penetrating the past of [his] people was deepened and intensified."
>
> (pp. 11–12)

The knowledge and relationships fostered in Jones' tearoom would lay the foundation for Woodson's unquenchable thirst for Black history. This intellectual curiosity, combined with the stories of his grandfather, father, and uncle as unruly and rebellious champions of their freedom, would become the foundation for Woodson's identity throughout his life. Woodson's effort at seeking truth was linked to the liberation of Black people. The unruly spirit of his family and his early intellectual development informed his efforts toward that mission. Like the character Alice in *Alice in Wonderland*, Woodson would "go down the rabbit hole" never to return. Black history became his life.

The Nadir: Understanding the Racial Milieu of Woodson's Racial Project

Rayford Logan (1997[1954]) referred to the period from 1877 to the early twentieth century as the "nadir." This was a period when many of the civil rights gained during Reconstruction were lost. Through the creation of Jim Crow policy and extralegal racial violence, African Americans entered into a new racial contract where racial terror and strident racial policies were used for Whites to regain social control. This also involved the disenchantment of World War I veterans, whose return back to the US was not filled with goodwill for their sacrifices but with contempt and in some cases racial violence (Davis, 2008; Williams, 2007). However, this was also a period when the image-making about African Americans was used to support the new southern ideology of racial repression (Fredrickson, 1987).

In this sense, coercion was not the only means to suppress Black life. Image making also served a similar purpose during the early twentieth century. During this period, there were at least four prominent mechanisms for shaping the imagery of African Americans. In the section that follows, we draw attention to the effects of academia, science, media, and school knowledge as four spaces in which a metanarrative about African Americans took shape. Woodson's racial project emerged within this context.

The Context and Confluence of Racial Imagery

Outlining the confluence of image-making mechanisms during the early twentieth century is important for making sense of the racial projects that emerged at this time. Du Bois argued that the racial other took form through a confluence of discourses (Brown, 2013). Du Bois stated:

> The theory of human culture and its aim has worked itself through warp and woof of our daily thought with a thoroughness that few realize. Everything great, good, efficient, fair and honorable and is "White." Everything mean, bad, blundering, cheating, and dishonorable is "yellow," brown and Black. The changes on this theme are continually rung in picture and story, in newspaper heading and moving picture, in sermon and school book, until, of course, the king can do no wrong—a White man is always right, and the Black has no rights which a White man is bound to respect. ... All through the world this gospel is preaching; it has its literature, it has its priests, it has its secret propaganda, and above all—it pays.
>
> (Cited in Ephraim, 2003, p. 79)

During the early parts of the twentieth century, much of the dominant academic discourse about African Americans focused on their biological composition. Historian Daryl Michael Scott (1997) refers to these discourses as *racial conservatism*: "biologists, physicians, and race psychologists pointed out the physical differences that explained the alleged cultural and intellectual inferiority of Black peoples" (pp. 1–2). He notes that during this period, ethnologists posited theories about the backwardness of African people.

Historian George Fredrickson explains that there were two prominent groups writing within the social sciences during this period: the accommodationalists and the competitive racists (Scott, 1997). The competitive racists believed that people of African descent "could not be assimilated into modern civilization" (Scott, 1997, p. 11). Common knowledge held that the biological composition of Blacks, including their skull shape and brain size, made them incapable of functioning as citizens. From the psychologists to natural scientists, scholarly discourse of the early twentieth century enclosed Black Americans and people of African descent into a metanarrative of racial lack. The accommodationalists on the other hand argued that African Americans could assimilate into U.S. society until they "arrived at the same stage of civilization as Whites" (Scott, 1997, p. 12).

The discipline of history, which Woodson studied in his doctoral education at Harvard, also shared in reproducing a racial narrative of White supremacy. Universities did not teach about the full scope of African American experiences and often treated the history of African Americans as non-existent. Historians also noted the pervasive ideology of White supremacy through Woodson's experiences in graduate school at Harvard (Goggin, 1993; Hine, 1986) where his history seminars were nothing less than contentious and dismissive of African Americans' contributions to American history. Goggin (1993) stated: "Although Woodson had believed that Channing was liberal on racial issues, he later recalled that in seminar Channing not only belittled the Negro's role in American history but also argued that the Negro had no history" (p. 21). Every facet of the field of history treated Black history as defined by bondage and, in many cases, suggested that the experience of Africans in America was beneficial because it provided them with Christianity and helped to curtail their "uncivilized ways." The ideas of paternalism and slavery were also promulgated by the well-known historian U.B. Phillips, whose ideas about slavery were also to become part of the pro-South ideologies pervasive in U.S. textbooks (Reddick, 1934).

During the early 1900s, scholars were well aware of the power and influence of textbooks in promoting a negative imagery of the African American child. The narrow casting of Black imagery in textbooks catalyzed activism aimed at redressing the racial imagery of African Americans. In the 1930s and 1940s, the National Association for the Advancement of Colored People (NAACP) convened a textbook committee that met at local branches to examine depictions of African Americans in history, literature, and civics textbooks (Zimmerman, 2002, 2004). Walter Benjamin's commentary at the twenty-ninth annual conference of NAACP provides a clear picture of the importance of textbooks within the racial discourse of this time:

> Because this tremendous, overshadowing importance of the dark complexioned people in the United States goes home so directly to the most intimate problems of human existence and has so much bearing upon them, it is of the utmost importance that the young people in our schools today, laying the foundation of their future lives, should have complete and accurate account of this most extraordinary chapter in human history.
>
> They should have it exactly as it is, true, dependable, without color or bias. But what do they get? They get a mingling of accepted fallacies, or errors that have been passed from one uninstructed writer to another, of assumptions of prejudice that have become imbedded in literature as fact, of misunderstandings and misrepresentations, often honest, always disastrous.
>
> (NAACP, 1939)

In the foreword of the NAACP publication *Anti-Negro Propaganda in School Textbooks*, Executive Secretary Walter White wrote:

> We want the great army of mothers and fathers of this country to know that the very textbooks which their children study in school are often germ carriers of the most vicious propaganda against America's largest minority, the Negro citizen.
>
> (NAACP, Foreword, 1939)

The findings from this work resulted in the publication, *Anti-Negro Propaganda in School Textbooks* (NAACP, 1939). This publication provided samples and political commentary about the implications of racial bias and "popular fallacies" about African Americans found in many U.S. textbooks.

Du Bois' (1935) classic text, *Black Reconstruction*, highlights the problems with textbooks. Du Bois noted: "One is astonished in the study of history at the recurrence of the idea that evil must be forgotten, distorted, skimmed over" (p. 722). The issue with textbooks was their lack of attention to historical accuracy. For example, in many cases, the narrative that the Ku Klux Klan stabilized power in the South was a common story line. The herofication of the Klan portrayed them as frontier patrolman called to employ necessary extralegal measures to vindicate the Southern way of life. In noting the utility of the Klan and other White supremacist organizations, textbook authors often drew on a common stereotype about Black fear and superstition. One textbook, with the subtitle, "The White Men Regain Control," stated:

> The South was threatened with ruin unless something was done to break the Negro control. To do this many White men joined secret societies.

These societies worked to frighten the Negro into staying away from the polls and to make him realize that the White man was still to run the South. Bands of men in White robes and with fiery crosses rode the highways at night. The superstitious Negroes feared the visits of the ghostly night riders who knocked at the cabin door at midnight and in solemn voice threatened the trembling negro with terrible punishments. The work of the secret societies had the desired results. Fewer and fewer of the Negroes went to the polls, and the White men gradually but surely regained control.

(Marshall, 1933, p. 458)

As Lawrence Reddick (1934) documented, textbooks during this time took a pro-South approach, consistent with the post-Reconstruction discourse of the *Lost Cause Movement*, which restored the imagery of the South through sites of memory and texts about the Civil War (Blight, 2003). David Blight explained:

As early as 1899, UDC chapters endorsed a pro-Southern textbook and began their decade-long crusade to fight what many perceived as a Yankee conspiracy to miseducate Southerners. When the UDC women took up the cause of history they did so as cultural guardians of their tribe, defenders of a sacred past against Yankee imposed ignorance and the forces of modernism. They built moats around their White tribe's castles to save the children from false history and impure knowledge.

(p. 278)

Other educational texts such as the *Coon Alphabet* and the children's song *Ten Little Niggers*, consistently depicted Black children as wild-eyed, incorrigible pickaninnies. The lyrics of *Ten Little Niggers* illustrated this point:

Ten little nigger boys went out to dine;
One choked his little self, and then there were nine.
Nine little nigger boys sat up very late;
One overslept himself, and then there were eight.
Eight little nigger boys traveling in Devon;
One said he'd stay there, and then there were seven.
Seven little nigger boys chopping up sticks;
One chopped himself in half, and then there were six.
Six little nigger boys playing with a hive;
A bumble-bee stung one, and then there were five.
Five little nigger boys going in for law;
One got in chancery, and then there were four.
Four little nigger boys going out to sea;
A red herring swallowed one, and then there were three.
Three little nigger boys walking in the zoo;

A big bear hugged one, and then there were two.
Two little nigger boys sitting in the sun;
One got frizzled up, and then there was one.
One little nigger boy left all alone;
He went out and hanged himself and then there were none.

(Taken from Anderson, 2009)

While it is not at all clear the extent to which the *Coon Alphabet* and *Ten Little Niggers* were used in schools, scholars still note that the production and circulation of these texts and songs were certainly consistent with the existing imagery of African Americans during this time (Martin, 2004).

The public media, via cartoons, movies and print, provided some of the most damaging images of Black life. For example, the same year that Woodson established the *Association* (1915), the critically acclaimed, controversial movie by D.W. Griffith, *Birth of a Nation* (1915), provided a racist and pro-Southern White supremacist take on history (Pitcher, 1999). The Black male legislators in the film were portrayed as destructive to the U.S. nation— depicted as incompetent and sex-crazed, with little care about governing the nation and more prone to eating, shucking, and jiving and pursuing White women through sexual advances. In the end, the movie portrayed the Ku Klux Klan as the "protectors" of a White Christian nation. They coalesced by repressing the votes of Blacks, thus realigning the racial contract of White racial dominance. This movie, however, was only one of many depictions of African Americans as child-like, chicken-eating "darkies." All through the early 1900s, ads found in tobacco, candy, and household appliances promoted an image of Black people in a sub-human characterization (Hall, 1997).

The characterization of African Americans as stereotypical images was a common trope, expressed in almost every facet of society, even children's television shows and cartoons. In these contexts, African Americans were depicted as scared, simple, watermelon-eating "darkies." This pervasive imagery of African American children was found in popular cartoons and children's songs, with Black children depicted through either parody or violence. The children's songs and counting games of the late nineteenth century and early twentieth century each provided the imagery of violence and/or parody, where Black life was stripped from its moorings in reality, and portrayed as sub-human and wild eyed, savage pickaninnies with water-melon smiles and animal-like features and limbs.

The cultural context of academia, science, media, and school knowledge produced an African American imagery that prevailed within every facet of African Americans' lives. There was little escaping the preponderance of images depicting African Americans as the savage, the clown, the brute, and the Sambo. One might dismiss these images as isolated cases where African American imagery was fashioned in a sub-human manner. However, this was not the case.

The cultural milieu of this time was to fashion Black people as having nothing to offer society except to toil and labor for White interests. The idea of not having a history beyond the paternalism of slavery and the post-Reconstruction context of poverty and emptiness became synonymous with Black people. It was clear that the confluence of discourses found in academic, popular, and scientific spaces helped to promulgate the superiority of whiteness and enclose the public imagery of African Americans within the most inaccurate and insidious images of the twentieth century. The production of these images, however, also met persistent resistance.

The New Negro and the Counter Narrative

Gates (1988) notes that a counter discourse of dissent and repudiation emerged from the moment enslaved Africans set sail to the new world in chains and bondage. Slave narratives, abolitionist conventions, letters, and speeches by free and enslaved African Americans indicate that an ongoing counter discourse took form in the fifteenth century and remained through the twentieth century. For example, while producing critical analysis of the textbooks; that is, outlining their biases and problems, Black scholars also produced scholarship and archives to counter the existing metanarrative of Black people. The counter discourse of African American imagery has been historically described through the trope of the *New Negro*.

The *New Negro* movement was the process African Americans took to restore and repudiate the prevailing negative images. Henry Louis Gates argues that the trope of the *New Negro* emerged out of two antithetical conceptions of "Black"— the historical construction of the Black Sambo in relation to the image of the *New Negro*. Gates (1988) goes on to describe the *New Negro*:

> The "New Negro," of course, was only a metaphor. The paradox of this claim is inherent in the trope itself, combining as it does a concern with time, antecedents, and heritage, on the one hand, with the concern with a cleared space, the public face of the race, on the other hand. The figure moreover, combines implicitly both an eighteenth century of utopia with a nineteenth century dream of an unbroken, unhabituated, neological self—signified by the upper case "Negro" and the belated adjective "New."
>
> (p. 132)

The notion of a revised neological self through the trope of the New Negro has largely been associated with the work of Alain Locke. Taken from his edited book in 1925, Locke outlined the context of the twentieth-century New Negro as moving through a new ontological space, where the conditions of time and space helped to bolster a "new psychology" about African Americans. He maintained that an interdisciplinary approach to revise the imagery of African Americans had to come through the arts, social sciences, and philosophies to construct a new imagery beyond the stock representations of Black life. (See Chapter 4 for more discussion on Locke's conception of the New Negro.)

This is the context of Woodson's project— the countervailing imagery of the Sambo and the New Negro. As we noted above, Woodson's project takes form at a time when African American imagery was shaped in the context of White supremacy. As we illustrate in the following section, Woodson and his colleagues developed a counter racial discourse that was philosophically derived and empirically included.

Woodsonian Curriculum Counter Narrative

Woodson's work confronted the prevailing ideologies about Black people during this time that African Americans were a people without history. During the early 1900s there was on ongoing discussion about Negro history as being solely defined by the interaction with Europeans or whether Negro history was informed by an ancient history from the continent of Africa. In addition, there also was an ongoing discussion on whether Black culture was informed by African and European influences or whether Negro American cultural forms were devoid of any influence from Africa. Woodson's project rested on the idea that African American history should be thought of in at least three ways.

Woodson's work pointed to the in-depth history of African antiquity (Woodson, 1928a). His historical studies and commentary in the *Negro History Week* provided a comprehensive and historically rigorous analysis of African history as responsible for advancing civilization. Woodson and Wesley's textbooks all provided stories, philosophies, political structures, and inventions that situated Africa's prominence in relation to the Western world. Here is an example taken from the textbook *The Negro in Our History*:

> In facing the forces of nature to wrest there from a livelihood, Africans have given a lesson to the so-called civilized world. In the industrial arts they have shown conclusively that they were once the greatest metal workers of the world. Developing as such, the Africans were the first to smelt iron and use the forge. To this race, therefore, belongs the credit for the gift of the most useful things to man.
>
> (Woodson & Wesley, 1922, p. 39)

Again, Woodson and Wesley (1928), in their text *Negro Makers of History*, illustrated the positioning of Africa in relation to European progress:

> The customs of the early Africans resembled very much those of the ancient nations around the Mediterranean Sea. The Africans were organized as

groups of families making up the tribe under the chief who with the assistance of a council of elderly men served his people as lawgiver, judge, military leader, and king. When ambitious, certain chiefs developed their possessions into large kingdoms and empires. In this way resulted the rise of Ghana (Kumbi), Melle (Manding), Mossi, and the Songhay Empire, following somewhat the golden age of Ethiopia which was once extensive enough to include Egypt.

(pp. 6–7)

Woodson and Wesley regularly challenged the myth that African and Western traditions and innovation evolved in a cross-cultural fashion. The following text taken from *Negro in Our History* illustrated this point:

The supposedly low depths of the native Africans emphasizes the so-called heights which Whites have attained. As a matter of fact, however, the African civilization does not suffer in comparison with the civilization of other members of the human family. All have intermingled and borrowed, the one from the other. In science, then, there is no such thing as races. Because of lack of opportunity in an unhealthy environment, some may have not accomplished as much as others more favorably circumstanced; but, wherever the climate conditions and opportunity for development have been similar, the cultures of various members of the human families have tended be very much alike.

(Woodson & Wesley, 1922, p. 4)

The intent of these authors was to point out how the development of civilization was collective and infused with culture from many parts of the world, as opposed to being solely defined by Western culture.

Second, Woodson's project examined Blacks' contributions to U.S. history. His work made clear that African American labor, creativity, poetry, and arts gave meaning and context to the narrative called "American History."

As Wynter (1992) argues, Woodson's project sought to transform the distortion of White racial rule, which placed people of African descent outside the record of human history. This idea of humanness is a core concept of Woodson's project, where he persistently challenged the dominant discourses of contempt and pity directed toward African Americans. Woodson's work went to great lengths to demonstrate that the life of Africans in the Americas was a symbol of honor, resistance, and human capacity. For example, Woodson's textbooks and the *Negro History Bulletin* would consistently provide images of African Americans in every facet of life—including the arts, sciences, and politics. Through the process of repetition and rigor, Woodson produced historical studies that he eventually retold through his textbooks, teacher journal, Negro History Week, and the *Home Study Program*, Woodson's teacher preparation program.

Third, Woodson's project pointed directly to the inhumanity of scientific racism and minstrelsy. Philosopher Charles Mills (1998) argues that White supremacy produced the racial classification of sub-person in relation to the normative category of whiteness. He further argues that the process of revising and repudiating the ontological meaning of "race" helps to challenge and transform enclosed racial categories, what he calls *revisionist ontology*. In this sense, Woodson's curriculum is a revisionist ontological project (Brown, 2010). Just as the process of constructing the racial Other requires production and reproduction through multiple planes of meaning, so does the process of revising and repudiating the onslaught of racial meanings that ontologically sealed Black life. William Ephraim (2003) stated:

> For the obvious aim of Woodson's endeavors—the motive of his Association and his book—was to debunk in scientific terms, the Eurocentric myth of Black inferiority, which was itself based on the enduring myth that Africa and Africans had no history and no culture.
>
> (p. 6)

Woodson's curricular project sought to give substance and history to a topic that had been enclosed in the imaginary of whiteness—"The Negro." Therefore, in this context, Woodson's project was not just about history, it was intertwined in juxtaposition to the prevailing stereotypes of Black people. Philosophers define ontology as the nature of being and existence. This is precisely what Woodson was trying to reconstruct through the *Association*. The process of gathering rigorous empirical data, writing and publishing scholarly works, all while making sure the findings were accessible to teachers, students, and the masses was the core of Woodson's curricular project.

In the same manner that Mills (1998) argues that the production of sub-persons was "manifested on several planes," Woodson found that the process of revising and repudiating the symbolic violence within history and curriculum of the Negro would require the development of a comprehensive curricular project organized on multiple planes—academic journals, textbooks, community gatherings, and teacher training. In a sense, Woodson's vision involved two planes of development. His project entailed the process of researching and *producing new knowledge* used in different educational and social settings. This racial project (Omi & Winant, 2015) involved developing sound empirical scholarship. Then there was the *dissemination of knowledge*. This process of dissemination was vital to Woodson's vision of making new knowledge available to the masses, particularly students and everyday citizens. Drawing on this two-prong approach, Woodson's work powerfully responded to the confluence of racial discourses during this time. In the section that follows, we outline how Woodson's work was in direct response to the systems of reasoning found within science, academia, history, K–12 curriculum, and the general image-making about the Negro.

Knowledge Production

As we have explained earlier in this chapter, Woodson's experiences at Harvard illustrated the manner in which Black history and the experiences of African Americans were rendered in the field of history. Black history did not exist in the field of history. The creation of the *Association* helped to provide a space—in a literal sense—to locate Black History. Woodson, however, understood that the barriers of White racial rule made it difficult for Black Americans to tell their own story and to do so under their own terms. Here, Woodson expressed these sentiments in a letter to Charles Wesley:

> The Negro faces another stone wall when he presents such scientific productions to publishing houses. They may not be prejudiced, but they are not interested in the Negro. We understand that the more serious the work is the less chance it has for reaching a large reading public. Yet scholarship must be advanced by these strictly scientific works. This represents a very dark prospect for the rapidly increasing number of young men and women who are prepared for creative work but receive no encouragement whatever. In this way the cause of Negro scholarship has dreadfully suffered in spite of the one-sided method of the foundations in trying to broaden the minds of Negroes teaching in their own schools. What is the use of knowing things if they cannot be published to the world? If the Negro is to settle down to publishing merely what others permit him to bring out, the world will never know what the race has thought and felt and attempted to accomplish and the story of the Negro will perish with him.
>
> (Cited in Wesley, 1951, p. 20)

Through the *Association*, Woodson developed a publishing press, K–12 curriculum materials, a teacher education correspondence course, a week devoted to Black History, and a Black History journal called the *Negro Bulletin*, all devoted to making history accessible to teachers, students, and the general public. However, much of this work came from the historians who had worked to develop his groundbreaking journal, the *Journal of Negro History*.

The *Journal of Negro History* helped to produce a clearinghouse for the history of people of African descent. What this did was give legitimacy to the field of Black History. Woodson believed that the project of Negro historical work needed to produce scholarship based on rigorous empirical analysis. Woodson wanted to place the history of people of African descent within the existing discipline of history. By making Black history a subfield of history, Woodson helped to produce a prominent counter narrative to the racist scholarship and imagery of African Americans found in academia during the early 1900s. The production of new knowledge was a direct response to the myriad untruths and silences concerning the history of African Americans. For example, the first six volumes of the journal confronted every possible silence or misconception concerning the history of the African Diaspora.

The first five issues of the *Journal of Negro History* gave a clear indication that, through Woodson's editorship and publications, the journal sought to produce a new body of knowledge about Black people. The experiences of African Americans in slavery and freedom, the culture and philosophy of Africa and the civic responsibility of the Negro American were explored through the journal. Woodson also regularly published historical biographies about doctors, poets, activists, and soldiers. Issue after issue, some aspect of the twisted and falsely constructed narrative of the Negro was implicitly deconstructed through the annals of the *Journal of Negro History*. The significance of the journal's prominence as revisionist discourse cannot be underestimated. Just as critical scholars have troubled the power of the dominant "archive" to inform social reality, Woodson understood that challenging the preponderance of ideas about the child-like and history-less Negro had to occur through the epistemological paradigm of the "academic journal."

If, as critical scholars note, academia helped to construct the social reality of African Americans, then the *Journal of Negro History* was an ideological rupture that reconceptualized the metanarrative of the "Old Negro." The focus on slave history, famous biographies, unsung biographies, and social histories would remain a common approach to other facets of the *Association's* efforts. However, beyond developing a rigorous archive of Black history, histories about Black people had to be accessible to the masses.

Knowledge Dissemination and Translation

All of the projects of the *Association* drew on two core precepts: translation and dissemination. The notion of "translation" was to make his work accessible and readable for the masses—including teachers and other laypersons interested in Black history. Then there was the idea of "dissemination" (Dagbovie, 2007a). While Woodson was a traditional historian in terms of how one should collect historical data, he felt strongly that rigorous historical scholarship must be made available to the masses in ways that were clear and relevant to their needs. Theorizing and repudiating the individual psychology of the Negro was a central theme of Woodson's revisionist ontological project (Brown, 2010). Woodson and many other African American scholars (see Chapters 1 and 4) understood that curriculum had the capacity to engender meaning in individuals' lives. The resolution was the production of textbooks that challenged theories about African Americans' worth as human beings.

Woodson believed that truth resided in overlooked historical studies. Therefore, the histories often cited in the *Journal of Negro History* would in part become infused in many of the stories presented in the textbooks. In essence, the elementary, secondary, and post-secondary textbook drew from the academic historical studies produced at the *Association* by Woodson and his co-author and protégée Charles Wesley, as well as other Black and White historians committed to the cause of producing rigorous Black historical work. What is important to note about Woodson's textbooks is that he was well aware of his audience—the Black child (Woodson & Wesley, 1922, 1928, 1935).

Although part of Woodson's project was to impress on the minds of White Americans the value and importance of Black history, it was clear that his audience was the Black child. The core argument in his book *The Mis-education of the Negro* was that Black people had been educated to have contempt for their own histories. For example, several chapters in *Negro Makers of History* sought to redress old theories about Black people's contributions to the US as well as highlight the achievements and agency of Black people in bondage and freedom. The textbook was a pedagogical device used to help promote a new racial imagery for African Americans, noting the voluminous contributions to U.S. society as scientists, lawyers, poets, philosophers, soldiers, politicians, business leaders, inventors, and artists. This presentation of "great" Black Americans was not just a tool employed to engender a new identity for Black children, it also served as a powerful counter discourse to the ideas that Negro capacities were enclosed by their biological composition.

This kind of history was also present in the *Negro History Bulletin*, where the target audience was mostly Black teachers and educators. The primary goal was to help Black teachers that possessed limited knowledge about Black history to supplement the White racist curriculum typically found in traditional schools. The *Bulletin* also allowed Woodson to discuss his philosophy of teaching and why African Americans needed an in-depth connection to history. Additionally, the *Bulletin* enabled Woodson to highlight possible lessons and activities that teachers and communities could employ to promote Negro History Week. Historian Pero Dagbovie (2007a) notes that Woodson also used this journal as a way for teachers and children to prompt conversations related to the education and the well-being of Black people.

Negro History Week however, was Woodson's crown jewel (Woodson, 1919, 1926[2002]; 1927). One indication of the importance of this event was expressed in the number of times Woodson highlighted the significance of the event in the *Association's* annual report (Woodson, 1923, 1925, 1928b, 1930, 1935). Woodson's vision was to use Negro History Week "as a stepping stone toward the gradual introduction of Black history into the curricula of educational institutions, from elementary school years through college" (Dagbovie, 2004, p. 376). As Lawrence Reddick (2002[1950]) explained:

> The intimate details of the precise time, place and circumstance under which the thought of Negro History Week first occurred to "the father of Negro History" has never been set down. We do not know whether this

"brain child" was born early in the morning or late in the night; during a stroll after dinner or a train traveling to New York. But we do know, at least, two of the conditions that surrounded its creation. One: a "week" to dramatize some broad idea or civic moment is an old American custom. Two: after producing the erudite *Journal of Negro History* for ten years with its necessarily restricted circle of readers, Dr. Woodson was convinced that a more spectacular gesture was needed to reach the larger public.

(p. 35)

As scholars explain, Woodson's Negro History Weeks were grand and comprehensive (Dagbovie, 2007a; Reddick , 2002[1950]); his "Negro History Week Circulars" involved a wide variety of pedagogical devices such as "banquets, breakfasts, speeches, parades, exhibits, and lectures" (Dagbovie, 2007a p. 50). Woodson's intent for Negro History Week was rather transparent. He regularly argued that Black people knew little to nothing about their history and events such as Negro History week were vital to re-educating Black people. Woodson, however, was smart about the dissemination of Negro History. He argued that the pedagogies of Negro History were intended to prompt a new racial consciousness beyond the prevailing discourses of inferiority. However, Negro History Week was just the beginning of a systemic process of engaging students, teachers, and principals in curricular projects. As Dagbovie (2007a) explains:

Woodson's vision of Negro History Week was optimistic and long-term. This seemingly token celebration was to serve as a stepping stone toward the gradual introduction of Black history into the curricula of educational institutions, from the elementary schools through college, through American communities Black and White.

(p. 376)

His work beyond Negro History week was to provide programs along with research and promotion materials to highlight the historical record of African Americans' achievements. He encouraged educational organizations to develop committees to help with fundraising, research techniques, and the preservation of Black documents. His entrepreneurial spirit, however, was always driven by his core educational philosophy: engendering a strong self-concept for Black people and challenging the existing ideas of race. Woodson (2002[1926]) explains the results of the first Negro History Week:

The important results of the celebration may be summarized as creating a demand for Negro pictures and Negro literature, disabusing the Negro mind of the idea of inferiority, and increased conviction among the Whites that racial bias undermines all truth, and the growing spirit of cooperation to the end of further extending the researches in Negro History that it may be popularized throughout the world.

(p. 27)

Woodson's revisionist project collectively spoke to an overarching racial philosophy: the deconstruction of the "Old Negro." As we stated earlier, the imagery of the Negro had been enclosed by a confluence of discourse: the sciences, the social sciences, media and school textbooks, which all made Black people into the dual imagery of the Sambo or the brute or what Sylvia Wynter (1979) calls the Nat/Sambo construct. The durability and regularity of this imagery presented a daunting task for Woodson and his colleagues.

Woodson had a profound philosophical belief that through historical and curricular revision, the imagery of African Americans could be altered. This however, was not just a theory of identity politics. Woodson believed that the way people of African descent had been rendered through history and curriculum helped to fuel the action of racial exclusion and violence. Before Franz Fanon's *Black Skin White Masks*, Woodson theorized the socio-psychological impacts of what he called "mis-education." However, unlike Fanon, Woodson located the context of curriculum and the classroom within the mind of African Americans. Taken from his oft-cited volume *The Mis-education of the Negro* he expressed the connection between imagery and the social realities of African Americans:

> No systematic effort toward the same economics, history, philosophy, literature and religion which have established the present code of morals, the Negro's mind has been brought under control of his oppressor. The problem of holding the Negro down, therefore, is easily solved. When you control a man's thinking you do not have to worry about his actions. You do not have to tell him not to stand here or go yonder. He will find his "proper place" and will stay in it.
>
> (Woodson, 1998[1933], p. xix)

Here, Woodson expressed the central theme of his project: the idea that curriculum has the capacity to transform the existing ideologies found in schools. The process of mis-education could be revised through a thorough and systemic counter-hegemonic discourse. In looking at the theoretical and practical substance of Woodson's work it is clear that his ideas have not received their just due within the history and foundations of educational thought. His ideas about curriculum and pedagogy predate many of the enduring theories of representation, class formation, and cultural relevance theories in the present. In the section that follows, we discuss how Woodson's project and theories of curriculum inform the contemporary theorizing of race, culture, and curriculum.

Ideas as Foundational to Critical and Progressive Educational Thought

Woodson on Culture

Since the Progressive Era, certain questions have endured within contemporary educational discourse. What is the purpose of culture in education? What kind of curriculum and pedagogy can best meet the needs of American labor? When thinking about these questions from a foundational standpoint, specific scholars often come to mind. For example, some of the earliest discussions about the significance of culture primarily emerged from anthropology and philosophy scholars such as Franz Boas, Melville Herkovitts, Ruth Benedict, and even John Dewey. Scholars will even situate the work of the Greeks and the Chicago School of Sociology as key spaces of intellectual thought for promoting advances in the idea of "culture." However, we would argue that Carter G. Woodson's ideas about culture are foundational to our ongoing concerns about context, culture, and relevance in schools. Beyond Woodson's ideas about culture only speaking to the needs of the "Negro," we argue that his ideas present a more global appeal for the theorization of culture.

Woodson conceptualized culture as a natural facet of society where a group's thoughts, practices, and inclinations interacted within their social environs. Throughout Woodson's scholarship is the documentation of the history of the Negro situated within a specific cultural context. Woodson's account of the history of Black education (Woodson, 1969, 1998 [1933]), the Black church (Woodson, 1921), or the military service of Black men (Woodson & Wesley, 1922) consistently noted the spatial and temporal contexts that informed the agency of Black people. For Woodson, the process of racial prejudice created the conditions for culture to change and adapt. Woodson's historical scholarship and K–12 materials alluded to the durability and transformation of African and Black cultures. Implicit to his work was the idea that culture is contextually specific, yet durable, even when confronted with issues of domination.

While recent scholarship has called for pedagogy to be *culturally sustaining* (Paris, 2012; Paris & Alim, 2014), Woodson's scholarship promoted the idea that cultures endure even if they are not acknowledged. This is a departure from the current concerns for cultural relevance and culturally responsive curriculum and pedagogy in that Woodson was arguing that whether schools acknowledge the presence of Black culture in schools or not, Diasporic influences of Black culture are "sustained" and improvised within the context of racial domination. Therefore, the process of transforming and challenging the traditional curriculum was less about "sustaining" and more about placing at the center the cultural forms and historical origins there were already present within the cultural milieu of Black life. Meaning, for Woodson, culture is "sustained" whether we give credence to the culture or not.

Woodson is certainly one of the earliest scholars to concretely understand the idea of *culture* and *relevance* within the school curriculum. Similar to recent concerns about the child's racial outlook, Woodson understood that school curriculum could reproduce racist ideas about the Black child. For example, the placement of Africa at the center of curricular decisions was not to replace one hegemonic discourse with another one, but instead it was to locate the masses of African American experiences and cultural forms within the context of a clear and distinct history and culture. The intentionality of African histories and philosophies was culturally relevant to the needs of African Americans because it disrupted the surrounding discourse that depicted African culture as irrelevant. In the same sense, however, Woodson understood that the varied spatial and temporal contexts in which people of African descent resided helped to produce different expressions of the African Diasporic experience. This conception of culture could be found throughout each of these projects within the *Association*.

Additionally, as cultural theorists in education note, Woodson recognized that the cultural knowledge one gained through curriculum was more than academic knowledge. It helped to produce a new psychology (Locke, 1997[1925]) or worldview that engendered a cultural and political consciousness—a key precept of Gloria Ladson Billings' (1995) theory of culturally relevant pedagogy. Woodson saw achievement and success among African Americans as mattering little if it engendered an ideology of contempt or pity for other African Americans.

His critique of "educated Negroes" was not to discredit the significance of achievement, because Woodson's textbooks and journal articles went to great lengths to showcase the achievements of African Americans. Therefore, the relevance of culture and curriculum was to produce a consciousness for Black people to internalize the significance of Africa not just as a "place" but also as a conceptual frame for generating responsibility to the causes and interests of Black people in Africa and throughout the Diaspora (Dagbovie, 2010).

What is important to note about Woodson's conception of culture is how his scholarship and curricular texts expressed the various subject positions of African Americans, particularly across class status and regional contexts. While one might see Woodson's project as essentializing in that he places all of his projects within the conceptual meanings of "Black people," the *Journal of Negro History* and his textbooks often highlighted the varied subject positions of Africans in America and across the globe (Woodson, 1916; 1941a, 1941b, 1941c; 1942). In addition, across all the projects in the *Association*, Black people were portrayed as radical, parochial, traditional, creative, business-oriented, scientific, and philosophical.

Woodson's conception of culture spoke to an enduring theoretical tension within education concerned with cultural essentialism and socio-political consciousness. Woodson understood that culture is contextual and fluid but also grounded on racial politics concerned with a collective conscious needed to overcome White supremacy.

What do these conceptions of culture mean to other racial projects? As we argue in this volume, the work of Black scholars is not just relevant to the conditions of African Americans; it provides key intellectual and practical insights about theorizing race and culture in a broader sense. Woodson's ideas about culture speak to its contextual nature. He felt that the production of curriculum had to address people's troubling conceptions of African Diasporic people. However, based on the variety of spatial and temporal contexts that Woodson drew from, it was clear that he understood that culture is fluid. A view of culture as contextually specific did not overlook the fact that curriculum needed to draw from some common cultural forms to help foster unity among African Americans. In this sense, Woodson could be thought of as a *strategic essentialist* (Spivak, 1988) who understood the contingencies of culture, but also incorporated a conception of culture in the school curriculum concerned with the political cohesiveness of Black people.

Woodson on Curriculum

As we have noted in Chapter 1, Woodson's ideas have had little to no recognition in the field of curriculum history (Brown & Au, 2014). In addition, his ideas are often cited only to speak to the conditions of African Americans. We contend, however, that Woodson's ideas about curriculum provide an important theorization of "curriculum" as a whole. In this section of the chapter we offer a concrete understanding of how Woodson conceptualizes curriculum.

A foundational question of curriculum studies and educational thought is: what constitutes "curriculum?" Scholars of the reconceptualist movement and critical scholars contend that curriculum is a body of knowledge imbued with ideological and epistemological assumptions (Au, 2012). In a similar sense, Woodson's curricular work and essays make clear that curriculum is not a neutral body of knowledge; on the contrary, it has an intentionality to produce a mindset that internalized a negative racial image of African Americans. In this imagery, a narrative of whiteness encloses Blackness. It attempted to normalize the material context of African Americans' lives as opposed to situating their condition as a blatant breach of a social contract among Americans. As Woodson (1998[1933]) explains:

> [T]o handicap a student by teaching him that his Black face is a curse and that his struggle to change his condition is hopeless is the worst sort of lynching. It kills one's aspirations and dooms him to vagabondage and crime. It is strange, then, that the friends of truth and promoters of freedom have not risen up against the present propaganda in the schools and crushed it. This crusade is much more important than the anti-lynching movement, because there would be no lynching if it did not start in the schoolroom.
>
> (p. 3)

In other words, curriculum not only created the conditions for racial and class hierarchies to remain in place, it fostered an entrenched racial consciousness. The ideological intentionality of a racialized curriculum produced and reproduced a racial self, in which Black children see their "face is a curse." In this sense, curriculum implants a mindset about blackness that not only causes African Americans to adhere to a system of reasoning about their personal identity, but also helps to hold in place the economies of racism (Brown & De Lissovoy, 2011) that conceptualize Black commerce, talent, and credentials as inferior. This is the crux of Woodson's thesis on "mis-education." As he explains in *The Mis-education of the Negro*, the history of curriculum is a central apparatus that discursively produced a racial narrative about a history-less people, while promulgating an ideology via the curriculum that sustains of class relations among African Americans and in the wider society. In the end, Woodson suggests "curriculum" is not simply a neutral body of school knowledge but is also ideological and propagandistic, able to construct identities and reproduce social stratification. In a sense, Woodson adhered to the theories of racial formation (Omi & Winant, 2015) via the production of knowledge.

Woodson understood that although curriculum has the capacity to implant an ideology of inferiority, it can also be repudiated and reformed through a multi-tiered and comprehensive process of historical, curricular, and pedagogical reform. Woodson understood, in large part, that the existing narratives circulating in school curriculum were informed by academics. Thus, the first step in the process of curriculum revision was to give credence to silenced narratives through the process of rigorous historical research. As we stated earlier in this chapter, the work of the *Association* produced voluminous historical studies and biographies that became part of the narratives of the *Negro History Bulletin* and Woodson's K–12 textbook materials. In addition his Home Correspondence Studies and teacher developed lesson plans helped to create the conditions for teachers to properly implement new historical narratives in the school curriculum.

The importance of these curricular innovations should not be taken for granted. In curriculum studies there is a rather significant gulf between the process of critical curricular analysis and what is possible in schools. Woodson implicitly knew that the overarching "propagandistic" nature of whiteness and White interests would subsume the master-narrative of U.S. history and African American people's experience. Thus it would require counter-hegemonic spaces to rethink and redefine the existing racial narratives.

This conception to curriculum is significant to ongoing debates about curriculum. If we use Texas or Arizona as a case, we see that curriculum decisions remain deeply imbued within ideological interests. Certainly, curriculum does not resemble the old racist stereotypes of yesteryear, but it is clear that the topics, questions, and content needed to reach historically under-served populations are thoroughly contested. There are two ways to make sense of and respond to the current concerns around curriculum. The first is to view curriculum reform as a contested space that requires ongoing activism. The other, however, is to consider how ideas of curriculum revision occur beyond the official spaces of curriculum authority, such as state governments and school districts.

While Woodson consistently critiqued the dominant narratives of curriculum, he also simultaneously set in place alternative spaces to challenge the curriculum. Thus, employing a Woodsonian approach to curriculum revision means recognizing the limitations of the curriculum choices that are made available to historically underserved groups and then pursuing a comprehensive counter-hegemony project from the academy to the classroom. So, what does that mean to us in the present? It means that our questions about curriculum must not only be engaged in official spaces, they must be taken up in local and grass root spaces including community centers, libraries, political organizations, and parents concerned with the insidious effects of curriculum. Similar to reconceptualist curriculum theories of the late twentieth century, Woodson understood the colonizing effects of curriculum. Just as activists understand the subtle effects of being co-opted, Woodson recognized that, in a White supremacist world that does not value the histories and experiences of people of color, their agency must occur within multiple planes.

Woodson's ideas about curriculum parallel and predate many of the key foundational theories of curriculum studies. In particular, the foundational ideas of the *null curriculum* and the *hidden curriculum* fit the core tenets of Woodson's ideas about the official curriculum. Eliot Eisner (1979) argued that the *null curriculum* had two dimensions— an intellectual process and the selection of subject matter. The dimension of the subject matter in the null curriculum involved the process of exclusions and omissions in the school curriculum. Eisner used the example of how exclusions and omissions occur within the discipline of History, where topics such as the history of science received little to no attention. The second dimension was the affective aspect of the curriculum, which involves "values, attitudes and emotions" (Flinders, Noddings, & Thornton, 1986, p. 35). As Flinders et al. (1986) explain, Eisner's framework accounts for the desire of schools to nullify certain feelings and emotions, through the selection of content. While the notion of this framework in the 1980s was groundbreaking, Woodson was essentially making the same argument 70 years before the publication of *The Educational Imagination*. Woodson wrote exhaustively about what is absent in the school curriculum and found that the discipline of History had excluded and omitted the histories of African Americans. In addition, Woodson's theorization of curriculum highlights how the propagandistic aspect of curriculum helped to nullify America's complicity in White racism and thus helped to reproduce attitudes and values about African Americans that were patently false. Placing Woodson's work within a *null curriculum* framework does not dismiss Eisner's theorization of curriculum, but it does highlight the kind of wholesale dismissal of Woodson's ideas in relation to the theorization of American curriculum.

Woodson's ideas about curriculum also have uncanny connections to the theorization of the hidden curriculum. While there are many instantiations of the hidden curriculum, our attention is given to those scholars that have been most concerned with how curriculum implicitly holds in places ideologies that support the reproduction of an economically stratified society (Anyon, 1981; Apple, 1990; Giroux, 1983). In this sense, the ways schools are organized in terms of the explicit objectives of learning and the manner in which a school day is structured will define a student's educational and job opportunities. These theories of reproduction have remained a defining foundational theory of curriculum studies. However, it is Woodson's ideas of curriculum that spoke to these concerns in the early 1900s. His critiques of the industrial-liberal arts debates around Black education poignantly outlined that each educational model reproduced the conditions for African Americans to not gain opportunities in trades and/or professions through either educational model. Even further however, Woodson argued that the explicit omission of Black history, and inclusion of falsehoods about Black people, helped to implant in Black and White people a negative mindset biased toward the contributions and capacities of Black Americans. Well before the reconceptualist movement in curriculum, which was concerned with the effects of ideology, Woodson made explicit the influence of White southern ideologies on American history in K–12 and higher education settings. Woodson explained that as a result of the "multiplication" of southern vindicationists' racial ideologies in academic studies, a new racial division theory was proffered. Woodson (1926) explained:

> Since one White man easily influences another to change his attitude toward the Negro, northern teachers of history and correlated subjects have during the last generation accepted the southern White man's opinion of the Negro and endeavor to instill the same in the minds of their students. Their position seems to be that because the American Negro has not in fifty years accomplished what the master class has achieved in fifty centuries the race cannot be expected to perform satisfactorily the function of citizenship and must therefore, be treated exceptionally in some such manner as devised by the commonwealths of the South.
>
> (p. 276).

Woodson was powerfully linking the world of ideas found in history discourse, as having ideological interests to reproduce White–Black racial division. Woodson's work thus is in striking alignment with theorists concerned with the hidden and ideological aspects of curriculum. Woodson's overall racial project, however, provides another important layer to curriculum theorizing: the processes of curriculum revision to counter the existing theories and histories about Black people. Overall then Woodson's tripartite critical framework understood the nullifying, hidden, and agentic aspects of curriculum.

Woodson on Teaching

Woodson's ideas about pedagogy were ahead of their time. An enduring issue of educational thought is what instructional practices can best tend to the issue of equity. How should teachers teach? What should teachers know? How do we teach teachers and students to understand new concepts and curriculum pertinent to changing contexts? Woodson's work tended to each of these questions.

The question of what teachers should teach was a question that emerged from Woodson's years teaching in the Philippines and his subsequent years in the US. This question was contingent on the cultural and racial context of the students in the classroom. For African Americans, Woodson understood that what was taught had to challenge the existing ideas, theories, histories, and silences that existed in the traditional schooling context. Thus the teaching of Black history and the cultural, political, creative accomplishments of African Americans was vital for changing the ontological meanings of Blackness that were pervasive in schools and society. As we stated before, these ideas about teaching and pedagogy provided the foundation to many of the theories of the twentieth century on culture and race that emerged.

The question of what teachers should know was a major concern to Woodson. As we noted earlier, central to Woodson's project was the dissemination of Black historical knowledge to the masses and students in particular. Therefore, Woodson spent a great deal of time interacting with teachers via his Home Study Program and the *Negro Bulletin*. The Home Study Program was a correspondence course for teachers who taught in a wide variety of histories, social sciences, and humanities topics under the tutelage of an African American scholar. As Michael Apple (2013) explains:

> But the problem of having teachers successfully engage in this struggle could not be solved by pronouncements alone. For Woodson, we must equip teachers with the knowledge and values that make the alternative of doing nothing unthinkable. Woodson redoubled his consistent attempts to reach out to teachers through his Association for the Study of Negro Life and History.
>
> (p. 43)

Woodson profoundly believed that teachers must have a deep interdisciplinary understanding of Black history in order to transform the curriculum. In other words, changing the content of textbooks was not enough for Woodson if teachers did not possess the historical and socio-cultural knowledge needed to carry out the curriculum. Similar to recent scholars' (Ball, 2006; Ladson Billings, 1995; Milner, 2010) concerns with what teachers know about equity and culture, Woodson had a profound belief that effective pedagogy came not only from a teacher's disposition and attitude toward their students, but also from their command of historical knowledge.

King and Brown (2015) maintained that Woodson employed three interrelated concepts related specifically to the teaching of Black history. They stated, "Teachers should develop their curriculum and pedagogy through approaching Black history as critical and scientific, practical and relevant, and global" (King & Brown, 2015, p. 27). Drawing from Woodson's ideas about teaching and learning, King and Brown (2015) developed a three-part conceptual framework about how teachers should teach Black History—what they call the *Woodsonian Conceptual Framework*.

The first part of this framework was that the teacher should learn Black history through a scientific process. Based on Woodson's lessons from the *Negro History Bulletin* and the context of his correspondence courses, the idea of "scientific" Black history was not necessarily the belief that teachers become academics but that their sources and acquisition of Black Historical knowledge must come from rigorous and reliable historical scholarship.

The second tenet of the framework was that teachers should teach Black history in a way that is relevant to the lives of Black students. As we mentioned previously in this chapter, the idea of "relevance" for Woodson was defined in two ways. The first and most significant was to reverse the existing ideas about race and culture about Black people. Second, Woodson illustrated relevance through his work by highlighting the diversity of African American experiences in textbooks and journals.

The third part of the conceptual framework was to emphasize the importance of a global context and people of African descent—what is often referred to as the African Diaspora. As King and Brown (2015, p. 28) state:

> Woodson avidly believed that no study of Black history could be effectively administrated without the teaching and analysis of the African Diaspora. Woodson insisted that if all students could hear and read about the contributions of African civilizations then they would have a greater appreciation of Black culture in America.

In some respects, the teacher was the example of what the student would become. Woodson poignantly argued that to be Black was not enough. The teacher had to possess an in-depth understanding of Black history and an ideological perspective taken to the teaching concerned with the transformation of African American students. Here Woodson (2000[1933]) made this point:

> With "mis-educated Negroes" in control themselves, however, it is doubtful that the system would be very much different from what it is or that it would rapidly undergo change. The Negroes thus placed in charge would be the products of the same system and would show no more

conception of the task at hand than do the Whites who have educated them and shaped their minds as they would have them function. Negro educators of today may have more sympathy and interest in the race than the Whites now exploiting Negro institutions as educators, but the former have no more vision than their competitors. Taught from books of the same bias, trained by Caucasians of the same prejudices or by Negroes of enslaved minds, one generation of Negro teachers after another have served for no higher purpose than to do what they are told to do.

(p. 23)

Woodson's analysis provided a critical perspective about the role and expectation of Black teachers.

This critique is relevant to contemporary questions about the inclusion of Black teachers in classrooms. In recent years, universities, foundations, school districts, and the U.S. Department of Education have been concerned about how to retain and recruit more Black teachers to the profession (Brown, 2012). However, Woodson's insights on this topic note that such discussions should be asking what kind of Black teacher should work in schools and for what purpose. Woodson understood that the Black teacher had to possess pedagogical content knowledge (Shulman, 1987) of the histories of African Americans that was both culturally relevant (Ladson-Billings, 1995) and humanizing (Brown, 2013). In this sense, his analysis transcended "race" as *the* sole criteria for "relevance."

A Summary of Woodson's Educational Thought

In summary, we conclude that Woodson's ideas about education were ahead of their time. His views on what curriculum can do and what can be done to revise the curriculum are at the very foundation of contemporary questions about curriculum. Woodson understood that within the racial project of Black freedom, the school curriculum played an insidious role in subsuming the mind with negative images of blackness. The relationship between the curriculum and the mind is of great value to contemporary questions about contemporary issues of achievement. His analysis raised important questions about how a system of beliefs or, as some educational theorists call it, a "hidden curriculum" (Apple, 1975; Giroux, 1983), reproduces African American students' educational conditions, even with the presence of an African American teacher.

Theoretical Extractions from Woodson's Project

There are a few key theoretical constructs that we can glean from Woodson's project. His approach to critique was grounded on three theoretical principles.

The first was to ground his critique in the *contexts* of Africans in America. While his work had a Diasporic Black focus, his analysis of the problems with education focused on the racial realities of the "Negro" in the US. Woodson was what historians today would call an "African Americanist." His questions and critiques focused on the existing conceptions taken to African American history in the US. Why is this important? Woodson was not trying to answer the question of "Black people" in a conceptually flat manner. His questions and critiques of U.S. curriculum challenged the arc of the historical narrative and how this narrative mis-educated the Negro. Therefore, in taking up a Woodsonian critique of curriculum one's theoretical questions must be contextual and empirically derived. What this means is that if a scholar is concerned with the education of Native Americans, their analysis must be contextualized within a space in where curricular and pedagogical questions are being assessed, as opposed to exploring a single context of Native American life and then assigning universal meaning to problems of "Native American education." In short, *context matters* to how problems are assessed and how curriculum revisions can be addressed when employing a Woodsonian approach.

The second principle was to deconstruct the duality of debates in education that provide either/or alternatives. As it has been duly noted in the Black educational histories (Anderson, 1988; Watkins, 2001), the Du Bois and Washington debate was a prominent and perennial discussion around the future of Black education. From Booker T. Washington's standpoint, education was about training and trades, without much concern for liberal educational thought and social agitation, whereas for Du Bois, it was about providing a liberal education for African Americans that would enable them to have a broad and interpretive analysis of their social environs.

In *The Mis-education of the Negro*, Woodson provided an alternative way to look at the education of African Americans beyond the existing discourses of industrial and liberal education. Woodson critiqued both models by accounting for a more insidious problem—the mis-education of the Negro. Mis-education essentially is a mindset that produces a sense of self-contempt for Black histories and Black people. Another classic either/or educational question involves whether students of color should remain in integrated or segregated education. A Woodsonian approach to this would ask whether each space, regardless of Black teachers or Black curriculum, actually provides the pedagogical and curricular possibilities to enable Black children to gain a worldview beyond the barriers of mis-education.

The third and most compelling theoretical dimension of Woodson's work was to ensure that the critiques leveled against education helped to prompt focused action—what we are calling Woodson's *praxis*. Woodson's goal-oriented action first provided substantive critiques to the archive of Black people in the US. Woodson understood that problems of silence and inaccuracy with the history of African Americans was a systemic problem informed by a confluence of factors including the scholarship found in academia, most notably the institutional capacities of universities and academic journals to shape the historical narrative.

Woodson understood the hegemonic capacities of White institutions to consistently tell the story about Black people either as in bondage or as the proverbial Racial Other. The curricular space of the *Association* provided a counter hegemonic space to challenge the reproductive capacities of schools and institutions that employed anti-Black pedagogies.

Woodson concluded that the desire and capacity to change the narrative would be to create alternative institutional spaces that would give vindication to the dominant discourse surrounding Black people's lives. This obvious counter hegemonic practice has direct implications to our current day curricular concerns. In this sense, the work of communities to rethink and reform curriculum must come from local spaces that coalesce around their issues of curriculum and find multiple spaces to study, publish, and disseminate new knowledge. His entrepreneurial revisionist project was in some cases a matter of the racial realities that closed all possibilities for African Americans to name and define their experience in the US. This context helped to mobilize a project that could not rely on White textbook writers, historians, and publishers to do the right thing. Thus our efforts must be to think about the comprehensive and multidimensional aspects of our work across multiple spaces and beyond schools. For example, imagine professors, publishers, curriculum development companies, and non-profits committed to issues of equity in the curriculum, working together for the same cause. And then working to produce historical and curricular research intended to develop, fund, publish, and disseminate to teachers and communities through textbooks and other curricular materials. This was precisely what Woodson's praxis entailed—a project that was realistic and collective.

Woodson in Closing

It is hard to fully grasp the long-term effects of Woodson's project. His ideas about redressing the mis-education of African Americans are with us today—100 years removed from its inception. Scholars remain concerned with the deleterious impact of schools not meeting the needs of students of color. This body of work owes a debt to the foundational curricular discourse of Woodson, including his ideas about mis-education, his attention to rigorous historical scholarship, and, most importantly, his efforts to make new knowledge available to the masses. Woodson's work is central to the ideas of cultural responsiveness, cultural relevance, multicultural education, as well as the critical educational thought in curriculum studies. Any historical or contemporary attention to the problems and dilemmas of curriculum should view Woodson's work as foundational to such an analysis. The lessons curriculum scholars can gather from his scholarship are voluminous. However, we maintain that two aspects of Woodson's work should inform the work of multicultural curriculum scholarship and educational thought as a whole.

The first is that Woodson's scholarship is interdisciplinary. Woodson's historical scholarship and the programs connected to the *Association* drew from multiple disciplines such as history, sociology, anthropology, and the humanities. His teacher correspondence courses had teachers work with some of the most well-known African American scholars across multiple fields of study, including the likes of E. Franklin Frazier, Alain Locke, and Charles Johnson. The content of his Black history textbooks also engaged with topics about African American life across multiple fields of study including science, art, politics, and history. This also was a hallmark of Woodson's Negro History Week Programs. A person attending a Black History event hosted by the *Association* would be impressed by the variety of ways Black history was conveyed through plays, speeches, and art. In keeping with this approach, contemporary scholarship about Black history and multicultural education must engage the question of curriculum inclusion within multiple disciplines and intellectual traditions.

The second is that Woodson's scholarship is transdisciplinary. His historical scholarship engaged historical questions beyond the discipline of History. Although Woodson had established himself as a credible historian, he was thoroughly committed to the idea of accessibility for the masses. His ability to move beyond academia was a hallmark of Woodson's method. His textbooks, Negro History Week Circulars, and teacher correspondence programs all spoke to the pertinence of making Black historical scholarship transdisciplinary. In this regard, curriculum scholars must examine topics that incite the field of curriculum studies, while taking new knowledge and ideas about curriculum beyond the boundaries of academia.

Woodson's praxis-oriented approach to curriculum and pedagogy is of great importance to current educational climate. In some regard, the problems that informed Woodson's work are quite similar to the current day situation. With persistent backlash against multicultural education over the last 20 years, much of the school curriculum is devoid of the kind of humanizing socio-cultural knowledge (Brown, 2013) Woodson provided. However, Woodson understood that the process of curriculum and historical revision was never going to arise from an open invitation by White institutions. As history has shown, the concerns of Black curriculum have been produced through a preponderance of silences, untruths, and ideological backlash (Vasquez Heilig, Brown, & Brown, 2012). He understood that if change was going to occur, it had to start with our own efforts. This is quintessentially Woodsonian. In the end, Woodson committed his life to deconstructing the myths about Black life. As we stated earlier, freedom and persistence informed his life and shaped his work. Woodson's life was Black History and his ideas and philosophies of curriculum should help to support a renewed attention to social change in the school curriculum.

References

Alridge, D. P. (1999). Guiding philosophical principles for a Du Boisian-based African American educational model. *The Journal of Negro Education, 68*(2), 182–199.

Alridge, D. P. (2008). *The educational thought of W.E.B. Du Bois: An intellectual history.* New York: Teachers College Press.

Anderson, J. D. (1988). *The education of blacks in the south, 1860–1935.* Chapel Hill, NC: University of North Carolina Press.

Anderson, T. (2009) "Ten Little Niggers": The making of a Black man's consciousness. Available online: http://folkloreforum.net/2009/05/01/%E2%80%9Cten-little-niggers %E2%80%9D-the-making-of-a-black-man%E2%80%99s-consciousness/ (accessed May 1 2009).

Anyon, J. (1981). Social class and school knowledge. *Curriculum inquiry, 11*(1), 3–42.

Apatheker, H. (1997). Personal recollections: Woodson, Wesley, Robeson and Du Bois. *Black Scholar, 27*(2), 42–45.

Apple, M. (1975). The hidden curriculum and the nature of conflict. In W. Pinar (Ed.), *Curriculum theorizing: The reconceptualists* (pp. 95–119). Berkeley, CA: McCutchan.

Apple, M. W. (1990). *Ideology and curriculum.* New York and London: Routledge.

Apple, M. W. (2013). Can education change society? Du Bois, Woodson and the politics of social transformation. *Review of Education, 1*(1), 32–56.

Au, W. (2012). *Critical curriculum studies: Education, consciousness, and the politics of knowing.* New York and London: Routledge.

Ball, A. F. ([1950] 2006). *Multicultural strategies for education and social change: Carriers of the torch in the United States and South Africa.* New York: Teachers College Press.

Blight, D. W. (2003). *Race and reunion: The civil war in American memory.* Cambridge, MA: Belknap Press of Harvard University Press.

Brown, A. L. (2010) Counter-memory and race: An examination of African American scholars' challenges to early 20th century K–12 historical discourses. *Journal of Negro Education, 79*(1), 54–65.

Brown, A. L. (2012). On human kinds and role models: A critical discussion about the African American male teacher. *Educational Studies, 48*(3), 296–315.

Brown, A. L. & Au, W. (2014). Race, memory and master narratives: A critical essay on U.S. curriculum history. *Curriculum Inquiry, 44*(3), 358–389.

Brown, A. L., King, L. J. & Crowley, R. (2011). Black civitas: An examination of Carter Woodson's contributions to citizenship education. *Theory and Research in Social Education, 39*(2), 277–299.

Brown, A. L. & De Lissovoy, N. (2011). Economies of racism: Grounding education policy research in the complex dialectic of race, class, and capital. *Journal of Educational Policy, 26*(5), 595–619.

Brown, K. D. (2013). Trouble on my mind: Toward a framework of humanizing critical sociocultural knowledge for teaching and teacher education. *Race Ethnicity and Education, 16*(3), 316–338.

Crowder, R. L. (2005). Tribute to the pioneer patriarch of African American history: Carter G. Woodson (1875–1950). *Afro-Americans in New York Life and History, 29*(2), 67–71.

Dagbovie, P. G. (2004). Making black history practical and popular: Carter G. Woodson, the proto black studies movement, and the struggle for black liberation. *The Western Journal of Black Studies, 28*(2), 372–383.

Dagbovie, P. G. (2006). Strategies for teaching African American history: Musings from the past, ruminations for the future. *The Journal of Negro Education, 75*(4), 635–648.

Dagbovie, P. G. (2007a). *The early black history movement, Carter G. Woodson, and Lorenzo Johnston Greene*. Urbana, IL: University of Illinois Press.

Dagbovie, P. G. (2007b). History as a core subject area of African American studies: Self-taught and self-proclaimed African American historians, 1960s–1980s. *Journal of Black Studies, 37*(5), 602.

Dagbovie, P. G. (2010). "Among the vitalizing tools of the radical intelligentsia, of course the most crucial was words": Carter G. Woodson's "The case of the negro" (1921). *Journal for the Study of Radicalism, 3*(2), 81–112.

Dagbovie, P. G. (2011). "Most honorable mention … belongs to Washington, DC": The Carter G. Woodson home and the early black history movement in the nation's capital. *The Journal of African American History, 96*(3), 295–324.

Dagbovie, P. (2014a). Reflections on conventional portrayals of the African American experience during the progressive era or "the nadir." *Journal of the Gilded Age and Progressive Era, 13*(1), 4–27.

Dagbovie, P. (2014b). *Carter G. Woodson in Washington D.C.: The father of Black history.* Charleston, SC: History Press.

Davis, D. A. (2008). Not only war is hell: World War I and African American lynching narratives. *African American Review, 42*(3/4), 477–491.

Dilworth, P. P. (2003). Competing conceptions of citizenship education: Thomas Jesse Jones and Carter G. Woodson. *International Journal of Social Education, 18*(2), 1.

Du Bois, W. E. B. (1935). *Black reconstruction in America 1860–1880*. New York: Simon and Schuster.

Ephraim, C. W. (2003). *The pathology of Eurocentrism: The burden and responsibilities of being black*. Trenton, NJ: Africa World Press.

Eisner, E. W. (1979). *The educational imagination: On the design and evaluation of school programs*. New York: Macmillan.

Fenderson, J. (2010). Evolving conceptions of pan-African scholarship: W.E.B. Du Bois, Carter G. Woodson, and the "Encyclopedia Africana," 1909–1963. *The Journal of African American History, 95*(1), 71–91.

Flinders, D. J., Noddings, N. & Thornton, S. J. (1986). The null curriculum: Its theoretical basis and practical implications. *Curriculum Inquiry, 16*(1), 33–42.

Fredrickson, G. (1987). *The Black Image in the White Mind: The Debate on Afro-American Character and Destiny, 1817–1914*. New York: Harper & Row.

Gates, H. L. (1988). The trope of the new Negro and the reconstruction of the image of the Black. *Representations, 24*, 129–155.

Geertz, C. (1973). Thick description: Toward an interpretive theory of culture. In C. Geertz, *The interpretation of cultures: Selected essays* (pp. 3–30). New York: Basic Books.

Giroux, H. (1983). Theories of reproduction and resistance in the new sociology of education: A critical analysis. *Harvard Education Review, 53*(3), 261–293.

Goggin, J. (1985). Carter G. Woodson and the collection of source materials for Afro-American history. *The American Archivist, 48*(3), 261–271.

Goggin, J. A. (1993). *Carter G. Woodson: A life in black history*. Baton Rouge: Louisiana State University Press.

Goggin, & Wilson, F. R. (1994). Carter G. Woodson. *The Journal of Southern History, 60*(4), 832–832.

Greene, L. & Strikland, A. E. (Ed.) (1996). *Selling Black history for Carter G. Woodson: A Diary, 1930–1933*, Columbia, MO: University of Missouri Press.

Hall, S. (Ed.). (1997). *Representation: Cultural representations and signifying practices* (Vol. 2). London: SAGE.

Hine, D. C. (1986). Carter G. Woodson, white philanthropy and negro historiography. *The History Teacher, 19*(3), 405–425.

King, L. J. & Brown, K. (2015). Once a year to be Black: Carter G. Woodson, curriculum and teaching during Black History Month. *Negro Educational Review,* 65(1–4), 23–43.

King, L. J., Crowley, R. M., & Brown, A. L. (2011). The forgotten legacy of carter G. Woodson: Contributions to multicultural social studies and African American history. *Social Studies, 101*(5), 211–215.

King, L. J., Davis, C. & Brown, A. L. (2012). African American history, race and textbooks: An examination of the works of Harold O. Rugg and Carter G. Woodson. *Journal of Social Studies Research, 36*(4), 359.

Ladson-Billings, G. (1995). Toward a theory of culturally relevant pedagogy. *American Educational Research Journal, 32*(3), 465–491.

Levine, D. (2000). Carter G. Woodson and the Afrocentrists: Common foes of mis-education. *The High School Journal, 84*(1), 5–13.

Lindsay, A. G. (1950). Dr. Carter G. Woodson as a teacher. *Negro History Bulletin, 13*(8), 183–183.

Locke, A. L. (1997 [1925]). *The New Negro.* New York: Simon & Schuster.

Logan, R. W. (1997[1954]). *The Betrayal of the Negro, from Rutherford B. Hayes to Woodrow Wilson.* New York: Da Capo Press.

Logan, R. W. (1945). Phylon profile VI: Carter G. Woodson. *Phylon (1940–1956), 6*(4), 315–321.

Marshall, T. M. (1930). *American history.* New York: Macmillan.

Martin, M. (2004). *Brown Gold: Milestones of African American Children's Books, 1845–2002.* New York: Routledge.

Meier, A. & Rudwick, E. (1984). J. Franklin Jameson, Carter G. Woodson, and the foundations of black historiography. *The American Historical Review, 89*(4), 1005–1015.

Mills, C. (1998). Revisionist ontologies: Theorizing White supremacy. In C. Mills (Ed.), *Blackness visible: Essays on philosophy and race.* Ithaca, NY: Cornell University Press.

Milner, H. R. (2010). *Start where you are, but don't stay there: Understanding diversity, opportunity gaps, and teaching in today's classrooms.* Cambridge, MA: Harvard Education Press.

National Association for the Advancement of Colored People. NAACP (1939). Anti-Negro propaganda in school textbooks [pamphlet]. New York: NAACP.

Omi, M. & Winant, H. (2015). *Racial formation in the United States.* New York and London: Routledge.

Paris, D. (2012). Culturally sustaining pedagogy: A needed change in stance, terminology, and practice. *Educational Researcher, 41*(3), 93–97.

Paris, D. & Alim, H. S. (2014). What are we seeking to sustain through culturally sustaining pedagogy? A loving critique forward. *Harvard Educational Review, 84*(1), 85.

Pitcher, C. (1999). D. W. Griffith's controversial film, the birth of a nation. *Organization of American Historians Magazine of History, 13*(3), 50.

Pressly, T. J. (2006). "The known world" of free black slaveholders: A research note on the scholarship of Carter G. Woodson. *The Journal of African American History, 91*(1), 81–87.

Reddick, L. D. (1934). Racial attitudes in American history textbooks of the South. *Journal of Negro History,* 19(3), 225–265.

Reddick, L. D. (2002 [1950]). Twenty-five Negro history weeks. *Black History Bulletin,* 65(1/2), 34.

Rashid, K. (2005). Slavery of the mind: Carter G. Woodson and Jacob H. Caruthers-intergenerational discourse on African education and social change. *The Western Journal of Black Studies, 29*(1), 542–546.

Scott, D. M. (1997). *Contempt and pity: Social policy and the image of the damaged black psyche, 1880–1996.* Chapel Hill, NC: University of North Carolina Press.

Shulman, L. S. (1987). Knowledge and teaching: Foundations of the new reform. *Harvard Educational Review, 57*(1), 1–23.

Spivak, G. C. (1988). Can the subaltern speak? In C. Nelson & L. Grossberg (Eds.), *Marxism and the interpretation of culture.* Chicago, IL: University of Illinois Press.

Strong-Leek, L. (2008). bell hooks, Carter G. Woodson, and African American education. *Journal of Black Studies, 38*(6), 850–861.

Vasquez Heilig, J., Brown, K.D. & Brown, A.L. (2012). The illusion of inclusion: A critical race theory textual analysis of race and standards. *Harvard Educational Review, 82*(3), 403–424.

Warren, C. (2007). Multicultural service learning as authentic assessment: Carter G. Woodson's Mis-education of the Negro revisited. *Black History Bulletin, 70*(2), 4.

Watkins, W. H. (1993). Black curriculum orientations: A preliminary inquiry. *Harvard Educational Review, 63*(3), 321–339.

Watkins, William H. (2001). *The White architects of Black education: Ideology and power in America, 1865–1954.* New York: Teachers College Press.

Wesley, C. H. (1951). Carter G. Woodson-as a scholar. *Journal of Negro History, 36*(1), 12–24.

Wiggan, G. (2010). Afrocentricity and the black intellectual tradition and education: Carter G. Woodson, W. E. B. Du Bois, and E. Franklin Frazier. *Journal of Pan African Studies, 3*(9), 128.

Williams, C. L. (2007). Vanguards of the new negro: African american veterans and post-World War I racial militancy. *The Journal of African American History, 92*(3), 347–370.

Woodson, C. G. (1916). The Negroes of Cincinnati prior to the civil war. *Journal of Negro History, 1*(1), 1–22.

Woodson, C. G. (1919). Negro life and history in the schools. *Journal of Negro History, 4* (3), 273–273.

Woodson, C. G. (1921). *The history of the Negro church.* Washington, D.C. Associated Publishers.

Woodson, C. G. (1923). Annual report of the director for the year 1922–23. *Journal of Negro History, 8*(4), 466–471.

Woodson, C. G. (1925). Annual report of the director. *Journal of Negro History, 10*(4), 590–597.

Woodson, C. G. (1926). Negro History Week. *Journal of Negro History, 11*(2), 238–242.

Woodson, C. G. (1927). The celebration of Negro history week. *Journal of Negro History, 12*(2), 103–109.

Woodson, C. G. (1928a). *African myths, together with proverbs.* Washington DC: Associated Publishers.

Woodson, C. G. (1928b). Annual report of the director. *Journal of Negro History, 13*(4), 403–412.

Woodson, C. G. (1930). Annual report of the director. *Journal of Negro History, 15*(4), 391–400.

Woodson, C. G. (1935). Annual report of the director. *Journal of Negro History, 20*(4), 363–372.

Woodson, C. G. (1941a). The Negro in New England. *Negro History Bulletin, 5*(1), 4.

Woodson, C. G. (1941b). The Negro in New York. *Negro History Bulletin, 5*(2), 28–.

Woodson, C. G. (1941c). The Negro in the West Indies. *Negro History Bulletin, 4*(4), 76.

Woodson, C. G. (1942). *Negroes in Brazil.* Washington, D.C. Association for the Study of African American Life and History, Inc.

Woodson, C. G. (1968). *The education of the Negro prior to 1861.* New York: Arno Press.

Woodson, C. G. (1969). *Negro orators and their orations.* New York: Russell & Russell.

Woodson, C. G. (1998[1933]). *The mis-education of the Negro.* Trenton, NJ: African World Press.

Woodson, C. G. (2002 [1926]). Observances of Negro history week. *Black History Bulletin, 65*(1/2), 21.

Woodson, C. G. & Wesley, C. H. (1922). *The Negro in our history.* Washington DC: Associated Publishers.

Woodson, C. G. & Wesley, C. H. (1928). *Negro makers of history.* Washington DC: Associated Publishers.

Woodson, C. G. & Wesley, C. (1935). *The story of the Negro retold.* Washington DC: Associated Publishers.

Wynter, S. (1979). Sambos and minstrels. *Social Text, 1*(1), 149–156.

Wynter, S. (1992). *Don't call us Negroes: How multicultural textbooks perpetuate racism.* San Francisco, CA: Aspire.

Young, M. F. D. (1971). *Knowledge and control: New directions for the sociology of education.* London: Collier-Macmillan.

Zimmerman, J. (2002). *Whose America? Culture wars in the public school.* Cambridge, MA: Harvard University Press.

Zimmerman, J. (2004). *Brown*-ing the American textbook: History, psychology, and the origins of modern multiculturalism. *History of Education Quarterly, 44,* 46–69.

4

TO CAPTURE THE ELUSIVE
Alain Locke on Diversity, Cultural Knowledge, and Race

"Too few well understood or adequately appreciated Locke"—Ralph Bunche on Alain Locke on the occasion of his memorial.

(Carter & Harris, 2010)

Introduction

"Locke's intellectual sojourn as a philosopher is in less need of explanation than appreciation" (Harris, 1989b, p. 10). We choose these words to open this chapter on Alain L. Locke, an extraordinary intellectual who equally claimed the role of scholar, philosopher, and aesthete.

In many ways Locke was an anomalous figure for his time. He was highly educated and unusually accomplished, a point made even more poignant as a Black man in early twentieth century US. He was also a gay man, a fact that he did not hide but that was less openly acknowledged in the context of early work produced about him. In fact, some scholars have suggested that Locke's sexuality may have played a role in the limited attention he was given as a contributor to American education thought and in his overall positioning as apolitical (Porter, 2012). Locke was most often associated with the Harlem Renaissance and the role he played in supporting and grooming the Black arts movement of the early twentieth century. For many years, this aspect of Locke's scholarship threatened to eclipse his other scholarly areas of interest, including cultural pluralism, race, and adult education. Locke wrote extensively about the Black arts, spanning across the genres of writing, visual, music, and performance.

For all of his contributions the scholarly community as a whole has paid limited attention to his work. A corpus of scholarship devoted to Alain Locke has emerged since the 1990s with much of this focused on Locke's philosophical ideas related to values, culture, art, and race. Edited books (e.g., Carter & Harris, 2010; Harris, 1999; Molesworth, 2012a), bound collections of Locke's lectures, essays, and reviews (Harris, 1989; Stewart, 1992), several biographies (Buck, 2005a; Cain, 2003; Harris & Molesworth, 2008), and an expansive number of journal articles and dissertations comprise this burgeoning body of work. Most of this work was produced in academic fields outside of the field of education. Aside from a few articles and dissertations written in the area of adult education, and one dissertation focused partially on Locke's intellectual ideas related to Blackness and critical theory (Porter, 2012), virtually no scholarship exists on Locke and education, specifically critical educational thought.

In presenting Locke's intellectual thought in this chapter we begin by first providing a brief biography of his life, highlighting the early schooling and educational experiences that framed his professional career. From here we move to a discussion in three parts of Locke's intellectual ideas. Each part addresses an issue of relevance to education in the US and how Locke's thought speaks to this concern. In doing this we seek to illuminate the relevance of Locke's work on critical education issues. Part one begins with a discussion of the context of schooling in the multicultural U.S. society. We focus on the ongoing challenges that U.S. schools face in providing an education that is equitable and multicultural. We follow this with a discussion that focuses specifically on Locke's intellectual contributions to the areas of culture, value theory, and cultural pluralism. Here we illustrate how these ideas formed the foundation of Locke's thinking around culture and the normative nature of values, two concepts that figured prominently across the span of Locke's scholarly trajectory and that speak to enduring concerns around diversity and pluralism in U.S. schools.

Part two considers the endemic problems around cultural knowledge and teaching. We ground these concerns in the ongoing dilemmas with providing students a curriculum and teaching experience that is affirming, relevant, and transformative. We then reflect on Locke's ideas around knowledge and culture through the subject matter of Black Art. Here we illustrate how Locke viewed culture and knowledge as key components in creating a Black art aesthetic that would both serve liberating ends for Black Americans and help to usher a more racially equitable U.S. society. For Locke, a culturally authentic Black art aesthetic, reflected cultural knowledge that was not a part of the dominant construction of "valid" art. He recognized the power that knowledge played in strengthening the identities of Black Americans, while also transforming dominant, deficit-based knowledge that failed to recognize the beauty and value of these individuals.

Part three focuses on the topic of race and racism. We open this section with an outline of the tensions and key considerations and theories that address race and racism in the context of education. We illustrate how race and racism exist in schooling but often go unacknowledged in school practice. Following this discussion we examine how Locke theorized the construct of race as a socially constructed, non-essentializing phenomena that operated in historically contingent ways. Finally, we close the chapter by considering the impact Locke's work has had and could have in education discourse and practice around the broad issues of diversity, knowledge, and race as they impact U.S. schooling.

Biography of a Scholar and Public Intellectual

Alain LeRoy Locke, a scholar described by biographer Charles Molesworth (2012b) as "the most exquisitely educated African American of his generation" and a "public intellectual in the tradition of American pragmatism" (p. xi) was born on September 13, 1885, to parents Pliny Locke and Mary Hawkins Locke. While given the name Arthur by his parents, Locke changed it to Alain LeRoy (Menand, 2001). Locke spent his formative years in Philadelphia, Pennsylvania under the doting and watchful eyes of his mother, Mary Hawkins Locke, with whom he shared a close relationship until her death in 1922. Locke was an exceptionally strong and accomplished student. He graduated from Central High School in Philadelphia and went on to complete a B.A. degree at the Philadelphia School of Pedagogy where he graduated first in his class (Harris & Molesworth, 2008; Harris, 1989a).[1] In 1904, he went to Harvard College, earning a B.A. degree, graduating *magna cum laude* and with honors in Philosophy. While at Harvard he was admitted to Phi Beta Kappa, received the Bowdoin Prize (a Harvard College English Language undergraduate student award), and was selected as the first African American to receive a Rhodes Scholarship. As a Rhodes Scholar, Locke secured admission to and studied at Oxford University in 1907. This experience proved challenging, one in which Locke experienced incredible disillusionment around the issue of race. Locke left Oxford without taking a degree and spent two years, from 1910–1911 at the University of Berlin.

Upon his arrival back to the United States, Locke completed a Ph.D in philosophy at Harvard in 1918 and landed a faculty position in 1912 in the Teachers College at Howard University where he enjoyed a 40-year career. Locke served as a professor of the Teaching of English and Instructor in Philosophy (Harris, 1989a). Aside from his unwarranted brief dismissal by Howard President J. Stanley Durkee in 1926, Locke enjoyed an illustrious career as a professor and Dean at Howard. Locke maintained a robust scholarly life, traveling and speaking extensively both nationally and abroad, participated on many national and international committees related to Black arts, adult education, and the study of Africa. Locke was connected to the Progressive Education Association. He edited a pivotal text associated with the intercultural movement entitled, *When Peoples Meet: A Study in Race and Culture Contact* (Locke & Stern, 1942). The intercultural movement was a precursor to what is commonly recognized as multicultural education (Banks, 1995). Additional archival data confirms that Locke was invited to participate in both research projects (Bow, 1945, March 16) and speaking engagements (Hinton, 1944, April 17; Locke, 1946, May 28; Holden, 1947, April 3) related to K–12 schooling. Additionally he published on the necessity to view teaching as a profession, rather than as solely an art. He expressed concern about people making the choice to become a teacher because it was the only job opportunity they perceived having. He also advocated that teachers receive higher compensation for their work (Locke, 1923). He enjoyed a long relationship with *The Opportunity* periodical, the official organ of the National Urban League, where he published widely. Locke also was a longtime member of and contributor to the Bahá'í Organization, a spiritual movement recognized for "their acceptance of all racial groups, their consideration of racism as religious sin, the integration of cultures as reciprocal sources of values and their democratic governance" (Buck, 2005b; Harris & Molesworth, 2008).

Never married or noted for having a long-term personal relationship, Locke lived a life as a bachelor and had no children. Perhaps this was related to the overwhelming focus he placed on his work. Throughout his life, Locke possessed an optimistic belief in the power of societal change through self-definition and the radical deconstruction of fundamental concepts like values, culture, and race. Yet at the core, Locke maintained a dogged commitment to addressing the daunting challenges of living equitably in a multiracial society.

Part One

The Discontents of Living and Learning in Multicultural America

Since its founding in 1774, the United States has faced the challenge of creating and maintaining a society that is inclusive of all its inhabitants. Its colonial past, purporting to offer true freedom and liberty to all, existed alongside the taking of Indigenous lands and the conquest of Indigenous and African peoples conveniently positioned as savage and sub-human, respectively. While contributing to the social, cultural, and political landscape of the country, the labor and lands of these groups were foundational, propelling the wealth of individuals and companies that continue to flourish economically to this present day (Bell, 1989–1990). This legacy continued in the twentieth century with the practices of U.S. imperialist domination; both nationally, through its maintenance of racially segregated worlds, and globally as it simultaneously laid imperial claim to foreign lands and the peoples and resources these spaces possessed (Winant, 2001). This history was at once paradoxically characterized both by democracy and violence. It was one where White supremacy reigned, granting sanction and value only to certain bodies, knowledge, and ways of being. One's location in or close alignment to Whiteness—recognized as a set of privileges, cultural practices, and ways of understanding the world (Frankenberg, 1993) and secured through domination (Leonardo, 2004)—afforded material benefits to those situated within its symbolic and legal boundaries. Nowhere was this history more evident than in the context of schooling.

The quest for education, specifically for Black Americans, often pursued under the threat of death or loss of limb (Williams, 2009) or of one's notion of self and community (e.g., see this volume, Chapter 3; Brown, 2013; Woodson, 2000) reflected a fully humanizing endeavor. The quest to realize the full promise of the United States was often viewed alongside gaining an education (Perry, Steele, & Hilliard, 2003). Yet schooling for enslaved Africans prior to the ending of slavery in the U.S. in 1865 was illegal (Carter, 2012). Schooling created by the White dominant society for indigenous peoples was designed to further colonize presumed savages by remaking the Indian into the image of the White, Protestant Anglo-Saxon, all while justifying the pilfering of indigenous land for the advancement of democracy (Adams, 1988; Tuck & Yang, 2012). Other groups of color, including those of Mexican and Japanese descent, while at times seeking recognition as legally White (San Miguel, 2000; Lopez, 1994) generally were placed outside both the boundaries and privileges of Whiteness.

For Black Americans living in the U.S. south, the ending of slavery did not lead to full and equal access to formal education even as it was widely desired. Anderson (1988) noted that at the conclusion of slavery, Black Americans vigorously sought an education previously denied them. They built and funded their own schools prior to the intervention of missionary societies and other philanthropic groups that got involved in education for the Negro. These early twentieth-century efforts, while helping to develop the burgeoning assemblage of historically Black colleges and universities (HBCU) that remain in existence, concomitantly faced challenges in setting the agenda for and control over schooling for Black Americans in the US (Locke, 1989d[1925]). Debates also ensued regarding the purposes of schooling for Black Americans. On the one hand some Black scholars recognized the value of a select few race leaders in the Black community pursuing the highest levels of education, as promoted by W.E.B. Du Bois in his early thinking around the talented tenth. Other thinkers like Booker T. Washington argued for an education that would bring immediate economic benefit to Black Americans, particularly those living in a southern, post-Reconstruction, Jim Crow racist society that restricted even the basics of personal rights and livelihood. Across his scholarship one noted that Alain Locke recognized the utility of both of these approaches, while also questioning the extent to which either were ever fully realized anywhere in the country (Locke, 1989d[1925]).

The advent of the industrial revolution, coupled with the tyranny of White supremacy and the concomitant White racial violence that characterized life in the south for Blacks (Marable & Mullings, 2003), ushered a mass migration of Black Americans to the North, Midwest, and West. Urban cities proliferated, swelling from the mix of new immigrant groups from Southern and Eastern European countries and the recent Black migrants from the U.S. south. Schools in these new areas, while more racially integrated, failed to offer Blacks equitable access (Franklin, 1979; Mabee, 1979; Tyack, 1974), including entry to professional opportunities following schooling (Blascoer, 1915). As noted in Chapter 3, school curriculum was generally not inclusive or affirmative for Black students. Too often this body of knowledge grossly misrepresented Black Americans or ignored their contributions. Additionally, the lack of Black teachers in these schools was of concern as it was presumed they held cultural knowledge that Black students needed to acquire (Franklin, 1979; Mabee, 1979). For example, Du Bois (1935) posed the question, "Does the Negro need separate schools?" Here, he argued the necessity for Black students to attend racially segregated schools and colleges/universities in light of the dehumanizing, racially hostile culture they would encounter in racially integrated settings, whether in the U.S. south or in the U.S. north. In both contexts Du Bois questioned whether Blacks could acquire a proper education that would equip them for full citizenship. He stated:

> If the public schools of Atlanta, Nashville, New Orleans and Jacksonville were thrown open to all races tomorrow, the education that colored children would get in them would be worse than pitiable. It would not be education. And in the same way, there are many public school systems in the North where Negroes are admitted and tolerated, but they are not educated; they are crucified. There are certain Northern universities where Negro students, no matter what their ability, desert, or accomplishment, cannot get fair recognition, either in [the] classroom or on the campus, in dining halls and student activities, or in common human courtesy.
>
> (Du Bois, 1935, p. 329)

Highlighting alternative scenarios of race and schooling that at the time did not exist, or did so in limited fashion, Du Bois argued that Black students would experience racism in schools dominated by a White cultural logic (Goldsby, 2006) embodied in the practices of staff, curricula knowledge, and/or valued ways of being that aligned with Whiteness. The crux of his argument was simple: Black students encountered unsafe (even, violent) conditions when attending racially integrated schools that failed to disrupt cultural practices that supported White supremacy.

These conditions bespoke of the racially alienating cultural environments students of color encountered and continue to face when attending dominant, White schools. Drawing from a Bourdieuan framework, Carter (2012) argued that in the contemporary context, students of color who attend such schools encounter a set of cultural practices sanctioned by and aligned with those in power, or a set of social relations that place privilege on knowledge and ways of being adopted by the dominant social class in society. The result is that school officials:

> May either establish school rules or implicitly enforce racial, ethnic, and class segregations within schools (and even curricula) that limit or deny

students the opportunities to acquire awareness and share some of the cultural tastes and historical sensibilities of their non-White peers. Such practices signify an aspect of organizational (in) flexibility that bars reciprocity in cultural exchanges among students within schools.

(Carter, 2012, p. 13)

Describing a context of racially integrated schooling similar to that of Du Bois, Carter (2012) noted the alienating conditions students of color encountered in these schools but extended the discussion by highlighting how they were not inescapable or inevitable. Rather, these practices were embedded in the institutional arrangements and daily practices of schools. These were both integrally tied to larger societal relations of power. Yet agentic opportunities did exist for "increased social interactions among different groups of students, across social identities, and across social boundaries [that] should, in theory, compel them to expose each other to "new" cultural practices and tastes" (Carter, 2012, p. 13). Here, Carter points to the unrealized project of multicultural education in the US. Multicultural education first emerged in the early twentieth century through the work of scholars and activists of color, was expanded upon as part of the intercultural movement of the 1940s, spoke to the optimism and social upheavals of the Civil Rights and Black Power Movements of the 1960s and 1970s, and challenged the culture wars of the 1980s and 1990s. We recognize that various typologies ensued (Banks, 1995; Sleeter & Grant, 2006[1986]) and debates emerged in the field of multicultural education around the focus of this work—e.g., *focus on one or multiple sociocultural markers*, including race, social class, gender, religion, sexuality; *target particular or various elements of the schooling experience*, including curriculum, pedagogy, school organization; and *place emphasis on curriculum* emphasizing celebrating difference, expanding official knowledge, or transforming school and societal relations through knowledge creation. However, regardless of the differences in form and focus, at its heart, theories of multicultural education move from an optimistic stance that wishes to transform relations of power that curtail equitable opportunities for all students, regardless of background to educationally flourish. In accomplishing this task, a key element was to respectfully, yet critically, engage across difference.

Writing some 77 years apart, the words of Du Bois (1935) and Carter (2012) point to a longstanding concern around multiculturalism in education. They consider if and how a multiracial society, marred by inequitable, dehumanizing conditions that sustain the privilege of one racially dominant group, might equitably school all students. Yet these two positions—the latter decidedly more hopeful than the former—ultimately ask that we consider the challenges posed by culture and race in schools. Unlike Carter (2012), Du Bois, who wrote in 1935, had no knowledge of (and could not envision at the time) the eventual passage of *Brown v. Board of Education* in 1954 that dismantled legally sanctioned racial segregation in the US. He was also unaware of (but perhaps might have foretold) the snail's pace that schools in the south took toward racial integration immediately following passage of *Brown*, the present retrenchment of racial segregation in schools across the US (Orfield, 2001), and the stronghold of neoliberal practices (e.g., charter schools, vouchers, standardized testing, alternative teacher certification) that currently threaten to undermine public schooling in the twenty-first century (Apple, 2014; Watkins, 2012).

Striking in their stability over time, these conditions mark the difficulties encountered when seeking to meet the educational needs of diverse communities in a multiracial society. These tensions figured prominently in the intellectual work of Alain Locke. His ideas stand to offer clarity to these pressing issues that continue to plague U.S. schools.

Alain Locke on Culture, Cultural Pluralism, and Value Theory

Trained as a philosopher, Locke expressed a special concern in explicating how values operated among different groups living in a multiracial society. The challenge, as he saw it, was accounting for cultural value systems in a way that did not normatively privilege values expressed and supported by a White, European worldview. Value theory is a branch of philosophy concerned with the nature of values and valuation processes in society. It goes back to the earliest development of philosophy and is associated with the study of axiology or ethics. Why, how, and the extent to which people value people and things in society form the basis of this work (Lemos, 1999). Eschewing an essentialist notion of values that approached these entities as universal and timeless, Locke recognized all values as situated in particular contexts that informed their emergence and function in society. Locke (1989a) positioned values as of vital importance to individuals in their lives. Values informed how people understood themselves, others, and the social world. The societal context in the United States provided a robust space to explore these ideas. Locke, recognized as a pragmatist (even a radical pragmatist by some—e.g., Harris, 1999), felt deeply that philosophic ideas could speak to pressing social concerns (Fraser, 1999). He was hopeful that racial harmony could, in fact, exist in the US, despite its legacy of White supremacy and racism. He envisioned and believed it was possible to erect a new racial society in the US—one that engaged intercultural social relations between racially different people with the goal of transforming dominant White cultural discourses and practices.

Race sat at the heart of Locke's pragmatic views on values (Porter, 2012; Fraser, 1999), with these ideas concomitantly informed by his belief in the need to build a culturally pluralist society. The notion of cultural pluralism was coined and theorized by Horace Kallen, who first served as a teaching assistant in a Greek philosophy course taught by George Santayana and taken by Locke in 1906 or 1907 at Harvard (Menand, 2001). Kallen also later attended Oxford during Locke's time there as a Rhodes Scholar. Kallen has credited Locke with assisting him in the burgeoning ideas of cultural pluralism (Harris & Moleworth, 2008; Kallen, 1957), the perspective that a unified societal relationship could exist between culturally different people. Kallen (1957) noted that cultural pluralism is "intended to signify … towards friendship by people who are different from each other but who, as different, hold themselves equal to each other" (p. 120). Cultural pluralism acknowledges that individuals should be viewed equally, regardless of whether they hold different experiences, knowledge, and/or beliefs that constitute the value systems to which they adhere and practice. Kallen (1957) stated:

> [T]he basis of our communion is our difference. Let us exchange the fruits of our differences so that each may enrich the other with what the other is not or has not in himself. In what else are we important to one another, what else can we pool and share if not our differences?
>
> (pp. 120–121)

While Kallen and Locke both drew from the idea of cultural pluralism, scholars noted that differences existed between their ideas (Menand, 2001; Porter, 2012). Kallen approached the idea with a vision that included only ethnic Europeans in the pluralist project. He also held essentialist and deterministic perspectives on race. Conversely, Locke imagined a culturally pluralistic society that included all groups, including African Americans. One of the unique contributions Locke made to the theorization of cultural pluralism was his assumption that race and culture were fluid, socially constructed, and historically situated (Menand, 2001). Locke's approach to values lay at the heart of these ideas.

Kallen (1957) argued that Locke's views on cultural pluralism were informed by the racist experiences he encountered as a Rhodes Scholar at Oxford. Upon learning of Locke's acceptance, several southern White winners from the US threatened to revoke their awards if Locke was allowed to remain in the program.[2] Additionally, senior officials at the Rhodes Trust surreptitiously worked, unsuccessfully, to have Locke removed prior to his matriculation (Harris, 2010). This situation highlights how Locke was positioned tightly in an existing racialized frame that recognized him only as Black—a signifier of presumed inferiority and deficiency, regardless of his actual ability and accomplishment (Harris & Molesworth, 2008). It is not surprising that during these early years as a university student Locke struggled to assert himself as an individual unbounded by the fetters of his racial identity. Harris and Molesworth (2008) chronicled the frustrations Locke felt toward the tokenized treatment he received as an accomplished Black student at Harvard. Early in his life he often deflected his racial identity, wishing that he could simply be viewed as an individual. In a letter he wrote to his mother concerning the Rhodes Scholarship, Locke stated:

> I'm going to England as a Negro—I will leave the color question in New
> York ... [T]he only condition on which I will take up the Negro question
> again is the race leadership in America—Otherwise none of it for me.
>
> (Harris & Molesworth, 2008, p. 57)

Over time, as witnessed in his scholarship, however, Locke moved from a more
universalist outlook to one that rendered "acquiescence an inalienable right to his
difference ... [This] became the core of his value system" (Kallen, 1957, p. 123).
Locke's system of values reflected his stance that "all philosophies ... are in
ultimate derivation philosophies of life and not of abstract, disembodied 'objective'
reality; products of time, place and thus systems of timed history rather than
timeless eternity" (Locke, 1989a, p. 34). He argued that values played an
imperative role (Locke, 1989a) in guiding how people understand and act in
society. He felt that people often moved from a place of unquestioned certainty,
whether consciously realized, regarding personal value positions. To this end,
Locke (1989a) highlighted a fundamental problem regarding the existence and
operation of values in multiracial societies: the assumption that one universal,
perennial, and true set of values existed.

> The common man, in both his individual and group behavior, perpetuates
> the problem in a very practical way. He sets up personal and private and
> group norms as standards and principles, and rightly or wrongly hypostasizes
> them as universals for all conditions, all times and all men.
>
> (p. 36)

Locke recognized value theory, with its emphasis on examining how value
systems operated in society, as a useful tool for interrupting value universals. Yet
value theory was not without its own shortcomings, particularly around the
epistemic and metaphysical assumptions embedded within the theory. These gaps
in value theory resulted from what Locke (2010) called a "dominant and chronic
formalism" that undermined the unfolding of its full promise (p. 78). Here Locke
speaks back to approaches that focus on form over content and that move from
the assumption that meaning is gained by analyzing a direct product absent of
consideration of the context in which it sits. An example of this is interpreting a
text by looking only at the text, rather than the characteristics of the background
of the person or the context in which the piece was created in order to assist in
the meaning-making process.

Locke's recognition that values operated in normative ways required that he
disentangle the traditional approach to understanding values. Locke (2010)
looked to a functionalist approach that would allow for a more "critical and
comparative study of our basic values and value systems" specifically during a
time of value conflict and crisis (Locke, 2010, p. 78). Drawing from philosopher
Friedrich Nietzsche's notion of the "transvaluation of values" (Locke, 2010, p.

78), Locke saw the necessity to disrupt unquestioned, normatively held values in society. Locke's keen insight into the hegemonic way that values operated within a multiracial society gives an indication that he recognized how Whiteness reigned supreme as the socially acceptable perspective concerning ways of knowing and being.

Locke rejected a dogmatic view of values (Carter, 2010; Locke, 1989a). He felt that dogmatic approaches were a natural outgrowth when one placed specific emphasis on ethics, "the most categorical and authoritarian of the value fields … [as they] lead[ing] naturally to an emphasis on solution by definition" (Locke, 2010, p. 77). He also felt that any approach to valuation theory that placed more attention on individual value norms, while neglecting to consider how values operated with each other, led to less dynamic and contextual understandings. Interestingly while he felt all values were derived in context and reflected cultural practices, perspectives and functions that were important to the communities where they existed and were enacted, he did not subscribe to a radical relativist position that might suggest dispensing with the notion of values altogether (Locke, 1989a). Locke acknowledged that various value types existed across communities—what Locke thought of as value genres. On the surface these values might appear different, but in actuality, they held functional equivalence, making way for points of commonality across the specific values expressed. Locke noted the following with regards to this process:

> Indeed, the most illuminating evidence as to the nature of the value genres and their systematic end values promises to come from the examination of parallelisms in their functioning, as well as from case analysis of their occasional overlapping and interchangeability.
>
> (Locke, 2010, pp. 77–78)

Here we find that Locke felt that people often draw from the same category of values that parallel those held by others. An example of this would be holding the value of respect. While people from different cultural groups might hold the similar value genre of respect, they might also have diverse rules for giving respect. For example, one group might believe that students should give any person in an authority role respect, while another group might believe that respect is something that is gained through mutual interaction and relationship, rather than granted solely because of one's position or role.

Recognizing the contingent, contextual nature of values did not, for Locke, mean accepting that all values were of equal function in a diverse society. Locke did not subscribe to the belief that all values were of equal utility or resided outside of the realm of judgment (Collins, 2010; Locke, 1989b). Rather his approach sought a middle ground (Locke, 1989a) between a purely objective or subjective stance of valuation. His functional approach to values, then, was to approach them as socially situated, requiring interrogation in order to evaluate their usefulness in a pluralistic society. Locke formalized these ideas into a working set of propositions he termed *critical relativism*.

Locke's *critical relativism* (1989e), outlined in his 1950 publication, "The Need for a New Organon in Education," reflected an educational methodology that "surplant[s] formal logic" (Harris, 1989b) with the intention to disrupt dogmatic thinking related to normative knowledge.[3] Locke's critical relativism "is not a system of logical rules or criteria of truth conditionals," but rather is a "reasoning modality that conditions the possibility of communicative competency and reflections on facticity" (Harris, 1989b, p. 19). Six elements comprised the approach:

1. implement an objective interpretation of values by referring them realistically to their social and cultural backgrounds,
2. interpret values concretely as functional adaptations to these backgrounds, and thus make clear their historical and functional relativity. An objective criterion of functional sufficiency and insufficiency would thereby be set up as a pragmatic test of value adequacy and inadequacy,
3. claim or impute no validity for values beyond this relativistic framework, and so counteract value dogmatism based on regarding them as universals good and true for all times and all places,
4. confine its consideration of ideology to the prime function and real status of being the adjunct rationalization of values and value interests,
5. trace value development and change as a dynamic process instead of in terms of unrealistic analytic categories, and so eliminating the traditional illusions produced by generalized value terms—*viz.*, static values and fixed value concepts and "ideals,"
6. reinforce current semantic criticism of academic value analytics, with its unrealistic symbols and over-generalized concepts.

(Locke, 1989e, pp. 273–274)

The first element entailed objectively interpreting values by considering them in context to their social and cultural backgrounds; the second required interpreting values as adaptations serving a functional role with regards to their situated sociocultural background. One could pragmatically judge whether a value was sufficient or not in light of its functionality in context. The third component recognized that no validity exists for values not placed under the aforementioned framework. This attempted to counter dogmatic adherence to values as universal and timeless. The fourth recognized ideology to serve a fundamental function in rationalizing a group's adherence to certain values. The fifth asked one to trace out how values developed and changed in meanings over time and in concert with larger sociocultural context. Undertaking this task would bring light to the falsity of viewing certain value categories as fixed, timeless and/or as ideals.

Finally, the sixth element advocated that one remain vigilant in interrogating and critiquing existing, often unquestioned approaches to analyzing values, along with the symbols they engender, that overgeneralize their significance.

For Locke, *critical relativism* would offer a way for K–12 and adult education to help students acquire a more useful way to understand and use values in the context of living in a multiracial society. Indeed, as Harris (1989a) stated concerning Locke's stance on the importance of values in society, "Social life requires imperatives" (p. 32). Locke recognized the power of holding a functional and critical relativist stance as this encouraged challenging the normative frames that individuals and societies operated within and that lead to conflict. Locke (1989b) stated:

> No single factor could serve this end more acceptably and effectively than a relativistic concept of culture, which, by first disestablishing the use of one's own culture as a contrast norm for other cultures, leads through the appreciation of the functional significance of other values in their respective cultures to the eventual discovery and recognition of certain functional common denominators.
>
> (p. 77)

This suggests that at the base of any attempt to live in a nation composed of people from diverse racial and ethnic backgrounds is the recognition of how normative thinking, and the practices it informs, shape and are shaped by one's cultural experiences. Locke (1989c) interrogated the superiority of values presumed in Western philosophic thought when questioning the regard automatically placed on traditional value categories.

That Locke (1944) felt his ideas held traction in the everyday practices of schooling is evident in his suggestions for helping students gain the knowledge needed to better understand world cultures. Across his work, Locke held the strident position that all people, including African Americans, needed to acquire a cosmopolitan disposition to the world (Harris, 2009; Harris & Molesworth, 2008; Locke, 1944). Implicit in his work was the focus on explicating the insidious operation of Whiteness, both as a normative frame and arbiter of presumed cultural superiority. Locke was clear that such an education must move beyond a superficial, cursory level of knowledge acquisition. Rather, it entailed "giving up our own cultural egotism, with its chauvinistic provincialisms, to become one among many in order that we may achieve [a] workable unity" (Locke, 1944, p. 381). This knowledge was viewed as useful, humanizing, and insightful, in its efforts to provide "a new social learning" (p. 381). In an article published in 1935, Locke offers a particularly succinct and practice-oriented series of steps that a teacher might take in a classroom to help students critically reflect on and expand their value mind-set. The first is to "condition the child with a favorable emotional set towards other groups" (Locke, 1935, p. 144). He noted the usefulness in using music, folk songs, and pictures to stir the child's natural curiosity in engaging this work. The second focused on equipping students with the historical and cultural knowledge that contextualized the creation of the aforementioned cultural products. Third, he argued the need for students to have social experiences in the natural, everyday environments of people from minority groups. Fourth, students should have "social and personal contact" (Locke, 1935, p. 145) in schools with children from the representative groups found in the larger society.

Locke's work on cultural pluralism and value theory, while operating in the world of philosophy, clearly speaks to enduring concerns in schooling related to cultural diversity. Collectively the ideas espoused by Locke resonated with concerns taken up in the field of multicultural education. Writing well before the formal scholarly emergence of what we now recognize as the multicultural education movement, Locke advanced key ideas related to the field. This field of inquiry is both expansive and interdisciplinary, with its focus on issues of equity, diversity, knowledge production, teaching, and schooling practices. In his focus on values, Locke moved from a hopeful place, focusing on how to transform society in such a way that it embraced difference in unity. He moved against *a priori* knowledge that presumed one timeless, universal set of knowledge, experiences, and perspectives existed. He acknowledged the challenges presented from living in the diverse, multiracial U.S. context. Yet the transformation he envisioned was not one focused simply on one group recognizing and valuing another, or what multicultural education scholars have called a "human relations" approach (Sleeter & Grant, 2006[1986]). Rather he imagined a culturally pluralistic society where difference was acknowledged and allowed to flourish. While values across cultural differences should be given consideration, they also needed to stand up to scrutiny and judgment, particularly concerning their functionality and utility towards enacting a more egalitarian society. When they do not work towards these ends, they require transformation.

Locke also recognized that knowledge existed outside the boundaries of White hegemonic value systems. Harris (1989b) pointed out that from Locke's philosophical standpoint, "Western culture hid itself from its own theoretical limitations" and thus "cannot be used to escape those biases" (p. 18). This suggests that Locke realized the inherent cultural biases of knowledge and how power dynamics further exacerbated the process of interrogating and intervening on values in service of cultural pluralist aims. His early work appears prescient in light of contemporary anxieties in education around the viability of the culture construct (Gutiérrez & Rogoff, 2003). Locke viewed knowledge as socially constructed and partial (Gonzales, 2005). He did not move from an admitted poststructuralist standpoint as he held some faith in science and rationality to contradict the pseudo-scientific, biogenetic explanations of race identity that were in vogue at the time[4] (Locke, 1992; St. Louis, 2002). Yet while he saw utility in applying a scientific approach to the study of culture and race, the *critical relativism* he advocated embodied a spirit of critical deconstruction; an approach that held healthy skepticism toward unchallenged normativity that sought to mask the unacknowledged, yet present value systems that reified and privileged Whiteness.

At the same time, Locke's work was analytically compelling in its divergence from the mainstream pragmatic and progressive thinking of the time. His approach to explicating the nature and role of values, which to his thinking formed the basis of thought and action in society, deftly moved between absolutist and relativist epistemic frames, while retaining both a functional and salient stance on values. He astutely recognized that values operated at the micro and macro level through his acknowledgment that values were imperative to the functioning of society, while also rooted in the contingencies of time and space. Finally, Locke's work was simultaneously suited to the everyday concerns of those interested in bridging the cultural gap across racially and ethnically different communities both in society and in school settings. The emphasis he placed on schools as a key site to intervene in cultural intolerance speaks directly to the role education is presumed to play in creating a more equitable, socially just world. This concern, approached in the opening of this Part as both historic artifact (Du Bois, 1935) and a present-day reality (Carter, 2012), elucidates the relevance and potential for enacting a Lockean approach to multicultural education.

Part Two

Curriculum and Teaching for All*? An Overview of the Enigma of Cultural Knowledge and Teaching*

Schools have long faced the challenge of providing an equitable education to all students. Nowhere is this more evident than in the areas of curriculum and teaching, two fundamental elements that frame the everyday practices of schools. While the notion of curriculum is complex and contested, in the context of schools it is often understood as the knowledge made available to and drawn upon by students and teachers. When this knowledge is sanctioned by school authorities and required for all students to acquire, it is understood as official curriculum (Apple, 2014). Examples of official curriculum would include state adopted content/subject area standards and textbooks, as well as other classroom resources and materials to which students have access. This compendium of knowledge is significant because of its sheer visibility and expansive accessibility to students.

This, however, is not the only knowledge made available to students in schools. As discussed in Chapter 3, there also exists both a hidden curriculum and a null curriculum. The hidden curriculum (Apple, 1971) refers to the unintended knowledge that students have access to and consequently learn in school. The hidden curriculum is often located outside of the sites of formal curriculum, transferring knowledge through the cultural arrangements, organizational patterns, and other institutional practices of schools. An example of the hidden curriculum can be found in the case of instructional grouping in the classroom. The practice of dividing students into similar ability levels is a longstanding instructional strategy. Yet while this practice may be positioned as an effective, appropriate teaching approach, it simultaneously transmits to students' knowledge about learning, teaching, and student ability: the idea that ability is hierarchical and learning occurs when students are grouped with similarly capable students. Another example is found in the ordering of students' bodies when moving from one space to another in a straight line. When students are taught to "line up" in school, they learn that their bodies are generally out of control until conforming to a strict, efficient, and orderly formation. The insidiousness, then, of the hidden curriculum rests in its ability to transmit knowledge in the most subtle of ways, often unbeknownst to the teacher.

The hidden curriculum also emerges in the confines of official curriculum. Students learn which societal groups possess important forms of knowledge on the basis of what knowledge is transmitted through school curriculum. Without receiving any direct instruction on the topic, students learn fairly quickly which groups in society are of the most value and worth. Finally there is the null curriculum, or the knowledge that is not included in the curriculum (Eisner, 1979; Flinders, Noddings, & Thornton, 1986). This knowledge is left out because it is presumably nonexistent or is viewed as inappropriate to offer to students in schools.

The trouble with curriculum is exactly this: What counts as valid, worthwhile knowledge and who gets to decide? (Apple, 2014). This question is significant as they get to the heart of the problem regarding school knowledge. It also speaks to longstanding concerns around the nature of curriculum in schools and its role in opening or curtailing opportunities to learn. An underlying assumption, here, is that knowledge matters. What students and teachers have access to in the classroom makes a difference in what students learn and think they know about themselves, others, and the larger social worlds they inhabit. This, perhaps, is the reason why school curriculum has long remained a key site for debate and struggle (Gay, 1979; Hare, [1971]2007; Kliebard, 2004; Woodson, 2000).

Just as Black Americans fought (and continue to fight) to secure equitable access to schooling in the US, a considerable part of this work has focused on the nature of knowledge found in schools (Banks, 1975; Cooper, 1892; Gordon, 1997; Woodson, 2000). This was particularly the case as African Americans increasingly attended racially integrated schools—at both the university/college and K–12 levels—and were taught by White, rather than Black, teachers. Scholars have documented the differences in approaches taken to curriculum and teaching in schools populated and staffed by African Americans. These educational spaces, while often suffering disparate material inequities with regards to antiquated curricula materials and dilapidated buildings, nevertheless transmitted important knowledge to students. This knowledge was embodied in the high expectations teachers and school leaders held for Black student achievement, as well as in the nurturing wisdom and support students received from their educators (Ladson-Billings, 2009[1994]; SiddleWalker, 1996).

Yet in spite of the safe spaces that racially segregated Black schools provided students, larger systems of Whiteness curtailed what knowledge counted as valid, particularly at the level of schooling (King, 2004; King & Wilson, 1990) and in the larger society that students negotiated during and after completing their education. Blackness, recognized as an expansive body of knowledge, practices, experiences, and ways of knowing and being associated with African diasporic peoples has and continues to be assaulted (Brown, 2013). The legacy of physical violence visited upon the Black body in the US is well documented (Brown & Brown, 2010; Goldsby, 2006; Shapiro, 1988). From the African Holocaust, estimated to have involved between 9–12 million people (Curtin, 1969; Inikori, 1976; Lovejoy, 1989), to the brutal institution of chattel slavery, the lynching practices erected at the dawn of the Jim Crow era, and the unremitting police brutality that continues into the present, Black Americans know the pain and threat of physical violence. They also know a violence that if subtle in its appearance, is more deafening in its impact. Simmering like a slow burn, emotional and psychological violence seeps into the everydayness of life. Referred to as racial micro-aggressions, they manifest through slights, assumptions, and prejudgments that co-terminously accompany Black engagement in the social world (Pierce, 1974; Sue et al., 2007). Marginalization and invisibility as evidenced by external valuations of the Black self and the varied knowledge, experiences, and ways of being and knowing aligned with it, mark the ferocious landscape of Black life in the US. In this schizophrenic reality, Black people teeter between hypervisibility and obscurity, sometimes simultaneously. This makes for a complex engagement with the world.

This discussion illuminates how knowledge operates in non-neutral, normative ways with dominant, hegemonic forms taken for granted and positioned as natural and correct, and those residing outside this frame ignored or rendered invalid, partial, and/or biased. In a sweeping indictment of the problems with curriculum, King (2004) elucidated how all knowledge stems from cultural practices, or what she calls "culture-centered knowledge" that "represents divergent conceptions of 'difference'" (p. 360). Yet hegemonic forms enjoy the privilege of having their ties to these practices erased and unnoticed. They operate in common-sense frames (Apple, 2014) that serve politically different purposes. According to King (2004), knowledge, regardless of its positionality in dominant discourse, can operate in four ways, particularly in the context of curriculum transformation that include: marginalizing, invisibilizing, expanding, and deciphering. *Marginalizing* knowledge refers to knowledge that "distorts the historical and social reality that people experience" (King, 2004, p. 361). This knowledge is recognized as biased and filled with omissions. Knowledge that is *invisibilizing* "obliterates the historical presence, unique experience, contributions, and perspectives of diverse people in the development of the United States and Western civilization" (King, 2004, p. 362). *Expanding* knowledge is akin to additive approaches to curriculum transformation that seek to "incorporate[s] multiple narratives and rotating standpoints from which to view and interpret social reality" (King, 2004, p. 362). This approach, however, does not change the underlying dominant narrative or cultural model of being (King, 2004) upon which the knowledge itself rests. Finally, *deciphering* knowledge speaks to curriculum transformation that aims to both change consciousness and allow for cognitive autonomy from dominant, hegemonic cultural values and rules of acceptability. King (2004) recognized that while such knowledge could not change society, it was a necessary catalyst to emancipate the minds of those who would undertake necessary social action. This is akin to American funk band Funkadelic's popular lyrics in the song bearing the same title: "Free your mind and your ass will follow" (Clinton, Davis, & Hazel, 1970).

It is not surprising that across the twentieth century scholars and activists have placed particular attention on interrogating and transforming the curriculum at multiple levels—official, hidden, and null. These efforts were fully invested in a sociopolitical context that focused on the larger projects of racial vindication, including its earliest proponents (Du Bois, 1935; Woodson, 1919). As addressed in Chapter 3, Dr. Carter G. Woodson stood as an early emblematic figure in his efforts to transform curricula knowledge to account for the contributions of Blacks in the U.S. historical arc. In practice, Anna Julia Cooper (see Chapter Two) worked at the school and classroom level to transform curriculum and make it significant to the lives of her students. The Civil Rights and Black Power eras of the 1960s witnessed the growth of Ethnic Studies as an academic field of study (Banks, 1995). These programs held revisionist aims regarding *deciphering* forms of curriculum transformation (Urrieta, 2007). From these efforts multicultural education advanced, focusing on the conditions both in and outside of schools that diminished equitable educational opportunities. Curriculum revision also figured prominently in these efforts. These calls to revise curriculum, similar to those undertaken in the early 1900s centered on providing more accurate and inclusive representations of historically marginalized groups (Butterfield et al. 1979; Brown & Brown, 2010; Grant & Sleeter, 1991; Zimmerman, 2002). This would include official sources of curriculum knowledge such as school textbooks (Grant & Grant, 1981; King, 2004), as well as materials that touched both schools and the wider society, including children's books and youth literature (Brown & Brown, in press; Bishop, 2012). While curricular changes were enacted, some of these occurred in superficial ways. "Color me brown" was the term coined to describe the practice of literally changing the color of a human representation from White to Black, whether in an illustration found in a children's picture book or of a toy figure such as a doll. The problem with this practice was that it reduced racial representation to simply skin tone, thus expressing a common, yet simplistic, *marginalizing* approach to multicultural education: racial differences are only skin deep. A resulting consequence is that while both the visual representations of characters in books (and toys) changed somewhat, alongside the purposeful inclusion of more narratives about people of color in school textbooks, the larger systems of knowledge that condoned and reified these practices in the first place remained untouched (Brown & Brown, 2010; Grant & Sleeter, 1991). This meant that on one level, these efforts whitewashed the very difference they were designed to illuminate. Yet at another level, in their failure to attend to the markers of cultural knowledge that emerged in the everyday, lived practices of racially different people, these practices fell short in transforming the official canon.

The recognition that curriculum knowledge played an important role in the education of marginalized students existed alongside increasing concerns around pedagogy, the methodology of teaching. Similar to how normative, hegemonic values framed what counted as valid curricula knowledge, it is easy to see how teaching as a mainstream cultural practice also existed in dominant frames that both reified norms of Whiteness and marginalized or rendered invisible alternative perspectives on the practice.

Across the 1970s anthropologists in education pointed to the relationships between teachers and students, paying close attention to how they operated at the micro, everyday, level of classroom interaction. What they noted were marked differences between these two groups. This condition, it was theorized, often led to cultural clashes or mismatches between the value and discourse orientation of teachers and students, particularly when the teacher was White, or came from a culturally dominant background and the student was of color.[5]

Compelling as it was to recognize the challenges that existed when teachers and students from culturally different backgrounds met in the classroom, this scholarship often failed to attend to larger, macro-level societal conditions that informed these encounters (Ladson-Billings, 1995; Rist, 1970; Rosenthal & Jacobson, 1968; Villegas, 1991). In her influential work on culturally relevant pedagogy, Ladson-Billings (1995) noted how education theorists neglected to account for the role that culture and power relations played in a teacher's effectiveness as a pedagogue. She looked to the extant literature on culture and teaching and argued for pedagogy that recognized the integral role that culture had on teacher (in)effectiveness. Using the case of effective teachers of Black students, Ladson-Billings (1995) highlighted how effective teaching was a sociocultural activity that required teachers attend to students' growth in academic achievement, cultural competence, and sociopolitical consciousness. Ladson-Billings (1995) recognized each of these three elements as integral to students' learning. Effectively this meant that students had to experience academic achievement in a way that upheld, rather than diminished, their cultural identities and that did not lead to the adoption of an assimilationist position that ignored the role of power and the existence of inequities in the larger social world.

Along with Ladson-Billings' research on culturally relevant pedagogy, other scholars also advanced theories on cultural approaches to teaching that took into account both micro- and macro-level concerns with cultural mismatch and its location in social arrangements and patterns that exist outside of the classroom (Foster, 1989; Irvine, 1989, 1990). These theories took on various monikers, including culturally congruent curriculum (Au & Jordan, 1981), cultural synchronization (Irvine, 1990), and culturally responsive teaching (Gay, 2010[2000]; Irvine, 2003, 1992; Villegas, 1991; Villegas & Lucas, 2002). Common to these approaches is their reliance on the cultural knowledge and ways of being and acting that students bring to the classroom. They also expanded what counts as valid knowledge by questioning normative, taken for granted expectations of school, while engaging and affirming their students' cultural identities in ways that lead to empowerment and transformation of both students and the knowledge encountered in and beyond the classroom. African-centered education, to which Ladson-Billings (2009[1994]) drew upon in her work on culturally relevant teaching, also placed culture at the center of its approach. African-centered education (Murrell, 2002) is associated with the larger body of Afrocentric thought, which argued the need to adopt epistemic and ontological approaches that decenter Western cultural orientations while simultaneously re-centering the ways of knowing and being to African diasporic peoples (Asante, 1988).

Paying attention to the role that culture plays in the teaching and learning process, then, speaks to theoretical ideas that recognize the integral role that both the social and the cultural play in societal relations, including both teaching and learning processes (Vygotsky, 1978). This perspective acknowledged that learning occurs in context, the outcome of interactions between people, environment, cultural artifacts, and tools. Learning, as well as teaching, is understood as occurring in these social networks of people, interaction, and culture.

As noted previously in this chapter, the construct of culture has faced harsh critique with regards to its presumed overgeneralizing and universalist tendencies in intragroup relations (Gonzales, 2005). A primary concern is that curriculum and teaching often position culture as static, monolithic and bounded, rather than adopting a stance to culture that views it as fluid, embedded in lived practices and hybrid as it moves in and across multiple identities and worlds. Recent scholarship has advocated for a transformed conception of culture in teaching that seeks connection and relevance to the lived experiences of students but that also allows for more fluid movement in and across cultural groupings. Here, Paris (2012) called for what he terms a "culturally sustaining pedagogy." This project asked teachers to teach in ways that recognize culture as a hybrid construct that bridges children and youth globally (Paris & Alim, 2014). While recognizing that cultural groups have never been static and that her original instantiation of culturally relevant pedagogy did not move from this assumption, Ladson-Billings (2014) acknowledged the utility in "remixing" culturally relevant pedagogy—what she called Culturally Relevant Pedagogy 2.0—to address the hybrid nature of culture in contemporary times. A contemporary instantiation of such teaching is theorized in the work of scholars that push for pedagogies that speak directly to youth culture, including those rooted in the cultural milieu of hip-hop (Emdin, 2010; Hill, 2009; Love, 2014; Petchauer, 2012). This work, though "remixed" to address the contemporary context of children and youth in U.S. schools, continues to voice the concerns of its predecessors, including Alain Locke, around the problem of cultural knowledge. As we will consider in the following section, Locke's early work on the transgressive, transformative power of a Black art aesthetic, through his role in the Harlem Renaissance, offers insight on the role cultural knowledge can play in providing more inclusive curriculum and teaching for students.

Alain Locke on Culture, Knowledge, and Black Art

A compelling aspect of Locke's scholarship was the attention he gave to power and the problematic of cultural knowledge in a multiracial society. His most recognized academic contribution resided in his work in the arts, specifically his edited anthology, *The New Negro*, and the movement of Black arts cultural renaissance, also referred to as the Harlem Renaissance, that it catapulted. This collection focused on themes related to Black culture and life, including essays, short stories, poetry, plays, illustrations, and an extensive bibliography. This work, clearly informed by Locke's philosophical orientation to values as socially situated and reflected in cultural practices, served as both statement and clarion call: a New Negro had arrived and he had much to say.

The term New Negro was not a new invention. Black race leaders had used the term as early as 1894, along with other Black writers, including Booker T. Washington, as well as Whites when describing Black people who transgressed their presumed social and political place in society (Gates & Jarrett, 2007; Harris, 1989b; Porter, 2012). Locke's New Negro, however, was born in and squarely situated in the world of the arts, with particular focus placed on nurturing the growth of a vibrant cultural standpoint. Toward this goal, some scholars have argued that Locke's instantiation of the New Negro repurposed the concept, stripping away its political, radicalized elements and replacing it with a focus on "romantic culturalism" (Gates & Jarrett, 2007). This claim speaks to the concerted efforts seemingly taken by Locke to not include pieces in his collection that pointedly addressed radical ideas (Foley, 2003) and his view that in reflecting an authentic Black cultural aesthetic, Black art should not be stifled by the need to specifically convey race propaganda (Locke, 1928). The tension between culture and politics reflects a longstanding debate in Black political thought (Watkins, 2006). This tension rests at the core of Locke's take on the New Negro. Locke (1928) noted, "my chief objection to propaganda [in art], apart from its besetting sin of monotony and disproportion, is that it perpetuates the position of group inferiority even in crying out against it" (p. 12). It is misleading to say categorically that Locke dismissed the import of political informed art. He saw its value, noting it in subsequent writings published post-*The New Negro* (Locke, 1931, 1939b). For instance, he stated: "art must first of all give beauty,—and somehow, too, a sincerely truthful version of life, if it is to last. That Negro art today is able to sustain a social function without ceasing to be good art is just all the more good fortune" (Locke, 1931, p. 102). Thus, Locke insisted that art serve culturally regenerative ends unimpeded by political impetus. This spoke as much to his belief in the transformative nature of art as it did to the freedom he felt Black artists should have to create unencumbered by the discontent of race in the US.[6]

Sweeping in its scope and claims, Locke (1997[1925]) boldly proclaimed in the opening of *The New Negro*:

In the last decade something beyond the watch and guard of statistics has happened in the life of the American Negro and the three norns who have traditionally presided over the Negro program have a changeling in their laps. The Sociologists, the Philanthropist, the Race-leader are not unaware of the New Negro, but they are at a loss to account for him. He simply cannot be swathed in their formulae.[7]

(p. 3)

With this proclamation Locke (1997[1925]) informed his readers that the New Negro, embodied by the vibrancy of the younger generation reflected "the new spirit [is] awake[ned] in the masses" (p. 3). This was "transforming what has been a perennial problem into the progressive phases of contemporary Negro life" (Locke, 1997[1925], p. 3). The Old Negro, opposite of the New Negro, embodied "more of a myth than a man" (p. 3). For Locke, the Old Negro was not rooted in reality, but was a fictional creation. It was a figure emblazoned by a White imaginary and reified by academic and popular discourses of Black depravity and deficiency.

Locke's admonition spoke directly to the larger ontological struggles that gripped Black thinkers concerning Blackness and Black people in the US. This was the idea that they were a problem. Locke (1997[1925]) stated:

So for generations in the mind of America, the Negro has been more of a formula than a human being—a something to be argued about, condemned or defended, to be "kept down," or "in his place," or "helped up," to be worried with or worried over, harassed or patronized, a social bogey or a social burden. The thinking Negro even has been induced to share this same attitude, to focus his attention on controversial issues, to see himself in the distorted perspective of a social problem. His shadow, so to speak, has been more real to him than his personality.

(pp. 3–4)

Seeking to shift the discourse from one in which Black people asked, as did W.E.B. Du Bois in 1903, "How does it feel to be a problem?" (Du Bois,

1994[1903]), Locke objected to this positioning. He set out to disrupt it by harkening to the burgeoning authenticity, courage, and self-determination expressed in an emergent Blackness that was rooted in Black creative expression. The New Negro represented a strong, unabashedly Black artist who reclaimed a culturally authentic Black aesthetic that rejected operating within assimilative White one.

At the time of his writing, Locke noted that several changes were occurring regarding African diasporic people[8] in the US. The hotbed of this action was Harlem, the heart of what would eventually become known as the Harlem Renaissance. This area boasted a budding community of Black people that included individuals from the African continent, the Caribbean Islands, and recently migrated Black Americans from the South. Regarding the latter, the Great Migration ushered upwards of six million Black Americans in the South to urban enclaves in the North, Midwest, and West regions of the country (Wilkerson, 2010). Locke (1997[1925]) noted that scholars attributed this movement to several conditions including the need for more workers during World War I, in light of the closing of foreign migration, farming, and crop difficulties due to boll weevil infestation and increased racial violence in the South and Southwest regions of the country. Though not discrediting these as contributing factors, Locke felt none of these explanations offered a full accounting of the movement. In his estimation:

> The wash and rush of this human tide on the beach line of the northern city centers is to be explained primarily in terms of a new vision of opportunity, of social and economic freedom, of a spirit to seize, even in the face of an extortionate and heavy toll, a chance for the improvement of conditions … the movement of the Negro becomes more and more a mass movement toward the larger and the more democratic chance.
>
> (Locke, 1997[1925], p. 6)

Locke makes his most vociferous claim here concerning the germination of the New Negro. It is one deeply connected to the most universal of urges: the quest for freedom.

The freedom that Locke spoke to through his framing of the New Negro entails autonomy and self-determination, a charting of one's own self and journey. It boldly disrupted the idea that Black people should remain hampered by a hegemonic White vision of who the Black person was and what the Black person—artist—could effectively become. Doing this, Locke pointed to the creative, courageous spirit of the New Negro: a Black person unafraid of his Blackness, harnessing it such that his overabundant intelligence and skill illuminated brilliantly.

Locke did not doubt the beauty, talent, and knowledge of Black people. If any problem existed, it was that the Black artist was too thoroughly saturated in the dominant, White normative value system. In their quest to achieve, they lost touch with their cultural selves, thus stifling the quality and value of their work. Locke called out the Black elite who had too long worked for accoutrements valued in the dominant White society as evidence of success. This was a problematic stance because Black people were denied a full seat at the banquet table of American society due to the White racism. These actions amounted to a "forced attempt to build [African American] Americanism," that was "impossible except through the fullest sharing of American culture and institutions" (Locke, 1997[1925], p. 12). Locke held out hope that a Black art aesthetic would marshal a fuller sharing (Locke, 1931), as well as usher the development of a liberated racial consciousness for Black people.

A key aim of the New Negro, then, was to reclaim and offer to the social world those fruits of a cultural identity that at present lay dormant. Indeed, as Locke (1997[1925]) noted, the New Negro did not simply "desire to be understood" by the dominant White society, but sought out a:

> fuller, truer self-expression, the realization of the unwisdom of allowing social discrimination to segregate him mentally, and a counter-attitude to cramp and fetter his own living—and so the "spite-wall" that the intellectuals built over the "color-line" has happily been taken down.
>
> (p. 9)

Predating theories of Black racial identity development by more than 40 years (Cross, 1971), Locke advanced ideas concerning the development of a Black race group consciousness, an integral component to the identity of the New Negro. Such development would entail movement from viewing Black Americans through a lens of self-pity and in need of special regard from Whites, to one that held deep racial pride for itself and refused hindrance to restrictive, normative discourses of deficiency. Locke (1997[1925]) stated:

> In this new group psychology we note the lapse of sentimental appeal, then the development of a more positive self-respect and self-reliance; the repudiation of social dependence, and then the gradual recovery from hyper-sensitiveness and "touchy" nerves, the repudiation of the double standard of judgment with its special philanthropic allowances and the sturdier desire for objective and scientific appraisal; and finally the rise from social disillusionment to race pride, from the sense of social debt to the responsibilities of social contribution, and offsetting the necessary working and commonsense acceptance of restricted conditions, the belief in ultimate esteem and recognition.
>
> (p. 11)

It is clear that Locke appreciated the power that holding a strong race-consciousness would have for African Americans as they navigated the racially turbulent US. Yet in accomplishing this task, Locke simultaneously felt that African Americans would need to turn their eyes both inward and outward towards the culture of their past—Africa.

Locke's writings on art indicated his insistence that a strong link existed between Africa and its diasporic communities, including Black Americans (Harris, 1988; Locke, 1939b). He moved from the perspective that the culturally authentic art produced by African Americans would possess features that were characteristic of the cultural repertoires of African peoples. Locke's (1929) strong affinity to Africa, informed his perspective that Black Americans, specifically youth, needed to learn more about the history and conditions in Africa as a means to disrupt an existing deficit knowledge about the continent. His belief that "the bonds between [Black Americans] and the Motherland have been rudely broken down" (Locke, 1929, p. 22) did not supplant the unique cultural continuities he felt existed between these two. While scholars have critiqued this perspective (i.e., see Epps, Huggins, Cruse, Murray, & Ellison, 1974; Harris, 1988), it is equally certain that Locke did not, at any point in his career, espouse a view of culture that was static and universal (Harris, 1988). Rather, he viewed culture, including the early ideas he developed regarding the cultural similarities between the New Negro and those indicative of African peoples, not as cultural essences, but as situated and contextual. This relationship was rooted in cultural practices that, while disrupted by the sociopolitical context of enslavement and the racially oppressive conditions that followed, still survived, and could be reclaimed.

Thus, even as Locke appealed for the cultivation of a Black art that was culturally authentic, in keeping with his philosophical orientation to culture and values, he challenged the idea that what comprised Black art, like the composition of the New Negro, did not have universal qualities.[9] Locke viewed Black art as culturally hybrid—the co-mingling of African and African American cultures and histories (Locke, 1939b; 1931). He argued that such art, in the temporal and spatial context that he wrote in was, "the result of the interaction of African factors on the Negro, in which the external factors have been as important as the internal" (Locke, 1931, p. 99). He also expected that the predilections and standpoints, informed by the cultural repertoires of practice of the New Negro, would likely change generationally.

In a piece published in 1925, Locke spoke directly to the young artists/writers of the generation who were advancing the knowledge and production of what he viewed as more culturally authentic work. He was impressed with their creativity, vitality, and energy. In them he recognized Black genius (Locke, 1927), individuals who were armed with "arresting visions and vibrant prophecies" (Locke, 2012, p. 183). In contrast to their predecessors who were positioned as race ambassadors these:

poets [who] have now stopped speaking for the Negro—they speak as Negroes. Where formerly they spoke to others and tried to interpret, they now speak to their own and try to express. They have stopped posing, being nearer the attainment of poise.

(p. 183)

Tapping into motifs that drew from what Locke recognized as the folkways of Black American cultural life—a cultural hybrid of knowledge and experiences born out of a uniquely African and African American cultural standpoint, according to Locke, this space spoke to the artists' "deepening rather than [a] narrowing of social vision" (Locke, 2012, p. 184). The challenge for the Negro artist was not "that of acquiring the outer mastery of form and technique," but rather "achieving an inner mastery of mood and spirit" that results from "self-consciousness, rhetoric, bombast, and the hampering habit of setting artistic values with primary regard for moral effect" (Locke, 2012, p. 184). Locke (2012) viewed these practices as "pathetic over-compensations of a group inferiority complex which our social dilemmas inflicted upon several unhappy generations" (p. 184). Indeed these young artists found intrinsic value and satisfaction in their craft; and "[i]f America [was] deaf, they would still sing" (p. 184).

By the 1930s and after the publication of *The New Negro*, Locke's emphasis on knowledge and art—via the excavation and elucidation of African diasporic cultural worldviews—expanded into the world of adult education. Locke's relationship with Arthur Alfonso Schomburg, a self-taught Black historian of Afro-Puerto Rican heritage, was mutually fulfilling. Both men held a zest for learning, especially in the area of cataloguing artifacts of Black history (Harris & Molesworth, 2008). In 1934 Schomburg solicited Locke to write a report for the American Association of Adult Education (AAAE) that examined the work of two community-based projects located in Harlem and Atlanta. A key finding from the study was that adult education for African Americans needed to focus on the study of Black culture.

When the AAAE decided to discontinue funding the Harlem and Atlanta programs, Locke created the Associates in Negro Folk Education (ANFE), a group connected to these programs and devoted to making Black cultural knowledge available to the masses. The aims of the program were to: prepare and publish study materials on the life and culture of African Americans; publish syllabi, outlines, and booklets for use in educational programs for African Americans; and influence a constructive program and policy in adult education (Gyant, 1999, p. 240). Members of the organization boasted several Black American luminaries including Arthur Schomburg, Charles S. Johnson, Eugene Kinckle Jones, Mary McLeod Bethune, Franklin Hopper, and Lyman Bryson. Out of this, Locke developed the Bronze Booklet Series, a collection of pamphlets published between 1936 and 1942. Cain (2003) noted that the series focused on different aspects of Black culture including: *Adult Education Among Negroes* (Ira

Reed, 1936); *Negro and Art: Past and Present* (Alain Locke, 1936); *The Negro and His Music* (Alain Locke, 1936); *A World of Race* (Ralph Bunche, 1936); *The Negro and Economic Reconstruction* (T. Arnold Hill, 1937); *The Negro in American Fiction* (Sterling Brown, 1937); *The Negro in Poetry and Drama* (Sterling Brown, 1937); and *The Negro in the Caribbean* (Eric Williams, 1942). A ninth book on Negro History, to be written by Carter G. Woodson, was proposed but never published (Cain, 2003).[10] A vast array of knowledge was reflected across the booklets as evident in the topics selected for inquiry. Of notable inclusion was the attention placed on the role and importance of acknowledging a de-essentialized, yet diasporic communal Black U.S. identity (e.g., *The Negro in the Caribbean*).

The entry of Locke into the world of adult education opened new avenues of exploration. This movement provided "another vehicle for achieving racial self-expression and identity" (Guy, 1996, p. 215). Locke's position harkened the promise to offer a culturally relevant pedagogy as a tool of racial uplift for the masses. It is also not surprising that Locke felt such an education would help Black Americans combat prejudice, and needed to engage the intellectual and cognitive development of students (Harris & Molesworth, 2008). This impetus to culture knowledge, both as a redemptive and pedagogic tool of freedom anticipated contemporary calls to make teaching and curriculum relevant in the lives of students (Ladson-Billings, 2009[1994]).

Unpacking Locke's take on art, culture, and knowledge requires navigating between his diverse and, at times, seemingly contradictory ideas. Locke was fully invested in the redemptive nature of art, specifically in the US that reflected an unrealized democracy due to its inability to appreciate racial difference. Locke read art as the primary vehicle to help usher in a transformed vision of the Black American. Art held the possibility of granting Black Americans a space in the American cultural milieu that was itself growing and looking for international acclaim (Locke, 1927). Looking back on Locke's romantic views on art with prescient eyes one might say he was naive on the durability of race in the US. However, a closer look suggests that Locke was not only purposive in his comments, but also astute and strategic in his assessment that the burgeoning Black artist had a potential opportunity to make an impact both nationally and internationally as a representative of the US. This viewpoint anticipates what critical race theorist Derrick Bell (1979) referred to as interest convergence: the view that the dominant group only enacts equity measures when they stand to benefit from the measure as well. The sections that follow will elaborate more in depth on the issue of race, specifically as it operated in the intellectual thought of Locke.

It is worth noting that 25 years after the publication of *The New Negro*, Locke reflected on the impact of the Negro/Harlem Renaissance movement. Locke acknowledged that the initial excitement about the possibilities of the movement to shift the creation and rendering of a new Black art aesthetic had waned. He noted several tensions including the fact that many Black artists increasingly became more self-indulgent in their work and the fact that on-going challenges existed around both creating art that was particular and universal, while also finding space to challenge the psychological bondage of trying to represent the race in positive ways (Locke, 1950). Along with noting that artists in the New Negro era at times proved themselves, "over-confident, vainglorious and irresponsible" presumably with regards to their creative outpouring (p. 391), Locke felt their work pushed beyond the boundaries of art that was social mimicry of White cultural values, culturally provincial and burdened by the dictates of racial superiority. Where the artists succeeded was in producing what Locke (1950) called a "third dimension of objective universality" that deftly merged the particularities of their narratives, often bearing racialist tones, with human universality (p. 392). Their work was both culturally germane and had appeal to a wide-ranging audience, regardless of its intimacy with the content. These cosmopolitan aims spoke directly to Locke's cultural pluralist tendencies. By way of criticism, Locke pointed to the struggles Black artists and intellectuals faced around respectability politics. Locke viewed this as especially harmful to creativity. He said:

> The Negro intellectual is still largely in psychological bondage. … Consciously and subconsciously, these repressions work great artistic harm, especially the fear of being accused of group disloyalty and "misrepresentation" in portraying the full gamut of Negro type, character and thinking. We are still in the throes of counter-stereotypes.
>
> (Locke, 1950, p. 393)

Art, for Locke, was not fully expressive of its power when, at the expense of producing culturally authentic work, it was more concerned with producing images that consciously challenged racialist discourses that affirmed Black inferiority. It is curious that Locke did not consider the extent to which his own hopeful stance toward the ability of quality, culturally authentic art to disrupt and transform racist discourse was itself enclosed in a frame that sustained the strident hold Whiteness had on Black intellectual and artistic production. His stance did not change the racialized game Black intellects and artists had to play; it only moved the game to another, daresay more challenging and vulnerable field of engagement.

Notwithstanding these challenges, if Locke was optimistic about the power of the artist to intervene and help to change entrenched deficit-based racist knowledge about Black people in the US, he was also clear that Black people needed to remove themselves psychologically and emotionally from the chains of racist, deficit-laden perspectives found in societal discourses. This was part of a project of race vindication and reclamation that entailed both release from Whiteness and the concomitant embrace of Blackness. This meant stepping outside of constructs and value orientations that reified hegemonic White cultural knowledge and calling forth knowledge from the wellspring of the African Diaspora. With this, Locke understood that Black Americans needed to develop a strong, independent group race consciousness. This frame of reference anticipated African-centered education with its approach to teaching and curriculum that centered the cultural repertoires of practice and storehouses of knowledge connected to West African peoples (Asante, 1988; Murrell, 2002). Asking the question, "Was Locke the premiere Afrocentric adult educator of the twentieth century?" Cain (2003) argued that Locke's scholarship seriously engaged ideas relevant to African-centered education, with its focus on centering Black cultural knowledge, even as he also advanced the seemingly opposite perspective of cultural pluralism. This provocative call speaks to the complexity of Locke's cultural knowledge work.

Simultaneously, Locke advanced ideas on cultural knowledge that predated and anticipated the anxieties scholars now express around the culture construct in the field of education (Gonzales, 2005; Gutiérrez & Rogoff, 2003; Paris & Alim, 2014). Locke appreciated the durable, yet fluid, contingent nature of culture. He also fully recognized what is commonly referred to as cultural hybridity and its role in identity formation. For Locke, African Americans reflected a culturally hybrid people, both American and of the African Diaspora. The social condition of moving across these spaces, collectively and individually, both historically and in the present, engendered a cultural knowledge that required articulation. This knowledge was informed by a set of cultural knowledge that did not reflect cultural essences but rather embodied a situated, lived practice. This was the cultural knowledge that Locke entreated Black artists to tap in to and for students to acquire through active cultivation and dissemination (Cain, 2003; Harris & Molesworth, 2008). Sociocultural learning theories that argue all learning involves sociocultural contexts in which the learner engages with cultural artifacts and tools (Vygotsky, 1978) seem particularly connected to fundamental assumptions Locke made concerning culture and learning in adult education. Also, Locke believed that in order for students to learn, particularly in the context of a society marred by racial prejudice, they needed knowledge that was relevant to their lives. This culturally affirming knowledge spoke directly to the goals of culturally relevant and responsive teaching.

Locating a voice that embodied this movement, while not relying on essentialist notions, allowed Locke to acknowledge how change was always an inevitable outcome of cultural work. The task of every generation was to reimagine an authentic Black cultural knowledge and voice, then, bring that to bear on living in the US. In recent years scholars have placed growing attention on youth culture as a site of knowledge production, possibility, and transformation (Duncan-Andrade, 2004; Ginwright & Cammarota, 2002). This work, riffing off themes laid down by Locke decades ago, recognizes the energy, vitality, and genius that resides in children and youth, especially those who are positioned as underachieving, deficient, and in need of remediation. The challenge of educators is to recognize the beauty of young people and encourage their critical engagement in the social world, rather than in self-defeating resistance that reinscribes existing inequitable power relations (Solórzano & Bernal, 2001).

On this point, Locke's example and reflections on the impact of the *New Negro* provide insight and a cautionary note. His concerns about the overindulgence of the younger generation speak as much to youthful zeal and the maturity that time brings as it does to the need to engage in critical reflexivity when gauging the limits of knowledge. Gordon (1997) articulated this beautifully when discussing the power and challenges of engaging youth in schools and communities. Even as these students both "see and experience injustice … they are constructing their own cultural contexts, unfortunately often without knowledge of their own cultural history" (p. 231). For Gordon, the potential gaps in this knowledge stood to impact how young people view themselves, others, and the social worlds they travel. These gaps also informed how youth engage with, move in, and act on the world. It is not enough, then, to venerate the vitality and spirit youth bring to the educative movement. We must listen in closely, supporting and helping them to see potential blind spots in their knowledge that inhibit their fuller recognition of injustice. Regarding this last concern, Locke was admittedly less anxious, particularly if in raising its awareness one's work was stymied, artistically or intellectually. A place of departure for us, then, and perhaps the lesson we can learn from both Gordon's insight and Locke's example is the danger of placing art, along with any other intellectual work, in a privileged space where it is free to disassociate from issues of power. Yet at the same time, in a moment where educators are asking that we capture and propel the energy of our youth in transformative ways, we, like Gordon and Locke, hold radical hope that those after us will access the cultural knowledge and courage needed to speak their own truths to power, even when that truth is discomfiting.

Part Three

Race, Racism, and Schooling in the US

Across the intellectual ideas of Locke we have encountered a rich body of work focused on key ideas that spanned the course of his scholarly life, including values, pluralism, culture, art, Blackness, and knowledge. Yet at the heart of these discussions, whether directly acknowledged or only merely hinted at is the ubiquitous issue of race. It is to this topic that we now shift our attention.

The election of President Barack Obama in 2008 saw a shifting discourse concerning race relations in the US. Journalists, media pundits, and academics wondered if the country had moved into a *post-racial* (St. Louis, 2002) moment. Behind the notion of *post-racial* was a presumption that the American political landscape had shifted from one where race played a fundamental, organizing role in social relations, at both the interpersonal and institutional levels, to one that was no longer relevant. While this presumption bespoke the possibility of a society released from the shackles of racism, it also intimated something else. It positioned race and racism of superficial consequence such that its legacy and lasting effects could shatter with the passing of one, albeit momentous, political moment (Brown, 2011).

The limitations of these presumptions are clearly obvious. Concurrent with claims that a post-racial moment had truly arrived, the country saw signs that called into question whether a race utopia had blossomed. Racist activities, including the hanging of nooses from trees in open school spaces and the rash of fraternity/sorority-themed parties and social events that focused on and drew from racist and stereotypical tropes of people of color became popular features on social media and in the news (Brown & Brown, 2010). Even more troubling were the multiplying deaths of Black people at the hands of police officers or neighborhood vigilantes, most of whom were White and received no punitive action (Brown & Johnson, 2015). Retaliatory violence, in response to these deaths also occurred with two Brooklyn police officers murdered while on duty and in their squad car (Mueller & Baker, 2014). Race, it seems, clearly matters.

To speak of the idea of race, in the context of schooling and education is a daunting and necessary task. As a term, race carries significant social meaning. It serves as both title and description. It is complex; pregnant with histories, practices, and frames of thought that shape and are shaped by the term itself. The challenge of speaking of race is that as a socially constructed term it is both created, while serving to create meaning. Positioning race in this way is a contemporary matter. This is to say, in the words of Omi and Winant (1993), that "race used to be a relatively unproblematic concept; only recently have we seriously challenged its theoretical coherence. Today there are deep questions about what we actually mean by the term race" (p. 3). Theoretically, race is generally understood as a social category that is imbued with meaning based on fluid processes that are political, and that can change meaning temporally and spatially (Bonilla-Silva, 2006; Omi & Winant, 2015[1986]). Racial formation is the term used by Omi and Winant (2015[1986]) to describe how meanings and understandings ascribed to race shift over time. This is also the case for racism, understood as the enactment of discriminatory practices based on race-based ascriptions. Recognizing the need to account for the shifting nature of racism, Holt (1995) advised casting this practice in the plural and reading and recognizing race-making processes as constructing *racisms*.

The paradox of race is that while it is recognized as a fully socially constructed artifice, it simultaneously exerts real, material, and social consequences. For example, based on the given social rules for racial classification in a given time and space, one's phenotypic characteristics are read and assigned meaning. If the racial category to which one is assigned is one that is highly venerated in society— recognized by positive ascriptions of value, status, ability, etc.— benefits accrue from assignment within this group. In the US the racial category of White is recognized for the historic position of privilege it enjoyed, socioculturally (i.e., by social practice and custom), politically (i.e., by law), and economically (Bonilla-Silva, 2006). By converse, the racial category of Black has historically resided in a place of disadvantage along this same axis. This positioning is not unique to only a U.S. context. It is part of a longstanding global system of reasoning or set of knowledge that has, at least since the emergence of Modernity and Enlightenment, recognized Blackness as the supreme non-human racial Other (Wynter, 2005). In his sweeping indictment of the history of race and racism in the US, Mills (1997) argued that the country was founded upon a racial contract in which the Black people, recognized as the Black, non-human Other, was placed effectively outside of the democratic social contract. This exclusion was not a breach or aberration, rather it was endemic to the conceptual apparatus and framing of the social contract itself. As a consequence, Mills (1997) posited, Black people had no rights from which to appeal their positioning as they were effectively shut out of the democratic social contract from its inception. Without fundamentally altering the systems of thought that epistemically and ontologically encased Black people as the less than human racial Other in the racial contract, they possessed no right to appeal for the rights granted in the democratic social contract.

The example above illuminates the complex interplay involved in reading race both as social construct and material effect. While it speaks directly to the material consequences of racial identity, in this case, an identity socially imposed upon a person, the construct of race, along with the benefits or disadvantages it offers, connects to but spreads beyond individual racial identity. Thus, in the case of a White person who receives material benefits on the basis of possessing a White racial identity, there is a related notion of Whiteness linked to the White racial identity that it engenders and embodies. Whiteness, then, both encompasses and speaks to a complex set of interactions composed of people, practices, histories, discourses, experiences, values, and ways of being and knowing that appeal to, align with, affirm, and maintain a system of White supremacy (Frankenberg, 1993; Leonardo, 2004). In a similar vein, a notion of Blackness exists that speaks to an analogous set of interactions that in a space dominated by normative, hegemonic Whiteness—and this is key—is recognized as the antithesis of Whiteness. In this context, Blackness is viewed as deficient and savage, what Wynter (2005) refers to as "the wrongness of being" (p. 107).

This discussion on the complexities of race directs attention to the insidious role it plays at the interpersonal and institutional levels in society. What, then, does this system say about schooling in the US? Race and racism, the system of discrimination to which race is attached, are salient and elusive in education. Voluminous scholarship and policy have documented racial disparities in schooling. Students of color, in particular Black students, underperform in relation to their White peers on all standard measures of school success, including: standardized tests, graduation rates, and college attendance (Carter, 2012; Nasir,

2012). Additionally, Black students are overrepresented in special education, school suspensions, and expulsions and underrepresented in talented and gifted programs and AP course enrollment (Howard, 2010). These conditions highlight, at the macro, societal level, the racialized differences associated with Black students in U.S. schools. Here, race as a descriptor allows one to see a pattern of educational disparities found in U.S. schools.

As pointed out in Chapter 1, scholars have long noted that in spite of the fact that racialized differences exist in schools, evidence suggests that concerns with race, particularly from a critical perspective, are given contradictory attention (Blascoer, 1915; Du Bois, 1935; Brown & Brown, 2010; Lewis, 2006; Pollock, 2004). Whether intentional or not, "seeing" race is as much about knowing what to look for as it is about holding a willingness to "notice" it in the first place. For example, in an examination of all the fifth, eighth, and eleventh grade Texas state adopted U.S. history textbooks, Brown and Brown (2010) found that the topic of racial violence targeted against African Americans was addressed in only superficial ways that positioned racism as both a relic of the past and as individual actions undertaken by aberrant people. Vasquez Heilig, Brown, and Brown (2012) found in their examination of the revised eleventh grade Texas American history state standards that the term racism is not mentioned at all. When race was invoked it was done so in ways that conflated culture with race and focused generally on the cultural contributions of various groups in the US. Additionally, the standards also provided a space for teachers to ignore or choose not to directly address the racialized nature of experiences and activism engaged in by individuals/ groups of color. In some instances knowledge related to certain groups—e.g., Asian American and Native America were missing altogether. At other times, the standards used the terms "including" and "such as" to refer to knowledge that students were expected to learn (i.e., including) and knowledge that teachers could, if they so desired, address in the formal curriculum (i.e., such as). The vast majority of knowledge related to people of color, when included in the standards, fell in the "such as" category.

Lewis (2006) found, in her research on three elementary schools with different racial compositions, that race mattered even when staff, parents, and students suggested it did not. Here, race was present, but not acknowledged in the decisions families made regarding the neighborhoods they chose to live in and send their children to school. It was also present in curriculum decision-making, particularly in the reticence to enact a multicultural curriculum in a school that was predominantly White and had very few students of color. In another study Pollock (2004) highlighted the complexities of race talk in a school ethnography that examined how staff and students in a multiracial high school talked about race. She noticed that race talk operated in complex and different ways. For example, it was deployed by staff when describing or discussing individual students but not in situations where the staff feared a situation might uncover potential racism or when they felt they might be personally viewed as racist. An example of the former is the reticence of teachers to speak about the strongly racialized patterns of under- and over-representation of students of color in the school. Pollock (2004) theorized this complicated race talk as a "colormute" discourse that closed off the possibility of talking about and addressing race inequity in potentially transformative ways.

What Brown and Brown (2010), Vasquez Heilig et al. (2012), Lewis (2006), and Pollock (2004) found in their studies is akin to what critical race theorists call colorblind ideology (Bonilla-Silva, 2006); the unwillingness to see or acknowledge race and any consequent role it might play in organizing social relations. As a broad theory, critical race theory (CRT) is concerned with explicating the myriad ways that race and racism operate in U.S. society, post *Brown v. Board*. Recognizing the enduring and primary role that race has occupied in patterning societal arrangements since the founding of the US, CRT (Crenshaw, Gotanda, Peller, & Thomas, 1995) offered a lens to understand the endemic nature of racism. CRT is a critical outgrowth of critical legal studies that, while concerned with how law helped to maintain societal inequity, failed to adequately address how race and the practice of racism specifically operated in these processes. Dixson and Rousseau (2006) noted several key tenets associated with CRT. Along with the pervasive role that race plays in society due to the historically linked relationship between property rights and human/civil rights in the US, CRT also contests dominant claims of objectivity, neutrality, color-blindness, and merit. It challenges ahistorical, decontextualized analyses of how the law operates, while simultaneously valuing the experiential knowledge of people of color in analyzing law and society. Finally, CRT recognizes the racial project of eliminating racial oppression as interdisciplinary work and part of a broader goal of ending all forms of oppression (Dixson & Rousseau, 2006). Scholars have adopted CRT in various disciplinary areas, including education, to explore the nature of race and racism found in schooling and other educative activities (Ladson-Billings & Tate, 1995; Solórzano, 1997).

The goal of CRT in education, then, is to excavate how race operates in society and in education, at both the structural and local, everyday levels. This is accomplished through strategies that include: (1) counter-storytelling, an approach that calls attention to the voices of marginalized people of color by listening to how their own experiences, and the knowledge that emerges from them, illuminate and disrupt dominant narratives about race, racism, and racial progress in society and schools (Solórzano & Yosso, 2001); (2) recognizing Whiteness as a form of property that offers to White persons and their interests various rights and privileges that include the right to disposition, the right to use and to enjoy, and the right to exclude (Harris 1993; Ladson-Billings & Tate, 1995; Vaught & Castagno 2008; Buras, 2011;); and (3) the nature, paradox, and limitations of interest-convergence (Bell, 1979; Donnor, 2005), or the strategy of addressing racial inequities in the context of remedies that serve and maintain dominant White interests. By centering race in the analysis of societal, school, and other educational relations, CRT in education offers a lens to understand the obvious, and more insidiously subtle, ways that race operates in the context of education. It should be noted that while CRT as a theory moves from a place of pessimism about the ability to ever extinguish racism from the U.S. social landscape (Bell, 1979), it is understood that this condition should not diminish the racial project of uncovering and working to dismantle racism (Yamamoto, Serrano, & Rodriguez, 2003).

It is clear that race exists in and plays a role in schooling. Whether at the level of curriculum or across everyday interactions with invested stakeholders, race is present silently or in obvious ways that many attempt not to see. What CRT, along with the earlier discussed constructs of racial formation, enduring racisms, the racial contract, and colorblind racism, provides is a set of theoretical tools to excavate and illuminate the elusive and ever-present nature of race in education. With this context in place, we turn again to Alain Locke to see what he had to say about race that might be of relevance to the field of education.

Alain Locke on Race and Racism

Just as Locke's work on art, knowledge, and Blackness drew from his philosophical orientation to values and culture, so did his work on race. In his most definitive work on the topic, *Race Contacts and Interracial Relations*, published posthumously in 1992, Locke offers an examination of race and racism in the social relations of the early twentieth-century U.S. milieu. This text is composed of five lectures Locke presented at Howard University in lieu of a course on race he proposed to teach but was rejected from doing so by the university trustees (Harris & Molesworth, 2008). Locke encountered considerable reluctance at the university around the lecture series. Harris and Molesworth (2008) noted that this "unwillingness to sanction a course on race" was presumably "representative of the wide-spread self-censorship and conservative anxiety that afflicted the Howard community" (p. 120). At this time Black colleges and universities, including Howard University, were often run by White administrators and advocated a conservative ideology that steered away from having students explore the topic of race. In spite of this resistance Locke garnered support for delivering the lectures from several organizations on the Howard campus. These sponsors included: the Howard chapter of the National Association for the Advancement of Colored People, the adult education section at Howard called the Teachers and the Commercial College and the Social Science club.

From 1913–1915, Locke prepared his lectures, pulling from the work of Georg Simmel, Franz Boas, and W.E.B. Du Bois, academics whose work focused on race and culture. Locke encountered this scholarship while a burgeoning scholar at Oxford and Berlin (Harris & Molesworth, 2008). Harris and Molesworth (2008) outlined three main points that emerged from the lectures—ideas that connected to Locke's larger perspectives on the nature of value and culture. The first addressed the idea that no scientific basis existed for race or the practice of racism. The second acknowledged the complex and hybrid nature of intergroup cultural interactions across history and space. The third point spoke directly to Locke's belief that, while normative cultural practices and values associated with the dominant group in a society—a civilization type—were often a stabilizing force in group identity, they were not innately the exclusive domain of a person located in a particular race group. The discussion that follows does not explicate each of the ideas specifically, but rather draws from them to elucidate Locke's thinking around race.

To be sure, a foundational element to Locke's thought on race was his assertion that no scientific basis existed for race (or racism). Rather, race was a cultural construction that enjoyed normative status in society and impacted societal relations as well. For example, early in lecture one, Locke posed the following rhetorical questions concerning the nature of race: "Meanwhile, what of a pure science of race? Is it necessary? Is it desirable? Is it possible if it were desirable and necessary? I fancy that in the present state of the sciences of [man,] it must be admitted impossible" (Locke, 1992, p. 7). Here, the question for Locke moves beyond one's desire to establish a scientific basis for race, to one that considers the verity of the idea itself. Through this exchange Locke asserted his belief that science cannot account for what is understood as race. Race, he goes on to note, is a construct fully vested in the cultural context in which it sits. It possesses diverse, varied meanings that science cannot fully account.

One of the reasons why science could not explain the nature of race in scientific ways was Locke's contention that the science behind the racial classification system of so-called "superior" and "inferior" races, produced by Monsieur de Gobineau, relied on flawed, circular argumentation (Locke, 1992, pp. 2–3). Locke asserted that while the methods scientists employed to support their claims of race difference may have accurately met the criteria of acceptable science, this research, in "seek[ing] to prove something which ha[d] already been made a basic assumption of the actual science" invalidated the research (Locke, 1992, p. 3). Locke (1992) posited that such research, no matter how elegant its design and execution:

> has devoted its [research and methodology not toward a] descriptive end [, but toward proving the existence of] certain superior race types and certain inferior race types, and [toward showing] that the whole history of man confirms the original classification, an original classification which de Gobineau introduced into the science of race thought.
>
> (p. 3)

Extending this idea, Locke (1992) drove home the point when speaking to the limits of a bio-scientific notion of race devoid of sociological considerations. He explained:

> When modern man talks about race[,] ... [he is really talking about the historical record of success or failure of] an ethnic group ... these groups from the point of view of anthropology, are ethnic fictions. This does not mean that they do not exist[,] but it can be shown [that these groups do] not have as [permanent] designations those very factors upon which they pride themselves. They have neither purity of [blood] nor purity of type. They are the products of countless interminglings of types[,] and they are the results of infinite crossing of types[.]
>
> (Locke, 1992, p. 11)

Locke spoke to a key theme that undergirded his theoretical ideas: dismissing with the notion of a fixed, essential race identity due to the cultural exchange and borrowing that intergroup contact facilitated historically. Having pointed to the historical contingencies that help to shape social meanings of race, Locke (1992) argued that, "until ... there shall come some scientific correlation between biological and sociological [factors,] we must realize that there is a limit placed upon the science of race" (p. 8). This claim set up the additional point Locke wished to emphasize on the social effects of race on social relations in the US. Here, he acknowledged that a relationship existed between racial differences and racial inequalities that spanned different areas in society. One, however, should not presume on the face of this knowledge that biological racial differences were the cause for these disparities. He questioned thinking that presumed Black people faced more inequitable conditions in society on the basis of their race identity. Locke (1992) pointed to social research that recognized the role that "historical, economic, and social factors" played in explaining the relationship between "race differences and racial inequalities" (p. 9). With this, Locke affirmed his position that race, as a social construct, is both shaped by and helps to shape racialized meanings and experiences that lead to real, material social conditions.

In her analysis of *Race Contacts and Interracial Relations*, Fraser (1999) argued that Locke's attention to explicating the socially constructed nature of race and racism connected with his concurrent recognition of how "the history of domination and of international political economy" (p. 5) operated in U.S. race relations. Speaking directly to Locke's redemptive hope in cultivating an authentic Black aesthetic, Fraser (1999) challenged accusations that Locke was "naive in emphasizing Black cultural production as opposed to economic interests and political struggle" (p. 4). To this point, in his lectures Locke (1992) acknowledged the role power played in race relations, both nationally and abroad. He also recognized how colonization and Empire were implicated in the economic, political, and social dominance of race, specifically around Whiteness. On this point Locke (1992) said:

> The civilization of Europe, then, thrives, from the imperialist point of view, upon an economic basis of an adoption of the goods of European

civilization through a false imposition of European civilization upon the social life of whatever group may come within its control and influence. The competitive and industrial basis, then, of modern systems has made almost all empires adopt this practice which was foreign, largely to ancient empires, namely [that of] insisting that any conquered or subjugated group immediately adopt to the dominant civilization markers of empire.

(p. 26)

In Locke's description, the practices of European colonization and Empire supported the colonizer in elevating his cultural values as supreme to all others. The colonized were expected to adhere to these value systems, even as they were positioned outside their limits of acceptability. Perhaps anticipating critique that some colonizing projects held "nobler and more ideal causes" (p. 26) than the acquisition of economic and political advantage, Locke turned his attention to missionarism, something he witnessed personally with the creation and administration of HBCUs (Locke, 1989d[1925]). Locke recognized missionary efforts as part of the larger project of imperialism. While he noted that outside the context of modern imperialism "[the missionary movement] would have been quite innocent in themselves" (Locke, 1992, p. 27), it was the "very profitableness of empire [that] made it possible for European civilization to indulge in missionarism to the extent that it has" (p. 27). Indeed, Locke (1992) did not believe that a "benevolent imperialism—a justification of the exploitation of peoples" could exist (p. 27). From these histories and practices, a sense of Anglo-Saxon superiority emerged as "a trademark of modern empires as well as the first commandment of modern empire" (Locke, 1992, p. 29).

Locke's analysis of the early twentieth century race conditions in the US—a bridging of imperialist histories of Western Civilization and the race-based apartheid conditions found in the US, especially in the South, brilliantly synthesized his foundational ideas on race (Fraser, 1999). Notwithstanding Fraser's (1999) critique of Locke's egregious claim that the United States was not an imperial power (circa 1916), Locke's ideas on the placement of race in the body politic illustrated how race was socially situated, historically contingent, and culturally informed by dominant normative values that thwarted democracy. Locke did not want to dispense with race, but rather recast it into a more useful construct.

In light of these conditions, Locke turned to his cultural pluralist perspectives to articulate a vision to attain Black American racial parity in the US. Locke argued that all societies possessed a civilization type that was emblematic of dominant cultural expectations for thought and action in a society. A feature of modern societies was that it required its inhabitants to socially assimilate to the civilization type (Menand, 2001). Social segregation in this context amounted to social subordination. Locke (1992) noted that even in 1916 some Black Americans had found ways to operate within the U.S. civilization type. Important to note, however, was Locke's insistence that gaining access to this space should not rely on cultural annihilation as a means to achieve complete conformity to the type. To this idea, Locke (1992) stated:

It is remarkable] that modern society is so essentially irrational that it [requires complete conformity to type.] To live in modern society means such an orthodoxy of living[,] as well as [such an] orthodoxy of social belief that it seems to threaten the freedom[,] the mental and moral freedom[,] of people.

(p. 92)

Locke accepted that movement toward the advancement of the Black race would entail efforts to align with the type. He also felt that movement toward the type should occur from a place of cultural power and strength. The arts served as an optimal site of possibility and transformation for Locke in this regard. In reclaiming one's cultural self—a self not based on the assimilative mimicry of a dominant White one—a strong group racial consciousness would flourish. In this space, Blacks would be poised for movement. Yet this movement could not occur only one way. Locke (1992) asserted that "there must be two parties to social contact" (pp. 93–94), leading to engagement with a process he called, "culture-citizenship" (p. 99). The culture-citizenship process embodied a fluid, active form of race-making of the citizen that was dissatisfied with adhering to a prefabricated model of cultural pluralism. Culture-citizenship was transgressive, forging toward a space of new meaning, possibility, and engagement through collective negotiation in and across racial difference and unity (Garcia, 2014). Interestingly, Locke (1992) noted that while the dominant group possessed power and could presumably decide not to engage in the process of culture-citizenship, they did not have the power to stop the "will of individuals and the collective will of the alien [non-dominant] group" that sought to move toward the type independently (p. 94). The costs for doing this, however, were of grave consequence, amounting to "social suicide" for the alien group (p. 94) should they choose to travel down this road by way of a one-way, rather than two-way, street.

What, then, was the effect on the dominant group if it chose not to pursue cultural pluralism? Locke recognized this as self-defeating behavior. In an article he published in 1927, Locke argued that serious change of social attitude toward Black Americans would shift when the country recognized the costs they incurred. Locke recognized the social investment that White Americans had in maintaining a racist society, as well as the problems it presented nationally and on an international stage. In keeping with his pluralist ideas, Locke felt that change would only occur if the dominant group recognized it was in their best interest to change, speaking directly to the CRT tenet of interest convergence (Bell, 1979; Donnor, 2005). For the US, what it stood to lose was its commitment to democracy and the continued cultivation of a racially polarized society.

Conversely, what it stood to gain by changing was a stronger sense of identity and unity across racial difference. It would also secure a place for the US on the international stage as a cosmopolitan and cultured society—something Locke (1927) felt it sorely lacked and could gain from embracing a culturally authentic Black art aesthetic.

In considering Locke's perspectives on race and racism it is clear that he rejected all attempts to locate race in an essentialized, monolithic way. Locke challenged the idea of essences—cultural and racial—as abiding and perennial characteristics innate to a person or group. Locke's positioning of culture and race as social constructions that operated in historically contingent and material ways across the everyday, lived experiences of the individual is as relevant in the twenty-first century as it was in 1916. Locke's keen analysis on the ascent of racism as a consequence of the international political economy and practices of domination enacted via race science, colonialization, empire, and the now defunct system of legal racial apartheid illuminated his breadth and depth as a scholar. Similarly, Locke's radical de-essentialist and deconstructionist stance predates the work of critical theorists, specifically those writing from a poststructuralist lens and/or postcolonial framework. Regarding the latter body of scholarship, the notion of social mimicry (Bhabha, 1984) holds particular sway. In similar regard, when writing about the similarities between the work of Locke and cultural theorist Paul Gilroy, Garcia (2014) noted that both authors adhered to a notion of dynamic nominalism in their approach to understanding race. Dynamic nominalism is a term used by philosopher Ian Hacking to describe how "acts of labeling that come into historical being in tandem … with the people the labels are said to name" (Garcia, p. 172).

Additionally, links can also be drawn between Locke's perspectives on race and key constructs that undergird critical theories on race. The ideas of racial formation (Omi & Winant, 2015[1986]) and race-making (Holt, 1995), as explanatory frameworks to understand the nature of race in society speak directly to the early intellectual thought of Locke. Anticipating the emergence of key constructs in critical race theory including interest convergence, Whiteness as property, and counter-storytelling, one finds germinating ideas in Locke's scholarly corpus. Locke's stance that cultural pluralism was both in the best interests of cultivating a healthy democracy as well as the overall well-being and status of marginalized racial groups foretold a CRT understanding of interest convergence. Locke was well aware of the power that the cultural construct of Whiteness held in the US. It is not a stretch to consider it a civilization type, what Locke described as the dominant group value orientations found in a society to which all thought and action were judged and expected to align. Due to his perspectives on the normativity of values, Locke viewed this process as natural to societies, while also recognizing its boundaries as flexible enough to allow for change. The CRT construct of Whiteness as property (Harris, 1993; Ladson-Billings & Tate, 1995) speaks directly to Locke's notion of a civilization type when drawing attention to the conferral of privileges and material benefits following those who express values associated with the civilization type. Yet while the principle of Whiteness as property holds a pessimistic view regarding the disruption and transformation of Whiteness into a more inclusive value orientation, Locke felt that the historically situated civilization type was flexible enough for a pluralist rearticulation. This is a clear point of departure between the two ideas. Finally, the hopeful vision that Locke held that a culturally authentic Black aesthetic would strengthen a collective race identity for Black Americans simultaneously served as a powerful counter-story to longstanding tropes of Black deficiency. From this it is easy to surmise that Locke believed Black people, in spite of (and perhaps even because of) the social conditions in which they lived, possessed agency. This agency was clear in that people authored themselves and fashioned, through their social practices, the world around them. Since this was the case, was it unreasonable to believe they could also refashion a new, more pluralistic, democratic world?

There are many questions that one might pose regarding Locke's ideas on race and culture, particularly regarding the optimism he held for his cultural pluralist project. Was he too optimistic, naive even, regarding race relations in the US? Did he underestimate the power of empire and Whiteness? Considering these questions through the privilege of time colors the extent to which one might fully appreciate the transformative nature of Locke's ideas on cultural pluralism at the time of his writing (Menand, 2001). As a pragmatist, Locke did not theorize ideas without considering the implications they would have for people in their everyday lives. So regardless of where one might land when considering Locke's perspectives on race, racism, culture, and living in a unfilled democracy, what does remain clear is the depth and seriousness to which he pursued answers to what remains one of society's most vexing concerns.

Conclusion

The Curious Absence of Alain Locke in Education Thought and Scholarship

This chapter has illustrated the depth and consistency of Locke's ideas. Yet given the vigor of Locke's intellectual thought it is particularly curious that the education field has neglected to consider his intellectual contributions in any substantive fashion. Locke's scholarly contributions, spanning a wide spectrum of interests show both focus and coherence and align clearly with ongoing concerns in the field. For example, his ideas on the complex, multidimensional nature of culture as both lived and material practice, his views on the contingent nature of values, and his advocacy for a holistically beneficially cultural pluralism for both national and global communities seem particularly akin to longstanding concerns expressed in education. Additionally Locke's contributions to the scholarship on the importance of a Black art aesthetic as transformative cultural knowledge highlight the existing limitations and transgressive power of curriculum and culturally relevant pedagogy. He also sought to capture and engage the cultural knowledge of young people, thus anticipating current concerns around youth cultural studies. Also, Locke's deconstructionist stance toward both culture and race and his commentary on the lasting effects of empire, colonialization, and imperialism concomitantly speak to the theoretical impulse of both poststructuralist and postcolonial frameworks.

Though these examples do not speak to the entire breadth of Locke's work, including its complexities, controversies, and overall significance to education, they offer some key areas that scholars would do well to explore more in depth. Regarding critical multicultural education, Locke is surprisingly absent from the scholarship. For example, in the key handbooks devoted to the study of multicultural education—e.g., *The Handbook of Research on Multicultural Education*, Locke is mentioned only once briefly. This is also the case in the larger extant literature on this topic. His omission is also felt in the multidisciplinary education scholarship concerned with theoretical issues around culture, race, and power, including curriculum theory. As addressed in Chapter 1, these absences highlight a broader problem with canonical literature in the academy and its failure to include knowledge by scholars of color. The longstanding practice of ignoring the scholarly contributions of these thinkers has left a vacuous hole that requires continual filling. We think that the intellectual work of Alain Locke fills this chasm beautifully.

Notes

1 There is a slight discrepancy in the historical record regarding Locke's rank at graduation at the Philadelphia School of Pedagogy (Harris & Molesworth, 2008; Harris, 1989a). In two accounts he is recognized as graduating first and in one account second (Buck, 2005b, p. 9).

2 Locke shared a complex history with Horace Kallen. While evidence is clear that the men shared collegial relations, there is indication that while Kallen expressed feelings of disgust toward the White southern Rhode Scholars who refused to attend a Thanksgiving dinner if Locke attended, Kallen expressed similar racist ideas himself. Kallen wrote in a letter to Barrett Wendell, a professor of English at Harvard: "As you know, I have neither respect nor liking for his [Locke's] race but individually they have to be taken, each on his own merits and value, and if ever a Negro was worthy, this boy is" (Buck, 2005b, p. 11).

3 The term Organon is a Greek term meaning, "an instrument of thought, especially a means of reasoning or a system of logic" (*Oxford English Dictionary*). Locke's call for a New Organon in education cleverly speaks to two preceding calls by philosophers for the need to create new approaches to traditional (or presumed nonexistent) syllogism in logic. The first is to the call made by Francis Bacon for a New Organon, or *Novum Organum*. Published in Latin in 1620, Bacon's own work, *Organon*, argued the necessity

for a new system of logic; one that would replace traditional Aristotelian syllogism (Wedin, 1999).

4 St. Louis (2002) argues that Locke's faith in the power of science and rationality to change existing genetic and deficit-based knowledge about racial identity changed over time.

5 Cultural mismatch was also highlighted in an influential study that pointed to the clashes that existed between teachers and students who shared a similar racial identity (African American) but different socioeconomic status (Rist, 1970). This work informed a growth of scholarship that focused on explicating the cultural practices, orientations, and experiences of Black teachers, specifically in their work with Black students (Foster, 1989; Irvine, 1989, 1990).

6 Writing in opposition to the ideas about art and propaganda espoused by Locke, W.E.B. Du Bois (1928) approached this problematic from the perspective that "all art is propaganda and ever must be, despite the wailing of the purists" (Gates & Jarrett, 2007, p. 259). Du Bois made it clear that art was to serve the purpose of conveying propaganda, while also noting that "[he] [did] not care a damn for any art that is not used for propaganda" (p. 259). Ultimately his argument was one of both equality and utility. He believed that White art conveyed its own propagandized views and he felt that Black art should have the space to present and advocate political ideas in service of the community's interests without impunity.

7 The reference to norns in this passage draws upon Norse mythology to describe three females who control the destiny of gods and men. It is not clear why Locke selected this specifically gendered example to analogize the sociologists, philanthropists, and race leaders who helped to fashion and sustain a deficient image of the Negro (recognized as the Old Negro). However, it does bear noting that during his life, Locke was accused of holding misogynist views and not showing support for female artists and their work (Hull, 1987).

8 The term African Diasporic is used here to denote Locke's recognition that during this time Black people from various diasporic context, including from the U.S. south and the Caribbean were brought together in urban centers (Locke, 1997[1925]).

9 In some of his earliest writing on Black American art, Locke writes concerning the development of this genre by pointing out the limitations he sees with in the art produced by Black artists. In some cases, he views the work as mimicry of White art forms and in other instances, he hopes to see it develop across an hierarchical plane. Here the first stage is "realistic" where the work speaks to the White American mainstream cultural sensibilities. The second stage embodies a "spiritual dynamic" of awakened consciousness, and draws from the well-spring of African cultural repertoires approaches. The third and final stage is one of confidence; arrival to this place is indicative of "the first flush of creative conquest of the formal arts; [these individuals] rightly feel themselves to be the first generation of true Negro artists" (Locke, 1931, p. 101).

10 Cain observed that the successful creation and dissemination of the Bronze Booklets was not without controversy. Carter G. Woodson was initially asked to publish the last booklet. While giving some indication that he accepted the offer, he later went on to complete his own publication, "The Handbook of the Study of the Negro". Harris and Molesworth (2008) noted that Locke solicited Schomburg to complete the history

booklet, but he died in 1938 and the volume was never produced. Additionally, Locke had approached W.E.B. Du Bois to publish a booklet on what was originally called "Second Reconstruction" (Cain, 2003, p. 54). Upon its completion, Du Bois changed the title to "The Negro and Social Reconstruction". The text was ultimately rejected by Locke and not included in the series. Evidence has surfaced suggesting "discomfort with Du Bois's leftist and nationalistic perspectives to his rejection of the New Deal" (Cain, 2003, p. 54). Cain (2003) posited that the Carnegie Foundation might have actually exerted pressure on Locke not to include the piece in the series. The most explosive aspect of the work appears to center on Du Bois' discussion of the "American Negro Creed" that outlined a course of action to advance African Americans in the US.

References

Adams, D. (1988). Fundamental considerations: The deep meaning of Native American schooling, 1880–1900. *Harvard Educational Review, 58*(1), 1–28.

Anderson, J. (1988). *Education of Blacks in the south, 1860–1935*. Chapel Hill, NC: University of North Carolina Press.

Apple, M. W. (1971). The hidden curriculum and the nature of conflict. *Interchange, 2*(4), 27–40.

Apple, M. W. (2014). *Official knowledge: Democratic education in a conservative age*. New York and London: Routledge.

Asante, M. K. (1988). *Afrocentricity*. Trenton, NJ: Africa World Press.

Banks, J. A. (1975). *Teaching strategies for ethnic studies*. Boston, MA: Allyn & Bacon.

Banks, J. A. (1995). Multicultural education: Historical development, dimensions, and practice. In J. A. Banks and C. A. M. Banks (Eds.), *Handbook of research on multicultural education*. (pp. 3–24). New York: Macmillan.

Bell, Jr. D. (1989–1990). Racism: A prophecy for the year 2000. *Rutgers Law Review, 93*, 93–108.

Bell Jr, D. A. (1979). Brown v. Board of Education and the interest-convergence dilemma. *Harvard Law Review, 93*, 518–533.

Bhabha, H. (1984). Of mimicry and man: The ambivalence of colonial discourse. *October, 28*, 125–133.

Bishop, R. S. (2012). Reflections on the development of African American children's literature. *Journal of Children's Literature, 38*(2), 5.

Blascoer, F. (1915). *Colored school children in New York*. New York: Public Education Association of the City of New York.

Bonilla-Silva, E. (2006). *Racism without racists: Color-blind racism and the persistence of racial inequality in the United States* (2nded.). Lanham, MD: Rowman and Littlefield.

Bow, W. E. (1945, March 16). Correspondence to Alain Locke. Alain Locke Papers Box 164-15 Folder 20; Manuscript division, Moorland-Springarn Research Center, Howard University.

Brown, A. L. & Brown, K. D. (2010). Strange fruit indeed: Interrogating contemporary textbook representations of racial violence towards African Americans. *Teachers College Record, 112*(1), 31–67.

Brown, A. L. & Brown, K. D. (in press). The more things change, the more they stay the same: Excavating race and enduring racisms in U.S. curriculum. In A. D Dixson, J. K. Donnor, R. Reynolds and M. Lynn (Eds.), *Why the post-racial is still racial: Understanding the relationship between race and education*. NSSE Handbook. New York: Teachers College Record.

Brown, A. L. & Johnson, M. W. (2015). Blackness enclosed: Understanding the Trayvon Martin incident through the long history of Black male imagery. In V. Evans-Winters and M. Bethune (Eds.), *(Re)Teaching Trayvon Martin: Education for racial justice and human freedom* (pp. 11–24). Boston, MA: Sense Publishers.

Brown, K. D. (2011). Race, racial cultural memory and multicultural curriculum in an Obama "post-racial" U.S. *Race, Gender & Class*, 18(3–4), 123–134.

Brown, K. D. (2013). Trouble on my mind: Toward a critical humanizing sociocultural knowledge for teaching and teacher education. *Race Ethnicity and Education*, 16(3), 316–338.

Buck, C. (2005a). *Alain Locke: Faith and philosophy* (Vol. 18). Los Angeles, CA: Kalimat Press.

Buck, C. (2005b). Alain Locke: Race leader, social philosopher, Bahá'í pluralist. *World Order*, 36(3), 7–37.

Buras, K. (2011). Race, charter schools, and conscious capitalism: On the spatial politics of Whiteness as property (and the unconscionable assault on Black New Orleans). *Harvard Educational Review*, 81(2), 296–330.

Butterfield, R., Demos, E. S. Grant, G.W. Moy, P. S. & Perez, A. L. (1979). Multicultural analysis of a popular basal reading series in the international year of the child. *Journal of Negro Education*, 48(3), 382–390.

Cain, R. A. K. (2003). *Alain Leroy Locke: Race, culture, and the education of African American adults*. Amsterdam: Rodopi.

Carter, J. A. (2010). New moral imperatives for world order. In J. A. and L. Harris (Eds.), *Philosophic values and world citizenship: Locke to Obama and beyond* (pp. 217–233). Lanham, MD: Lexington.

Carter, J. A. & Harris, L. (Eds.). (2010). *Philosophic values and world citizenship: Locke to Obama and Beyond*. Lanham, MD: Lexington Books.

Carter, P. L. (2012). *Stubborn roots: Race, culture, and equality in U.S. and South African schools*. New York: Oxford.

Clinton, G., Davis, R. & Hazel, E. (1970). Free your mind and your ass will follow. [Recorded by Funkadelic]. On *Free your mind…* [CD]. Detroit: Westbound.

Collins, C. J. (2010). Multicultural education, metaphysics, and Alain Locke's post-metaphysical alternative. In J. A. Carter and L. Harris (Eds.), *Philosophic values and world citizenship: Locke to Obama and beyond* (pp. 111–122). Lanham, MD: Lexington.

Cooper, A. J. (1998). The voice of Anna Julia Cooper. In C. Lemert and E. Bhan (Eds.), *The Voice of Anna Julia Cooper* (pp. 51–347). Lanham, MD: Roman and Littlefield.

Crenshaw, K., Gotanda, N., Peller, G. & Thomas, K. (Eds.). (1995). *Critical race theory: The key writings that formed the movement*. New York: The New Press.

Cross, W. (1971). The Negro to Black conversion experience. *Black World*, 20(9), 13–27.

Curtin, P. D. (1969). *The Atlantic slave trade: A census*. Madison, WI: University of Wisconsin Press.

Dixson, A. D. & Rousseau, C. (2006). *Critical race theory in education: All God's children got a song*. New York and London: Routledge.

Donnor, J. (2005). African-American football student athletes in major college sports. *Race Ethnicity and Education*, 8(1), 45–67.

Du Bois, W. E. B. (1926). Criteria of Negro art. In H. L. Gates & G. A. Jarrett (Eds.), *The New Negro: Readings on race, representation and African American culture, 1892–1938*. (pp. 257–260). Princeton, NJ: Princeton University Press.

Du Bois, W. E. B. (1935). Does the Negro need separate schools? *Journal of Negro Education*, 4(3), 328–335.

Du Bois, W. E. B. (1994[1903]). *The souls of Black folk*. New York: Dover.

Duncan-Andrade, J. M. R. (2004). Your best friend or your worst enemy: Youth popular culture, pedagogy, and curriculum in urban classrooms. *The Review of Education, Pedagogy and Cultural Studies*, 26, 313–337.

Eisner, E. W. (1979). *The educational imagination: On the design and evaluation of school programs*. New York: Macmillan.

Emdin, C. (2010). *Urban science education for the hip-hop generation*. Rotterdam: Sense Publishers.

Epps, A., Huggins, N., Cruse, H., Murray, A. & Ellison, R. (1974). The Alain L. Locke Symposium. *The Harvard Advocate*, 107, 9–29.

Flinders, D. J., Noddings, N. & Thornton, S. J. (1986). The null curriculum: Its theoretical basis and practical implications. *Curriculum Inquiry*, 16(1), 33–42.

Foley, B. (2003). *Spectres of 1919: Class and nation in the making of the New Negro*. Urbana, IL: University of Illinois Press.

Foster, M. (1989). "It's cookin' now": A performance analysis of the speech events of a Black teacher in an urban community college. *Language in Society*, 18(1), 1–29.

Frankenberg, R. (1993). *The social construction of whiteness: White women, race matters*. Minneapolis, MN: University of Minnesota.

Franklin, V. P. (1979). *The education of Black Philadelphia: The social and educational history of a minority community, 1900–1950*. Philadelphia, PA: University of Pennsylvania Press.

Fraser, N. (1999). Another pragmatism: Alain Locke, critical "race" theory, and the politics of culture. In L. Harris (Ed.), *The critical pragmatism of Alain Locke: A reader on value theory, aesthetics, community, culture, race and education* (pp. 3–20). Lanham, MD: Rowman and Littlefield.

Garcia, J. (2014). Dynamic nominalism: Alain Locke and Paul Gilroy. In R. R. Fisher and J. Garcia (Eds.), *Retrieving the human: Reading Paul Gilroy* (pp. 161–186). Albany, NY: State University of New York Press.

Gates, H. L. & Jarrett, G. A. (Eds.). (2007). *The new Negro: Readings on race, representation and African American culture, 1892–1938*. Princeton, NJ: Princeton University Press.

Gay, G. (1979). On behalf of children: A curriculum design for multicultural education in elementary school. *Journal of Negro Education*, 48(3), 324–340.

Gay, G. (2010 [2000]). *Culturally responsive teaching: Theory, research and practice* (2nd ed.). New York: Teachers College Press.

Ginwright, S. & Cammarota, J. (2002). New terrain in youth development: The promise of a social justice approach. *Social Justice*, 29(4), 82–95.

Goldsby, J. (2006). *A spectacular secret: Lynching in American life and literature*. Chicago, IL: University of Chicago Press.

Gonzales, N. (2005). Beyond culture: The hybridity of funds of knowledge. In N. Gonzales, L. C. Moll and C. Amanti (Eds.), *Funds of knowledge: Theorizing practices in households, communities, and classrooms* (pp. 29–46). Mahwah, NJ: Lawrence Erlbaum.

Gordon, B. M. (1990). The necessity of African-American epistemology for educational theory and practice. *Journal of Education*, 172(3), 88–106.

Gordon, B. M. (1997). Curriculum policy, and African American cultural knowledge: Challenges and possibilities for the year 2000 and beyond. *Educational Policy*, 11(2), 227–242.

Grant, C. A. & Grant, G. (1981). The multicultural evaluation of some second- and third-grade textbook readers—A survey analysis. *Journal of Negro Education*, 50(1), 63–74.

Grant, C. A. & Sleeter, C. E. (1991). Race, class, gender, and disability in current textbooks. In M. Apple and L. Christian-Smith, (Eds.), *The Politics of the Textbook*. New York: Routledge & Chapman Hall.

Gutiérrez, K. D. & Rogoff, B. (2003). Cultural ways of learning: Individual traits or repertoires of practice. *Educational Researcher, 32*(5), 19–25.

Guy, T. (1996). Alain Locke and the AAAE movement: Cultural pluralism and Negro adult education. *Adult Education Quarterly, 46*(4), 209–223.

Gyant, L. (1999). Alain Locke and his contributions to Black studies. In L. Harris (Ed.), *The critical pragmatism of Alain Locke: A reader on value theory, aesthetics, community, culture, race and education* (pp. 235–249). Lanham, MD: Rowman and Littlefield.

Hare, N. ([1971]2007). Questions and answers about black studies. In N. Norment, Jr. (Ed.), *African American Studies Reader* (pp. 16–20) (2nd ed.). Durham, NC: Carolina Academic Press.

Harris, C. I. (1993). Whiteness as property. *Harvard Law Review, 106*(8), 1710–1791.

Harris, L. (1988). Alain Locke's atavism. *Transactions of the Charles S. Peirce Society, 24*(1), 65–83.

Harris, L. (Ed.). (1989a). *The philosophy of Alain Locke: Harlem Renaissance and beyond*. Philadelphia, PA: Temple University Press.

Harris, L. (1989b). Rendering the text. In L. Harris (Ed.) *The philosophy of Alain Locke: Harlem Renaissance and beyond* (pp. 3–27). Philadelphia, PA: Temple University Press.

Harris, L. (1999). Preface. In L. Harris (Ed.), *The critical pragmatism of Alain Locke: A reader on value theory, aesthetics, community, culture, race and education* (pp. xi–xxv). Lanham, MD: Rowman and Littlefield.

Harris, L. (2009). Cosmopolitanism and the African Renaissance: Pixley I. Seme and Alain L. Locke. *International Journal of African Renaissance Studies, 4*(2), 181–192.

Harris, L. (2010). Conundrum of cosmopolitanism and race: The great debate between Alain Locke and William James. In J. A. Carter and L. Harris (Eds.), *Philosophic values and world citizenship: Locke to Obama and beyond* (pp. 57–73). Lanham, MD: Lexington.

Harris, L. & Molesworth, C. (2008). *Alain L. Locke: The biography of a philosopher*. Chicago, IL: University of Chicago.

Hill, M. L. (2009). *Beats, rhymes, and classroom life: Hip-hop pedagogy and the politics of identity*. New York: Teachers College Press.

Hinton, C. (1944, April 17). Correspondence to Alain Locke. Alain Locke Papers Box 164-36 Folder 33; Manuscript Division, Moorland-Springarn Research Center, Howard University.

Holden, L. W. (1947). Correspondence to Alain Locke. Manuscript Division, Moorland-Springarn Research Center, Howard University.

Holt, T. C. (1995). Marking: Race, race-making, and the writing of history. *The American Historical Review, 100*(1), 1–20.

Howard, T. (2010). *Why race and culture matter in schools: Closing the achievement gap in America's classrooms*. New York: Teachers College Press.

Hull, G. T. (1987). *Color, sex, and poetry: Three women writers of the Harlem Renaissance*. Bloomington, IN: Indiana University Press.

Inikori, J. E. (1976). Measuring the Atlantic slave trade: An assessment of Curtin and Anstey. *Journal of African History, 17*(2), 197–223.

Irvine, J. J. (1989). Beyond role models: An examination of cultural influences on the pedagogical perspectives of Black teachers. *Peabody Journal of Education, 66*(4), 51–63.

Irvine, J. J. (1990). *Black students and school failure*. Westport, CT: Greenwood.

Irvine, J. J. (1992). Making teacher education culturally responsive. In M. Dilworth (Ed.), *Diversity in teacher education: New expectations* (pp. 79–92). San Francisco, CA: Jossey-Bass.

Irvine, J. J. (2003). *Educating teachers for diversity: Seeing with a cultural eye.* New York: Teachers College Press.

Kallen, H. M. (1957). Alain Locke and cultural pluralism. *The Journal of Philosophy, 54*(5), 119–127.

King, J. (2004). Culture-centered knowledge: Black studies, curriculum transformation and social action. In J. Banks & C. Banks (Eds.), *Handbook of research on multicultural education.* (2nd ed.) (pp. 349–378). San Francisco, CA: Jossey-Bass.

King, J. E. & Wilson, T. L. (1990). Being the soul-freeing substance: A legacy of hope in Afro humanity. *Journal of Education, 172*(2), 9–27.

Kliebard, H. M. (2004). *The struggle for the American curriculum, 1893–1958.* New York and Hove: Psychology Press.

Ladson-Billings, G. (1995). Towards a theory of culturally relevant pedagogy. *American Educational Research Journal, 32*(3), 159–165.

Ladson-Billings, G. (2009[1994]). *The dreamkeepers: Successful teachers of African American children* (2nd ed.). San Francisco, CA: Jossey-Bass.

Ladson-Billings, G. (2014). Culturally relevant pedagogy 2.0: aka the remix. *Harvard Educational Review, 84*(1), 74–84.

Ladson-Billings, G. & Tate, W. (1995). Toward a critical race theory of education. *Teachers College Record, 97*(1): 47–68.

Lemos, N. M. (1999). Value theory. In R. Audi (Ed.), *The Cambridge dictionary of philosophy.* (pp. 949–950) (2nd ed.). Cambridge, UK: Cambridge University Press.

Leonardo, Z. (2004). The color of supremacy: Beyond the discourse of "White privilege." *Educational Philosophy and Theory, 36*(2), 137–152.

Lewis, A. E. (2005). *Race in the schoolyard: Negotiating the color line in classrooms and communities.* New Brunswick, NJ: Rutgers University Press.

Locke, A. (1923). Professional ideals of teaching. *The Bulletin, 2*(2), pp. 8–10. Alain Locke Papers Box 164-124 Folder 20; Manuscript Division, Moorland-Springarn Research Center, Howard University.

Locke, A. (1927). Should the Negro be encouraged to cultural equality? *Forum, 78,* 500–510.

Locke, A. (1928). Art or propaganda? *Harlem, 1*(1), 12.

Locke, A. (1929). Afro-Americans and West Africans: A new understanding. *WASU, 17,* 18–24. Alain Locke Papers Box 164.105 Folder 29; Manuscript Division, Moorland-Springarn Research Center, Howard University.

Locke, A. (1931). The Negro in art. *Christian Education, 15*(2), 98–103.

Locke, A. (1935). Minorities and the social mind. *Progressive Education, 12*(3), 141–146. Alain Locke Papers Box 164-117 Folder 5; Manuscript Division, Moorland-Springarn Research Center, Howard University.

Locke, A. (1939a). Advance on the art front. *Opportunity, 17,* 132–136. Alain Locke Papers Box 164.105 Folder 9; Manuscript Division, Moorland-Springarn Research Center, Howard University.

Locke, A. (1939b). The Negro's contribution to American culture. *The Journal of Negro Education, 8*(3), 521–529.

Locke, A. (1944). Understanding world cultures. *Educational Leadership,* 381–382. Alain Locke Papers Box 164-128 Folder 2; Manuscript Division, Moorland-Springarn Research Center, Howard University.

Locke, A. (1946, May 28). On becoming world citizens. Commencement address at University of Wisconsin High School. Alain Locke Papers Box 164-123 Folder 8; Manuscript Division, Moorland-Springarn Research Center, Howard University.

Locke, A. (1950). Self-criticism: The third dimension in culture. *Phylon, 11*(4), 391–394.

Locke, A. (1989a[1935]). Values and imperatives. In L. Harris, *The philosophy of Alain Locke: Harlem Renaissance and beyond* (pp. 34–50). Philadelphia, PA: Temple University Press.

Locke, A. (1989b[1944]). Cultural relativism and ideological peace. In L. Harris, *The philosophy of Alain Locke: Harlem Renaissance and beyond* (pp. 69–78). Philadelphia, PA: Temple University Press.

Locke, A. (1989c[1945]). A functional view of value ultimates. In L. Harris, *The philosophy of Alain Locke: Harlem Renaissance and beyond* (pp. 81–93). Philadelphia, PA: Temple University Press.

Locke, A. (1989d[1925]). Negro education bids for par. In L. Harris, *The philosophy of Alain Locke: Harlem Renaissance and beyond* (pp. 240–252). Philadelphia, PA: Temple University Press.

Locke, A. (1989e[1950]). The need for a new organon in education. In L. Harris, *The philosophy of Alain Locke: Harlem Renaissance and beyond* (pp. 265–276). Philadelphia, PA: Temple University Press.

Locke, A. (1992). Race contacts and interracial relations. In J. C. Stewart (Ed.), *Race contacts and interracial relations* (pp. 100–110). Washington DC: Howard University Press.

Locke, A. (1997[1925]). *The new Negro.* In A. Locke (Ed.), *The new negro: Voices of the Harlem renaissance* (pp. 3–16). New York: Touchstone.

Locke, A. (2010[1945]). A functional view of value ultimates 1945. In J. A. Carter and L. Harris (Eds.), *Philosophic values and world citizenship: Locke to Obama and beyond* (pp. 77–81). Lanham, MD: Lexington.

Locke, A. (2012[1925]). Negro Youth Speaks. In C. Molesworth (Ed.), *The works of Alain Locke* (pp. 183–187). New York: Oxford.

Locke, A. & Stern, B. J. (Ed.). (1942). *When peoples meet: A study in race and culture contacts.* New York: Committee on Workshops, Progressive Education Association.

Lopez, I. F. H. (1994). Social construction of race: Some observations on illusion, fabrication, and choice. *Harvard Civil Rights-Civil Liberties Law Review, 29,* 1.

Love, B. L. (2014). Culturally relevant cyphers: Rethinking classroom management through hip-hop-based education. In A. Honigsfeld and A. Cohan (Eds.), *Breaking the mold of classroom management: What educators should know and do to enable student success* (pp. 103–110). Lanham, MD: Rowman and Littlefield.

Lovejoy, P. E. (1989). The impact of the Atlantic slave trade on Africa: a review of the literature. *The Journal of African History, 30*(03), 365–394.

Mabee, C. (1979). *Black education in New York State: From colonial to modern times.* Syracuse, NY: Syracuse University Press.

Marable, M. & Mullings, L. (Eds.) (2003). *Let nobody turn us around: Voices of resistance, reform, and renewal: An African American anthology.* Lanham, MD: Rowman & Littlefield.

Menand L. (2001). *The metaphysical club: A story of ideas in America.* New York: Farrar, Straus and Giroux.

Mills, C. W. (1997). *The racial contract.* Ithaca, NY: Cornell University Press.

Molesworth, C. (2012a). *The works of Alain Locke.* New York: Oxford.

Molesworth, C. (2012b). Introduction. In C. Molesworth (Ed.), *The works of Alain Locke* (pp. xi–xxxvi). New York: Oxford.

Mueller, B. & Baker, A. (2014). 2 N.Y.P.D. officers killed in Brooklyn ambush; suspect commits suicide. *The New York Times*. Available online: www.nytimes.com/2014/12/21/nyregion/two-police-officers-shot-in-their-patrol-car-in-brooklyn.html?_r=0 (accessed January 20, 2015).

Murrell, P. C. (2002). *African-centered pedagogy: Developing schools of achievement for African American children*. Albany, NY: State University of New York Press.

Nasir, N. S. (2012). *Racialized identities: Race and achievement among African American youth.* Stanford, CA: Stanford University Press.

Omi, M. & Winant, H. (1993). On the theoretical status of the concept of race. In C. McCarthy and Crichlow (Eds.), *Race identity and representation in education* (pp. 3–10). New York and London: Routledge.

Omi, M. & Winant, H. (2015[1986]). *Racial formation in the U.S.* (3rd ed.). New York and London: Routledge.

Orfield, G. (2001). *Schools more separate: Consequences of a decade of resegregation*. Cambridge, MA: The Civil Rights Project, Harvard University.

Oxford Dictionary. Available online: www.oxforddictionaries.com/us/definition/american_english/organon (accessed March 15, 2015).

Paris, D. (2012). Culturally sustaining pedagogy: A needed change in stance, terminology, and practice. *Educational Researcher, 41*(3), 93–97.

Paris, D. & Alim, H. S. (2014). What are we seeking to sustain in culturally sustaining pedagogy? A loving critique forward. *Harvard Educational Review, 84*(1), 85–100.

Perry, T., Steele, C. & Hillard, A. G. (2003). *Young, gifted, and Black: Promoting high achievement among African-American students*. Boston, MA: Beacon.

Petchauer, E. (2012). Sampling memories: Using hip-hop aesthetics to learn from urban schooling experiences. *Educational Studies, 48*(2), 137–155.

Pierce, C. (1974). Psychiatric problems of the Black minority. In S. Arieti (Ed.), *American Handbook of Psychiatry* (pp. 512–523). New York: Basic Books.

Pollock, M. (2004). *Colormute: Race talk dilemmas in an American school*. Princeton, NJ: Princeton University Press.

Porter, R. K. (2012). *Contested humanity: Blackness and the educative remaking of the human in the twentieth century* (Doctoral dissertation). Retrieved from Proquest (3526663).

Rist, R. (1970). Student social class and teacher expectations: The self-fulfilling prophecy in ghetto education. *Harvard Education Review, 40*, 411–450.

Rosenthal, R. & Jacobson, L. (1968). *Pygmalion in the classroom: Teacher expectation and pupils' intellectual development*. New York: Holt, Rinehart and Winston.

San Miguel, G. (2000). *"Let all of them take heed": Mexican Americans and the campaign for educational equality in Texas, 1910–1981*. College Station, TX: Texas A & M Press.

Shapiro, H. (1988). *White violence and Black response: From Reconstruction to Montgomery*. Amherst, MA: University of Massachusetts Press.

Siddle Walker, V. (1996). *Their highest potential: An African American school community in the segregated south*: Chapel Hill, NC: University of North Carolina Press.

Sleeter, C. E. & Grant, C. A. (2006 [1986]). *Making choices for multicultural education: Five approaches to race, class and gender* (5th ed.). New York: John Wiley & Sons.

Solórzano, D. G. (1997). Images and words that wound: Critical race theory, racial stereotyping and teacher education. *Teacher Education Quarterly, 24*, 5–19.

Solórzano, D. G. & Bernal, D. D. (2001). Examining transformational resistance through a critical race and LatCrit theory framework: Chicana and Chicano students in an urban context. *Urban Education, 36*(3), 308–342.

Solórzano, D. G. & Yosso, T. J. (2001). Critical race and LatCrit theory and method: Counter-storytelling. *International Journal of Qualitative Studies in Education, 14*, 471–495.

St. Louis, B. (2002). Post-race/post-politics? Activist-intellectualism and the reification of race. *Ethnic and Racial Studies, 25*(4), 652–675.

Stewart, J. (Ed.) (1992). *Race contacts and interracial relations.* Washington DC: Howard University Press.

Sue, D. W., Capodilupo, C. M., Torino, G. C., Bucceri, J. M., Holder, A., Nadal, K. L. & Esquilin, M. (2007). Racial microaggressions in everyday life: Implications for clinical practice. *American psychologist, 62*(4), 271.

Tuck, E. & Yang, K. W. (2012). Decolonization is not a metaphor. *Decolonization: Indigeneity, Education & Society, 1*(1), 1–40.

Tyack, D. B. (1974). *The one best system: A history of American urban education.* Cambridge, MA: Harvard University Press.

Urrieta Jr, L. (2007). Identity production in figured worlds: How some Mexican Americans become Chicana/o activist educators. *The Urban Review, 39*(2), 117–144.

Vasquez Heilig, J., Brown, K. D. & Brown, A. L. (2012). The illusion of inclusion: A Critical Race Theory textual analysis of race and standards. *Harvard Educational Review, 82*(3), 403–424.

Vaught, S. E. & Castagno, A. E. (2008). "I don't think I'm a racist": Critical race theory, teacher attitudes, and structural racism. *Race Ethnicity and Education, 11*(2), 95–113.

Villegas, A. M. (1991). *Culturally responsive pedagogy for the 1990s and beyond.* Washington, DC: ERIC Clearinghouse on Teacher Education & American Association of Colleges for Teacher Education.

Villegas, A. M. & Lucas, T. (2002). *Culturally responsive teachers. A coherent approach.* Albany, NY: State University of New York Press.

Vygotsky, L. (1978). *Mind in society: The development of higher psychological processes.* Cambridge, MA: Harvard University Press.

Watkins, W. (2006). A Marxian and radical Reconstructionist critique of American education. In W. Watkins (Ed.), *Black protest thought and education* (pp. 107–136). New York: Peter Lang.

Watkins, W. (2012). *The assault on public education: Confronting the politics of corporate school reform.* New York: Teachers College Press.

Wedin, M. V. (1999). Aristotle. In R. Audi (Ed.), *The Cambridge dictionary of philosophy* (pp. 44–51). (2nd ed.). Cambridge, UK: Cambridge University Press.

Wilkerson, I. (2010). *The warmth of other suns: The epic story of America's Great Migration.* New York: Vintage.

Williams, H. A. (2009). *Self-taught: African American education in slavery and freedom: African American education in slavery and freedom.* Chapel Hill, NC: University of North Carolina Press.

Winant, H. (2001). *The world is a ghetto.* New York: Basic Books.

Woodson, C. G. (1919). Negro life and history in our schools. *The Journal of Negro History, 4*(3), 273–280.

Woodson, C. G. (2000[1933]). *The miseducation of the Negro.* Chicago, IL: African American Images.

Wynter, S. (2005). On how we mistook the map for the territory, and re-imprisoned ourselves in our unbearable wrongness of being, of Désêtre. In L. Gordon and J. A. Gordon (Eds.), *Not only the master's tools: African American studies in theory and practice* (pp. 107–169). Boulder, CO: Paradigm Publishers.

Yamamoto, E., Serrano, S. K. & Rodriguez, M. N. (2003). American racial justice on trial—again: African American reparations, human rights and the war on terror. *Michigan Law Review, 101*, 1269–1337.

Zimmerman, J. (2002). *Whose America? Culture wars in the public schools.* Cambridge, MA: Harvard University Press.

EPILOGUE
On Black Intellectual Thought:
The Matter of Black Lives

Looking back on this project, each of us realizes that the contents of this volume fill a void that we have felt for years as graduate students and professors of curriculum and instruction, and as scholars who engage with and consider education policy in our work. Each of us at different moments in our careers has been left wanting and wondering why the ideas of African Americans were absent from the prominent theories of curriculum and pedagogy. Everywhere we turned within this discourse of critical theory was the overwhelming domain of [dead and old] White males, most of whom gave little attention to the education of African Americans and other people of color except to marginalize them or to indicate they did not fully belong through words and/or deeds.

For answers to questions about the socio-cultural nature of learning, John Dewey and Lev Vygotsky provided the key foundations of thought. To understand the histories of social Reconstructionism and social justice in curriculum theory the key works of Harold Rugg, George Counts, and Theodore Brameld were vital. Then we learned that Karl Marx provided the most important critique to capitalism and political agency. Furthermore, to better understand the application of Marxian analysis within various spheres of society we were encouraged to fill our shelves with the works of Herbert Marcuse and Theodor Adorno or what was called the Frankfurt School—the progenitors of *critical theory*. For a related strand of thought, the *sociology of knowledge*—the study of the relationship of human thought and the social context in which it develops—we were beckoned to the works of Karl Mannheim and the classic text *The Social Construction of Reality* by Peter Berger and Thomas Luckmann. To access the theories of hegemony and common sense we knew to turn to the Italian scholar Antonio Gramsci. Moreover, sprouting from these traces of thought was the requirement that we read and study the work of Paulo Freire, the forerunner of *critical pedagogy.* Then, even beyond theories that moved beyond Marxist-influenced schools of thought, it was Michel Foucault and Jacques Derrida and the *post* French thinkers that were essential reading. Black people indeed were not presented as the predecessors of critical educational thought.

This of course is not an issue only endemic within critical educational thought; the worlds of art, literature, social science, and science grapple with these issues of canonization. What was striking to us about this absence is that we knew all along that Black thinkers explored questions and concerns about curriculum and pedagogy during the last half of the nineteenth and into the first half of the twentieth century that were closely aligned with mainstream ideas and concerns, although from the standpoint of Black life. Furthermore, in some cases Black scholars such as Alain Locke were integral to progressive thinking in the 1930s and 1940s, even publishing an edited volume titled *Where People Meet* for the intercultural movement (Banks, 2004). Despite Locke's influence in the struggle for American curriculum, his ideas and contributions are almost nonexistent. Thus creating the context for a White canon to name, identify, position, and endure.

We should note however, that the process of learning about the importance of White male scholars and celebrating their work was both explicit and implicit. The process of learning and knowing about this canon occurred in our encounters with the ideas and theories cited in journal articles, books, and major studies. White male scholars shaped both the official and hidden curriculum of mostly every aspect of graduate school. In books listing the key schools of thought and theorists, the same names surfaced repeatedly. At national conferences, many graduate students and professors taught as they were taught, so consciously or unconsciously learning would take place according to established norms and values. An unquestioned master narrative had taken form.

The Civil Rights movements of the 1960s and 1970s (e.g., Blacks, women, gays, and lesbian) perhaps interrupted somewhat the White male canon but in no way was there a great interruption. Contemporary theorists in critical educational theory were overwhelmingly White and male—Henry Giroux, Paul Willis, Michael Apple, William Pinar, and Peter McLaren became the key theoretical interpreters of curriculum, hegemony, resistance, agency, and power in schools. There were some exceptions to this narrative, but overall White males explored broad education questions about schooling, while women and folks of color only spoke to questions germane to their cause.

Despite the durability of this canon, we each knew something was not right. We all had backgrounds in Black studies, and in our work as multicultural scholars and teachers we took every opportunity to add the work of Ralph Ellison, Carter G. Woodson, Frantz Fanon, Toni Morrison, W.E.B. Du Bois, and a whole host of great thinkers from the traditions of Black thought. We also added the work of more contemporary Black scholars such as Geneva Gay, Carol Lee, Arnetha Ball, Gloria Ladson-Billings, Joyce King, Beverly Gordon, and William Watkins.

In addition, we moved to include the work of other scholars of color and women (e.g., Ronald Takaki, Carlos Castaneda, Mario Garcia, Angela Valenzuela, Mary Wollstonecraft). However, even with these efforts, we remained at a loss, staying in conversation with each other, sharing with wonderment and surprise new discoveries of ideas, articles, and histories of African American thinkers and others whose ideas were speaking to many of the core ideas in critical educational thought. It was surprising to find scholars who wrote so powerfully and substantively about theories of pedagogy, curriculum, and identity were so often absent from the extant literature in critical educational thought.

Exchanges would sound something like this: "Hey Carl, have you read this piece by Du Bois about curriculum?"; "Keffrelyn, did you know Woodson had a correspondence course for teachers to learn Black history?"; "Anthony, did you know Sylvia Wynter wrote a piece in 1979 about whiteness?" As time passed, we realized that the theories and ideas that are foundational to critical educational thought had also been explored by Black thinkers. Ideas such as social reproduction, agency, hidden curriculum, democracy, null curriculum, intersectionality, hybridity, genealogy, and strategic essentialism were contained within the annals of Black thought. So one day Carl asked: "Why does this not exist in the literature?" We had no specific answers at the time but we realized that if we did not do this work, who would? Carl thus brought us together to pursue this project and from that day forward we heeded Arthur Schomburg's (1992[1925]) call to "dig up our past."

As we mentioned above, we dug into sites of memory (Nora, 1989) not commonly examined within circles of critical educational thought. We soon realized two things. The first is that these sites of memory and ideas contained within them are voluminous. One response to the void found in critical educational thought might be that Black scholars did not write much about education thought. Such a statement is patently false. The more we dug, the more we found. From these excavations surfaced theoretical, historical and sociological, anthropological, philosophical theories of curriculum and pedagogy. The second thing we discovered was that while there was a lot to sort through among many scholars, books, archives, and journals, the process of focusing on a single thinker yielded fascinating findings about the nuances of their ideas. With each of the authors explored within this volume, there existed some general thoughts about their work, as we have noted in Chapters 2, 3, and 4, but their work spoke to a broad range of ideas. We also recognized that while these scholars are not foreign within Black studies in terms of their lives and contributions, their theories of education had received limited attention. Our contribution was to get at the nuances of this work and how they bear on the enduring theoretical questions in educational thought. Woodson's, Cooper's, and Locke's ideas and contributions should encourage scholars of educational thought to pause and ask: "What other scholars explored these theoretical concerns?" And, to believe that others have.

Key Themes: The Ties that Bind

So, now that we are on the other side of this journey, we have discovered that three important themes tie these authors together. Collectively these threads patch together a quilt of ideas and discourse that has been historically silenced by the presiding ideas in educational thought.

The first is that each scholar was thoroughly committed to the ideas of humanity. They each were writing at a time when African Americans' humanity was deemed questionable through the sciences, theology, and social science. Their ideas and body of work also focused on understanding the function and capacity of American democracy and citizenship. They also each remained committed to the idea that knowledge acquisition was vital to African American education. It is for this reason that we describe each scholar as adhering to what we call a revisionist ontological project (Brown, 2010, and Mills, 1998). In the section that follows, we lay out the way these threads surfaced across each author's ideas about educational thought.

Humanizing Thought

The slogan and hashtag "#BlackLivesMatter" has received a considerable amount of attention in recent years. In the wake of numerous deaths of Black males from law enforcement officers and citizens, it helped to spawn an anti-racist cross-cultural movement. However, here we pause to consider what the term "Black lives matter" means as a historical phenomenon. To say that Black lives matter is to imply that someone in society does not see Black life as mattering. The phrase in this historical moment means a right to live and not die, which is a statement of basic human and civil rights. However, while *this* movement is new, the tenets of this claim existed in the very beginning of Black intellectual thought. David Walker's Appeal, Frederick Douglass' 4th July speech in 1852, and Claude McKay's poem "The Lynching" each reflect this sentiment. For example, in his speech, Douglass (1852) indicated the meaning and spirit of American democracy:

> What, to the American slave, is your 4th of July? I answer; a day that reveals to him, more than all other days in the year, the gross injustice and cruelty to which he is the constant victim. To him, your celebration is a sham; your boasted liberty, an unholy license; your national greatness, swelling vanity; your sounds of rejoicing are empty and heartless; your denunciation of tyrants, brass fronted impudence; your shouts of liberty and equality, hollow mockery; your prayers and hymns, your sermons and thanksgivings, with all your religious parade and solemnity, are, to Him, mere bombast, fraud, deception, impiety, and hypocrisy—a thin veil to cover up crimes which would disgrace a nation of savages. There is not a

nation on the earth guilty of practices more shocking and bloody than are the people of the United States, at this very hour.

(Taken from: www.historyisaweapon.com/defcon1/douglassjuly4.html)

Just as racial violence has been a durable aspect of Black life, Black thinkers have consistently petitioned against this kind anti-Black violence. Moreover, while it is clear that the work of Anna Julia Cooper, Carter G. Woodson, and Alain Locke spoke to the idea that Black lives matter, it also tended to the notion that life mattered beyond a fundamental right to live. For Cooper, Woodson, and Locke, "life" was invigorated by a renewed spirit of Black people having a right as humans to living a flourishing life filled with freedom, happiness, well-being, love, and compassion. Mainstream scholarship often credits Aristotle's notion of "human flourishing," but these sentiments reside in the earliest forms of Eastern thought. In addition, this sentiment of Black life mattering was a fundamental aspect of Cooper, Woodson, and Locke's vision for Black education.

Across their ideas about education was an acute attention to what was possible as opposed to what was not possible for Black people to live a flourishing life. Whether expressed in the histories of Woodson's textbooks or Cooper's ideas about humanistic curriculum or Locke's ideas about culture and values, their education vision reached beyond the minimum aspects of human existence. This is an important aspect of contemporary concerns of Black education that tend to focus on the deficits in schools, which in turn enclose the kind of questions we can pursue. For example, if schools are only asked to focus on the question of why Black males are disproportionately expelled and suspended from school then our attention can only focus on the dehumanizing aspects of these learning spaces. In other words, if our attention to Black lives mattering in schools only focuses on losses and deficits, then questions will never be pursued that reach beyond the depths of low achievement and marginalization. Drawing on the sentiments of Cooper, Woodson, and Locke, the human capacities of Black children must be imagined beyond the discourse of impediments. This kind of broad and far-reaching sentiment was also reflected in their ideas about American democracy and civic engagement.

Democratic Theory and the Making of Citizens' Thought

Cooper, Woodson, and Locke had a profound belief in American democracy and the role and capacity of the Black citizen. They each believed in the general ethos of American democratic ideals, while providing a persistent criticism of White America's exclusion of African Americans from the body politic. Their visions of Black education each appealed to a conception of citizenship that embodied certain habits and dispositions to civically engage. In this context, the process of citizen making entailed a belief that America could never live up to its highest ideals without the full inclusion of the Black Americans. Each of the scholars' education vision sought to produce a kind of political and cosmopolitan consciousness.

For Woodson, education would engender a civic consciousness poised to engage the Negro problem and to view Black people without contempt or pity. Cooper's ideas also appealed to the ideals of racial uplift, calling for an education that stimulated a balance of head and heart, ready to redress the race problem in the US. Locke's conception of the New Negro imagined Black citizens helping to fulfill and extend the ideals of American democracy. The New Negro in this sense would be the miner's canary, helping to gauge the health of the body politic, no longer encumbered by the race questions. As Locke (1992[1925]) states, "To all of this the New Negro is keenly responsive as an augury of a new democracy in American culture" (p. 9).

This kind of comprehensive aspect of Black education is important to contemporary conceptions of the Black child's inclusion and devotion to an American nation. Cooper, Woodson, and Locke conceptualized education as engendering a kind of citizen capable to function and redress the race problem and the dilemmas of American democracy. However, what sits at the foundation of the process of citizen making is the knowledge one acquires, another theme across the authors. We explain in the next section the overarching theme of knowledge acquisition and how each author generally tended to this topic.

Knowledge Acquisition

Two implicit questions inform each author's ideas: *What will Black people learn through curriculum? What should knowledge stimulate in a Black consciousness?* For Cooper, Woodson, and Locke, a critical acquisition of knowledge will enable Black people to achieve the ideas of human flourishing and civic engagement. Hence, knowledge acquisition and epistemological questions of knowing are at the foundation of all three authors' educational visions.

Cooper, for example, understood that a curriculum that developed the whole person (e.g., knowledge, character, judgment, disposition, taste) was preferable to a curriculum solely focused on training for work. As we note in chapter 3, Cooper understood that curriculum had to achieve two goals. The first was to challenge the existing theories about Black inferiority. In addition, to shift the existing ideas that Black girls could be both a lady and a scholar. The core aspects of curriculum were to implant in Black people a Social Gospel needed to actively address the conditions of Black life.

Woodson similarly argued that curriculum had to envelop the Black child with histories, stories, biographies, and academic discourse that challenged the existing norms of race and the African and African Diasporic experience—as we express in Chapter 3. His ideas of miseducation provide a clear indication of Woodson's vision of knowledge acquisition being more than mastery of skills and matriculation through the highest level of academic achievement. In fact, the hallmark qualities of miseducation for Woodson were a Black person that matriculated to the highest ranks of education, yet held negative beliefs about African and African Diasporic people and histories.

So, like Cooper, curriculum and knowledge acquisition for African Americans had to actively precipitate identity and consciousness. His textbooks and articles in *The Negro History Bulletin* give some indication that Woodson believed that the African American child must understand and internalize different professions and talents of African Americans. This suggests that Woodson understood that knowledge implants in Black people an imagery that could provoke a conception of self tied to different subject positions of life.

Locke also believed that knowledge acquisition should incite a new way for African Americans to see themselves. As we have discussed in Chapter 4, Locke's conception of the New Negro highlights the connection between knowledge and the renewed ontology of Black people. What is implicit to Locke's treatise about the renewed Black self is the idea that knowledge should engender a new identity. In Locke's (1992[1925]) words:

> Similarly the mind of the Negro seems suddenly to have slipped from under the tyranny of social imitation and to be shaking off the psychology of imitation and implied inferiority. By shedding the old chrysalis of the Negro problem we are achieving something like a spiritual emancipation.
>
> (p. 4)

What this quote highlights is a conception to knowledge acquisition consistent across both Woodson and Cooper, which is that knowledge produces a mind set or, as in Locke's words, a set of values needed to engage and meet the social circumstances of Black life.

Black Intellectual Thought and Beyond

How does looking back help us to explore our contemporary questions of Black intellectual thought in education? First, we are at a point in time that requires that we ask philosophical questions about the meaning and purpose of education. In looking back, it could create the opportunity to explore the historical context of our concerns and whether specific ideas, questions, and philosophies are durable over time. As we have shown in this volume, the questions and ideas explored through the key works and ideas of Cooper, Woodson, and Locke rest right at our doors in 2015. As we contemplate the meaning of the phrase "Black lives matter," Black intellectual thought has the potential to guide us to consider whether we are asking the right questions. What Cooper, Woodson, and Locke offer by way of orientations of thought are insights to our present concerns in education. Their ideas require us to consider not just whether life matters, but what life can look like and how education can stimulate a flourishing life. They ask us to consider: *What is the meaning and purpose of education?*

We believe that *Black Intellectual Thought* provides such a conceptual space. Cooper, Woodson, and Locke's critical educational thought implores us to ask questions that are philosophical, historical, and perceptive to the complexity of our causes. As we close, we find that Woodson's (1926) hopeful words about history provide a poignant reminder that, when asking the question of whether Black lives matter, we are asking a human question of universal proportions.

> Let the light of history enable us to see that "enough of good there is in the lowest estate to sweeten life; enough of evil in the highest to check presumption; enough there is of both in all estates to bind us in compassionate brotherhood, to teach us impressively that we are of one dying and one immortal family." Let truth destroy the dividing prejudices of nationality and teach universal love without distinction of race, merit or rank. With the sublime enthusiasm and heavenly vision of the Great Teacher let us help men to rise above the race hate of this age unto the altruism of a rejuvenated universe.
>
> (p. 241)

References

Banks, J. (2004). Multicultural education: Historical development, dimensions, and practice. In J. A. Banks and C. A. McGee (Eds.), *Handbook of research in multicultural education* (2nd ed., pp. 50–65). San Francisco, CA: Jossey-Bass.

Douglass, F. (1852, July 5). The meaning of fourth July for the Negro. Retrieved February 12, 2015: http://www.historyisaweapon.com/defcon1/douglassjuly4.html

Locke, A. L. (1997 [1925]). *The New Negro*. New York, NY: Simon & Schuster.

Mills, C. (1998). Revisionist ontologies: Theorizing White supremacy. In C. Mills (Ed.), *Blackness visible: Essays on philosophy and race*. Ithaca, NY: Cornell University Press.

Nora, P. (1989). Between memory and history: Les lieux de mémoire. *Representations, 26*, 7–24.

Schomburg, A. (1992[1925]). The Negro digs up his past. In A. Locke (Ed.), *The new Negro: An interpretation* (pp. 231–237). New York, NY: Arnon.

Woodson, C. G. (1926). Negro history week. *The Journal of Negro History, 11*(2), 238–242.

INDEX